Le Bron

BASKETBALL

AND

FOOTBALL

I devoted a
whole chapter
to you ⸺

George Thomas Clark

Tom Clark

8-29-17

ISBN: 978-0-9967492-8-2 – Trade Paperback
Copyright 2017 by George Thomas Clark

GeorgeThomasClark.com
Bakersfield, California
webmaster@GeorgeThomasClark.com

Books by George Thomas Clark

Hitler Here
The Bold Investor
Paint it Blue
Death in the Ring
Echoes from Saddam Hussein
Obama on Edge
Tales of Romance
In Other Hands
King Donald
Basketball and Football

Introduction

In a rousing trip through the worlds of basketball and football, George Thomas Clark explores the professional basketball league in Mexico, the Herculean talents of Wilt Chamberlain, the difficulties and humor of attempting to play basketball in middle age, and observes that coaching at Caltech can be more painful than studying all night for a physics exam. We also peer into the minds of legends LeBron James, Phil Jackson, Kobe Bryant, John Wooden, Adolph Rupp, and numerous others.

On the gridiron Clark reveals the talent and tragedy of Donald Rogers, an All American at UCLA and a star for the Cleveland Browns, the challenges of attending a Seahawks game in Seattle, the thoughts of brilliant but tormented Bill Walsh, the glory and horror of O.J. Simpson, major college football players being exploited by the NCAA and university bureaucrats, the rise and fall of the USC Trojans, issues of alcoholism, substance abuse, and domestic violence, and more.

Half the stories are straight nonfiction and others are satirical pieces guided by the unwavering hand of an inspired storyteller.

Contents

BASKETBALL

ROUNDBALL ADVENTURES

Hoops on the Other Side

It's Saturday in art-rich and tourist-clotted Guanajuato, and soon I'll have a much anticipated chance to watch my first professional basketball game in Mexico, a land traditionally noted for boxing champions and skilled soccer players. Since Thursday I've been scouting the city as a potential new home and asking about cost of living – it's rather high by national standards – and the local basketball team. Where does Abejas play? Are the games usually sold out? Do I need to buy tickets in advance? What time do games start? Most people know who Abejas is, though not with the clarity Angelinos, fans or not, understand the Lakers. About a third think Abejas plays at the University of Guanajuato, an elegant colonial institution of limited space, while the rest correctly say the Municipal Auditorium several miles south of downtown. Some smile at the notion of basketball tickets being hard to get. No one I talk to knows what time games start or has ever been to one.

In the afternoon I call a taxi company and in comprehensible but inarticulate Spanish set an appointment to be picked up at six in front of my apartment, rented for one week, above a city boasting red, yellow, green, orange, and purple hillside homes. I arrive at the gym at six-thirty and see an attractive white building highlighted by a yellow Abejas logo. At the ticket window I learn tipoffs are at eight, but the young lady says, "There's no game tonight."

"Why?"

"It's been suspended."

"What happened?"

"The lights over the court aren't working."

"Here's my business card. I'm here to write a story about your team. Please let me talk to a team official."

She excuses herself and in a few minutes a young man approaches. I'm too concerned about the cancelled game to ask if he's a potential Pat Riley, and instead inquire, "Can't they fix the lights?"

"Not tonight," he says. "They'll play this game tomorrow."

"What time?"

"Two p.m. or nine a.m."

"In the morning? Which is it?"

"I don't know. We're talking to the league now. Check our page on Facebook. I'll be back in five minutes."

Boxes of candy, chips, sodas, beers, and hot dogs are stacked in front of the gym, and concessionaires start carrying them inside. I hope that bodes well, but the Abejas employee does not return so I ask to speak to someone else. A young woman steps outside and introduces herself as Karina Raya, manager of communications.

"I saw Abejas play Halcones of Xalapa on TV last night. But the game wasn't played last night, was it?"

"No," she says, "it was delayed a few days."

"Aren't your games on live TV and radio?"

"No. They're so expensive."

"Radio and TV should be paying you to broadcast your games."

"I agree. But it's difficult."

Indeed. Basketball in Mexico has the meager status of soccer in the United States forty years ago and needs time to become part of the culture. The National Professional Basketball League was founded only fourteen years ago. Forty franchises have folded. Three joined the league in two thousand twelve, Abejas three years earlier.

The lady from the ticket booth emerges and says, "There's going to be a game tonight."

"Muy bueno."

I buy a "VIP" ticket for a hundred forty pesos, about twelve bucks, and enter a congenial basketball facility. My seat is actually a sofa – all are black or white – and coffee tables rest in four spacious rows on each side of the first level. The next level, comprised of traditional red seats, overlooks the court all the way around and offers everyone good views of polished hardwood centered by the bright Abejas logo. Scoreboards at each end indicate ten-minute quarters and large video screens hang high on each side. This may be the most attractive basketball venue in the league, I'm told, though the capacity of about two thousand is the smallest.

I'd asked for a program but an employee said, "We don't have them."

I later turn to communications chief Raya who responds by laser printing two rosters that provide photos, names, numbers, nationalities – Mexican or extranjero (foreigner) – and league numbers certifying basketball competence, but no heights, weights, or colleges.

During warmups I think most of the Mexican players from Gansos of Mexico City have roughly the size and skills of junior college cagers in the United States. Each team is limited to three foreign players, in this case African Americans who look like they played in division one. Abejas enters with only eight relatively small players, all but one listed as Mexican citizens, and I sense Gansos is going to rout them, and hope kids in the crowd of about five hundred will enjoy the prowess of the big city guys. Wait, in warmups Abejas is dunking, one hand, both hands, reverses, alley-oops after self-addressed high bounces. They're also swishing three pointers. Maybe they'll hang with Mexico City awhile.

A fellow about twenty appears to take my order and soon delivers nachos with unexpected corn dispersed in cheese and chips.

"This is great," I tell the couple next to me.

"You can't get better than this for the price," he says. He's from Seattle, she from Guadalajara, and they've lived in Guanajuato five years.

"I'm amazed how pretty this place is."

"The owners keep improving it," he says. "Five years ago the roof leaked."

"You come often?"

"Quite a bit. This is the smallest crowd I've seen."

More fans should've come. Guard Roman Andrade plays racehorse all night, pushing the ball up court, creating regular layups, reverse layups, firing passes to teammates open inside and out. Mexico City needs to practice perimeter defense. Andrade and backcourt mate Steve Monreal, both under six feet, singe the nets with three pointers, and so does small forward James Sandoval, who's a fine leaper and penetrator.

"Andrade's exciting," I say.

"My favorite player," says the lady.

"He's from Albuquerque," adds her husband. "The other guard, Monreal, is from Los Angeles. I think they both have dual citizenship so they don't count against the limit."

I never see a stat sheet but don't need one to feel Abejas hit about seventy percent during a second half of gym-rocking cheers that foretell victory, a hundred five to eighty-five. Afterward, kids rush onto the court and shoot baskets at both ends. That's the way to make lifelong fans.

My post-game task, as a tourist without car or Mexican cell phone, is less gleeful. There's no pay phone in the gym, but I don't worry much. It's easy to get a taxi downtown, and I assume down here, too. I'll just walk down Villa Seca, a street of bumpy surfaces and rough-looking bars and restaurants. Many taxis pass. Most are full. I wave to all of them. Those empty must be heading toward calls. I still don't ask to use any phones on Villa Seca. Around the corner I head to an open-front, working class restaurant facing the main highway divided by a high chain-link fence.

"Can I use your phone, por favor, I don't have one?"

"Sorry. No."

Should've tried a tip first. I move to the next restaurant and offer a customer twenty pesos, about a dollar fifty, to use his cell phone. He appears ready to agree before saying his phone doesn't have enough time. This restaurant also lacks a public phone, and employees are uninterested in a stranded tourist. For fifteen minutes I stand roadside, waving and hollering as taxis race by. A young waiter comes over, cell phone in hand, and asks, "Who do you want me to call?"

I give him phone numbers of two taxi companies. He calls each three times and tells me, "Sorry, no one's answering. It's a busy week."

Saturday two days after Christmas in downtown Guanajuato is like a compressed San Francisco at rush hour aggravated by hordes of strollers. But this isn't city center. It's a hardscrabble suburb. People aren't on the streets hailing taxis. One is bound to stop. Fifteen minutes later, no one has. Maybe the other side of the freeway. No one's over there but it's well-lit and heads toward town. A few hundred yards ahead there's an overpass for pedestrians. Thinking don't do it, I do it. I walk up the structure, over the freeway, and down the opposite side and pick a bright spot to resume gesticulating and shouting. Here all the headlights are hitting me in the eyes. It's been about an hour since I left the gym, and I'm getting tired and impatient.

A short and slender fellow approaches, both hands in coat pockets. He's studying me and I him. What's he got in there? He's getting close. How old is he? Maybe eighteen. He's a handsome boy who could star on a TV show and is probably not dangerous.

"Hola, where are you going?"

"Toward downtown," I say.

"Me, too. I think a taxi will come soon."

What a soothsayer. In seconds a car eases over. On the windshield a sign promises "Taxi Seguro," secure taxi. There's no taxi company sign on the passenger door. I haven't seen the other side. The boy hops in the front seat. I get in back and the driver pulls away.

"How much to go to Privada de Portales, above the city?" I ask. All passengers, especially tourists, should establish prices before departure.

Suddenly, I'm no longer worried about money. I'm looking at the rearview-mirror reflection of a grim gray man who sneers, "We'll decide the price when we get there."

"I want to know now."

He accelerates to about seventy miles per hour and glances at the boy who taps the driver's right ankle with his left foot.

"I said, 'How much?'"

He ignores me. What a fool I am, an experienced traveler in Mexico, riding behind two men in the front seat of a speeding car. They can take me anywhere. I can't jump out now. But I can't let them get me to an isolated place where they, and accomplices in wait, may shoot or stab me. Maybe I should punch the driver in the head. Punch him and then punch the boy. Then I'll duck before the crash. But maybe I'll have an opportunity to jump out. I'll do that at the next red light. I'll kick the door open and flee.

"Listen, I don't want to go to my apartment. I only want to go downtown (el centro), to Teatro Juarez. Many people are there."

They don't respond. I listen for clues and swear I'll try something if he drives by any Centro signs. If I don't, this may be it. I feel sick.

Finally, the old man asks, "What time is it?"

"Eleven oh three," says the boy.

There's the Centro sign. What if he doesn't take it? Strike or jump out. Maybe both. He takes it. But maybe he's going to drive into some Guanajuato alley or up into hills of colorful houses now darkened.

"Stop right here," I order. "Let me out and I'll give you a hundred pesos."

He pulls over and I jump out and hand the boy the equivalent of eight bucks, and he gives it to the old man. Then the boy steps out and, heading for crowded streets in a Guanajuato night, says, "Hasta la vista."

* * *

Two days later, Monday afternoon, I call communications director Karina Raya, who hasn't arrived at work, and leave a message that I'd like some help getting a taxi after the game against the Soles of Mexicali that evening. When I arrive I smile at blonde and well-groomed Raya and say, "It's pretty hard to find a taxi here. I need a Mexican cell phone."

"Don't worry. I'll call one for you when I call taxis for the players."

"Muchas gracias."

This evening Abejas enters the arena with three more players, all from the United States. One is Steffphon Pettigrew, team leader in scoring and rebounding with twenty-one and eight. He and McHugh Mattis missed their return flights after excused holiday visits home. The third addition is team newcomer A'Darius Pegues, a center.

Abejas, with an eleven and fourteen record, needs this infusion of size and athleticism against seventeen-and-nine Soles. One would expect massive Mexico City to attract more talent than the dreary desert of Mexicali but that's not the case. In this league the Halcones of Xalapa, a moderate-size city in Veracruz, have been comparable to the San Antonio Spurs, winning four titles and thrice finishing second. Mexicali also has some Spurs in them, thrashing Abejas early as Matthew Bryan-Amaning swats shots and scores inside while sharp-shooting teammates strike from outside. Mexicali coach Ivan Deniz O'Donell then rescues his stunned opponents, inexplicably benching Bryan-Amaning for an extended second-quarter stretch during which the local big men score inside and swift guards Roman Andrade and

Steve Monreal either penetrate or nail threes to make a close game.

The Soles reassert themselves in the second half, and about fifteen hundred fans urge Abejas to battle a more talented opponent that leads by twelve in the fourth quarter. A'Darius Pegues, using his large body, plays good defense to prevent Bryan-Amaning from further dominating the game, but Mexicali leads eighty-four to seventy-eight with two-thirty to go. Steve Monreal then steals a pass and has an easy breakaway layup he declines by throwing the ball off the board so Stepphon Pettigrew can snare it en route to a slam generating one of the loudest roars I've heard, the small gym serving as an echo chamber. If I'd been the coach and that play hadn't converted, I'd have fined Monreal two games pay and Pettigrew one. I may have fined them anyway. Don't increase degree of difficulty when you're trailing late in the game. I'm not worried, though. I may be screaming, too.

Abejas soon ties the game at eighty-four and gets the ball back, fritters time, and, after Soles knocks it out of bounds, has an inbounds pass on the visitor's baseline with two seconds on the shot clock and forty-five in the game. Roman Andrade, as noted above, is under six-feet, yet he's assigned to throw the inbound pass while a big body and long arms obstruct his view. He overthrows Steve Monreal but even-shorter Steve dashes back and retrieves the ball just in front of half court on the left side and with his laser left launches a set shot that banks in, putting Abejas ahead by three. No exaggeration: bring ear muffs in case these guys are in a close game. Everyone's standing. Even Mexicali fans may be cheering that shot.

Soles gets no closer and Guanajuato wins ninety-three to eighty-nine in one of the most enjoyable games I've seen in years. Kids from this city of one hundred thousand, girls and boys, rush onto the court, pounding basketballs and rattling rims. I watch at courtside, as communications director Raya promised I could, waiting for the players to relax in their dressing room before most exit wearing uniforms under their warm-up gear. I see grim Mexicali coach Ivan Deniz O'Donell who must regret keeping shot-blocker Matthew Bryan-Amaning seated too long in the second quarter. I doubt he'll do so again. Right now I'm more interested in culture and introduce myself to the first player who comes out.

"I'm Greg Preer," he says, shaking hands. "Playing here is a great experience. I love talking to people in the community. I was raised in a bilingual family and am fluent in Spanish. My mother's from Mexico."

"I understand that taxis are taking you guys home. Do you drive here?"

"We don't drive. The team has a deal with a taxi company, and anytime we want to go somewhere we just call them."

"Do you pay rent?"

"No, our rent is free so we live on less than most people. You can live really well here on three thousand dollars a month. "

"Now, I'm not asking you personally, but about how much do some of the guys get paid in this league?"

"In Guanajuato we make six thousand dollars a month. Guys on some of the better-established teams make more."

"That's pretty damn good with all the perks."

"It sure is."

"Where are you from?"

"Akron. I played at St. Vincent St. Mary's High School, same school as LeBron James. I was still in junior high when he graduated. He's a good friend."

"Where'd you play college ball?"

"Whittier College. I averaged seventeen points a game. The last two seasons I played in Leon, about forty miles west of here, and averaged fourteen a game. I didn't play tonight, though."

Next I talk to A'Darius Pegues, a very large man.

"How do you like playing in Mexico?" I ask.

"I love it, but I've only been here three days. This was my first game."

"I've been here longer than that, five days. Where have you been playing?"

"I played five months in Latvia and averaged ten points, eight rebounds, and one block. We could've had a better team but our guards were only seventeen or eighteen. I also had a good Euro League game with eighteen points, eight rebounds, and three blocks."

"Where'd you play college ball?"

"Two years at Western Kentucky."

"You're kidding. I was born in Bowling Green."

A'Darius Pegues smiles and places a big hand on each of my shoulders and says, "That's great."

"Western has a helluva basketball tradition. I followed them back in the sixties when they had Clem Haskins. I lived in California by then but was still a fan."

"I'm very good friends with Clem. We talk on the phone a lot. I always look forward to that."

"They had a great team in sixty-seven," I say. "Haskins was a first-team All American, and Greg and Dwight Smith were outstanding players, too. Those guys integrated Southern basketball. Before then, division one ball was all white. After their success — two straight appearances in the NCAA Tournament — Adolf Rupp at Kentucky and other big schools in the South had to recruit black players.

"Early in Haskins' final season he broke his wrist, and after missing several games played with a cast on his right forearm. It made shooting difficult or they would've beaten Dayton and Don May in the tournament. Dayton ended up going to the Final Four and getting drilled by UCLA. Western would've definitely played better than Dayton with Haskins healthy, and I think could've given UCLA a good game. But nobody was going to beat the Bruins. Have you talked to Clem about the Smith brothers?"

"No," he says.

"Here." I write: "Clem, Dwight, Greg, integration, 1964-67."

"Just read that to Clem. That's all you'll need. He scored twenty points a game one season in the NBA and had a few other good years. Dwight was a year older than Greg, six-five, and a great all around player, offense, defense, rebounding. The Lakers drafted him in the second round when there were a lot fewer teams in the league. He would've been an excellent player for many years. After the sixty-seven season he was killed in a car wreck. Greg was driving. The roads had been flooded and their car went off the road. Their sister in the backseat also died. She and Dwight drowned in a rain-swollen ditch.

"Thankfully, Greg survived. He went on to play with Kareem (Abdul Jabbar) in Milwaukee and started at forward when the Bucks won the NBA title. He was a powerful rebounder for a guy six-five."

"Wait a minute," says Pegues. "Kareem played in Milwaukee? And won a title there?"

"Damn right. Nineteen seventy-one. Young people only associate him with the Lakers, but he got a ring in Milwaukee, too. By the way, good job tonight. There's no way Abejas wins without you. You slowed down Matthew Bryan-Amaning."

"The guy's a beast," Pegues says. "There are a lot of good players down here."

I look at huge, cut biceps expanding his warm-up jacket and say, "You're in damn good shape. Do you lift weights?"

"Yeah, I was only six-ten and one-ninety-eight when I got to Western and two-fifty when I left two years later."

I thank A'Darius Pegues, who redshirted his first year to concentrate on studies at Western Kentucky and just before the following season tore an ACL ligament. Frustrated, he transferred to two other schools before finishing his collegiate career at Campbellsville University in Kentucky. His international sojourn then began.

Now, what about the Mexicali phenom, Matthew Bryan-Amaning? He's six-ten, two-forty, has an eighty-seven-inch wingspan, and averaged fifteen points and eight rebounds for the University of Washington in 2011. That year he had college career bests of thirty points and seven blocks against Arizona State, in separate games, and fifteen rebounds versus Oregon State. He was projected as a late second round pick but went undrafted. Scouts praised his athletic ability, shot blocking, and scoring close to the rim, but some said he lacked a face-up offensive game, didn't handle the ball well, and was a "better off-ball defender than on-ball (and) too often allows his man to get where and what he wants."

He posted modest numbers for New Orleans and Chicago in recent NBA summer league play and averaged eight points and three rebounds in the Adriatic league two years ago and, this year, eleven and four for Olympique Antilles in France. He's been in Mexicali a couple of months and playing like he did in college, rejecting and disrupting shots, dunking, and scoring on short shots softly delivered. It's stunning a player so good can't play in the ultimate league and tempting to conclude NBA executives are wrong. But barring his entrance at power forward are incumbents Tim Duncan, Dirk Nowitzki, Anthony Davis, Blake Griffin, Zach Randolph, Kevin Love, LaMarcus Aldridge, Pau Gasol, David Lee, Greg Monroe, and plenty of others who, amazingly, are beastlier than Matthew Bryan-Amaning. That's impressive, and perhaps I should say scary.

January 2015

Wilt Would've Been Seventy

My friends and I, clever adolescents all, used to call our timid town "Sportamento" or "Hickramento," derisive references not merely to the absence of professional sports and division one college competition but as well to the backwoods community-wide conviction that Sacramento did not deserve the best in sports, would never be able to support pro teams and should not even dream about, much less act on, acquiring them because, after all, we could just drive down Interstate 80 to the regal Bay Area and see the big boys play. My family and I often traveled to wind-whipped Candlestick Park to watch Willie Mays, Orlando Cepeda, and Willie McCovey hit moon shots for the Giants and once ventured to rickety Kezar Stadium and saw the struggling 49'ers whip the legendary Green Bay Packers of Vince Lombardi.

During this era, as Lyndon Johnson escalated war in Viet Nam and the Beatles rocked Ed Sullivan on TV, Americans of average means could, without busting the budget, take their families to professional basketball games. And, in a delightful expression of quaintness, the San Francisco Warriors every year played one regular season basketball game in an otherwise forlorn Sacramento more attuned to professional wrestling than basketball and that had no facility larger than the even-then-ancient Memorial Auditorium. Nowadays NBA teams are considered philanthropic if they stage exhibition games out of town in arenas seating a paltry ten thousand. In late 1964 the Warriors took on the New York Knicks for real in the Sacramento High School gym accommodating no more than three or four thousand fans.

The place was about half empty; locals clearly preferred an evening of soap operas to witnessing the exploits of Wilton Norman Chamberlain. They made a bad choice. None of them, one confidently asserts, recalls even an instant of what appeared on the tube, yet it's likely everyone at Sac High that night remembers Chamberlain. Standing about seven-foot-three – forget the official listing a couple inches lower – he ran and jumped like a gigantic decathlete, soaring one foot, two feet, even three above the rim to block shots and capture rebounds with ease and decisiveness approaching supernatural. In another game, Chamberlain consumed fifty-five rebounds, which is the baseball equivalent of clubbing five or six home runs in a game. See how many rebounds players get today. Yes, competition is better now and battles for the basketball even more intense. Still, no contemporary player could travel back in time and approach Wilt's career average of twenty-three rebounds a game.

Despite his unequalled shot blocking and rebounding, Wilt Chamberlain is forever synonymous with offensive production. He averaged fifty points a game in 1962 and one night hurled in one hundred. That season he scored fifty or more points forty-five times and did so a hundred eighteen games in his career. He didn't hog the ball or force shots; he was in fact the most efficient of scorers, leading the league nine times in field goal percentage. One season he shot almost seventy-three percent from the field. In a single game he took eighteen shots without a miss. All the above statistics still preside as National Basketball Association records. There are many more, but Wilt Chamberlain should be celebrated not primarily for the way he filled a stat sheet but for what he produced visually and emotionally.

I know, and so do a couple of friends. We were lucky. At halftime we tentatively moved from our seats to the floor several feet behind the Warriors' offensive basket. Surely, they won't let us watch from so close, we assumed. But they did. For twenty-four minutes of action, about an hour on the clock, we studied Chamberlain as he dunked over two or three defenders, banked in soft fade-away jump shots, and held his right palm in the sky to softly roll the ball off fingertips down into the basket. We were also treated to the repartee of an NBA game. Knicks coach Eddie Donovan peppered referee Richie Powers with accusations he was letting Wilt manhandle the Knicks. Donovan knew where this could lead. He'd been the opposing coach the night Wilt scored a hundred. Powers finally tucked the basketball under his arm, stomped toward the bench, pointed at the coach, and shouted, "No shit, Donovan."

"Oh, that's good talk, Richie. That's good talk."

The complaints did not undermine Chamberlain. He scored

forty-four points, but his team lost. The Knicks' big left-handed rookie, about six-nine and two hundred fifty pounds, kept stroking in outside jumpers. Who the hell's that, we wondered? He was Willis Reed and would anchor the Knicks' championship teams in 1970 and 1973. Chamberlain already yearned for a title. Despite his astonishing play since entering the league in 1959, his teams (and all others) had been overwhelmed by Bill Russell and the talented Boston Celtics. Many fans accused Wilt of being a loser. The charge was ridiculous but tormented him, and early in 1965 – in the fashion of LeBron James and Kevin Durant today – he forced the Warriors to send him back to his hometown and the star-laden Philadelphia 76'ers. They improved the rest of the season before the Celtics defeated them in the Eastern Conference finals. In 1966 Philadelphia won the conference with a fifty-five and twenty-five record and looked like a champion until Boston took four playoff games of five and enabled coach Red Auerbach to light another victory cigar on the bench before striding into the front office. Bill Russell became coach and remained on the court as the ultimate team champion.

Responding with a stylistic overhaul in 1967, Wilt shot and scored less while passing more, and his teammates flourished: Hal Greer sizzled as a sharpshooter; Chet Walker operated smoothly at forward; Luke Jackson provided two hundred fifty pounds of force before they called his position power forward; Billy Cunningham, the "Kangaroo Kid," sprang from the bench, gunning and scoring; burly ex-marine Alex Hannum proved a shrewd and forceful coach. And the 76'ers compiled a sixty-eight and thirteen record, best in NBA history to that point. The Celtics still blocked the entrance to the top floor. This time Wilt's team hammered the Celtics four of five games to take the conference finals. At the buzzer he celebrated by punching the basketball into the rafters. The NBA finals also concluded in victory, over the Warriors of Rick Barry and Nate Thurmond, and Wilt rejoiced.

His reign would certainly continue in 1968 as the 76'ers again overpowered the league, finishing sixty-two and twenty. They began the Eastern Conference finals with a rush, winning three of four games to knock the Celtics to the edge of elimination. During that span the 76'ers averaged a hundred sixteen points a game. In the next three contests Boston, defending aggressively, slashed that output by fourteen points and, by the end of game seven, as Red Auerbach exhorted them from the stands, the Celtics had again prevailed.

That was enough. Wilt Chamberlain again demanded change, and the Los Angeles Lakers beckoned. When he put on his new golden yellow uniform, he joined a team that featured Jerry West and Elgin Baylor. The three superstars instantly created Showtime, a decade before Magic Johnson arrived, and the 1969 team rolled to a league-best fifty-five and twenty-seven record, earning home court advantage in the playoffs. The Celtics, meanwhile, had limped (by their standards) to a forty-eight and thirty-four mark, and logic indicated this would be Bill Russell's final year. Aching knees had undermined his jumping ability, and for the first time he scored less than ten points a game. Venerable Sam Jones, king of the bank shot, was also slowing at the end of his career.

Despite their antiquity, the Celtics opened the playoffs by hand-cuffing the Philadelphia 76'ers, winners of fifty games even without Wilt, and took the series four games to one. Next, the Celtics stifled the New York Knicks four to two. The Lakers throttled their opponents with comparable efficiency, and the premiere matchup in sports – Wilt versus Russell – would unfold a final time. This would be their second clash in the NBA finals; they'd already battled five times in the conference finals, and the Celtics had prevailed every year save 1967. Wilt couldn't permit Russell to win again and escape into glorious retirement. Jerry West and Elgin Baylor were perhaps even more determined; in the NBA finals they'd lost five times to the Celtics and never won.

The Lakers captured the first two games at home, but victory margins were only two and six points. Back in Boston Garden, the dreary slaughterhouse on an old parquet floor, the Celtics won games three and four by margins of four and one. The Lakers took game five by thirteen, moving to the cusp of victory. The Celtics didn't yield, winning by nine back in the Garden. In the first six games, the home team had won every time, and Lakers owner Jack Kent Cooke, confident that trend would endure, ordered thousands of celebratory balloons readied for release from nets high above the floor of the fabulous Forum.

The Celtics replied with a barrage at the start of game seven, nailing eight of their first ten shots to take a twelve-point lead. They still led after three quarters, by fifteen, and Wilt Chamberlain, who'd never fouled out of a game, already had five personals and would have to restrain himself. Fouls also troubled Boston: Sam Jones committed his sixth, and Bill Russell and John Havlicek each had five. With a little less than six minutes to play, Wilt jumped for a rebound and jarred his knee while landing, and asked coach Bill van Breda Kloff to take him out. The Lakers, spurred by Jerry West's scintillating scoring and passing, cut the deficit to two points with three minutes left, then to a single point. Wilt asked to be put back in. Van Breda Kloff, who before taking the job had declared he could "handle Chamberlain," waved the big man off, scoffing, "We don't need you."

They in fact did need Wilt Chamberlain, and a little good luck. Don Nelson, who last week announced he's returning to coach the Golden State Warriors at age sixty-six, fired a foul line jumper too long. The ball hit the back of the rim, bounced straight up, and instead of coming down outside the target, as it normally would, fell straight through the rim. I cursed the TV, as I had so many times during the sixties when fate blessed the Celtics. Nelson's unlikely shot proved the margin in a championship victory; it was Boston's eleventh crown in thirteen years. After the game Russell said Wilt had let his team down when he took himself out. Wilt was livid and for years refused to speak to the man he'd often invited to his mother's Philadelphia home for Thanksgiving dinner. The estrangement was an unfortunate postscript to dozens of stirring confrontations between two supreme players. The Celtics won sixty percent of the games despite Wilt averaging almost twenty-nine points and twenty-nine rebounds. Russell, by comparison, averaged about fourteen points and twenty-four rebounds.

More professional disappointment awaited Wilt Chamberlain in 1970 when the Lakers lost another seventh game of the NBA finals, but this time it was to the New York Knicks, and the decisive fourteen-point margin in the final game precluded pangs about what could have been. In 1972 the Lakers won thirty-three games in a row, still an

NBA standard, and handily beat all three playoff opponents en route to the championship, the second for Wilt and first for long-denied Jerry West. Elgin Baylor, due to injuries, had not played since early in the season. It's ironic that West, whose teams lost in the NBA finals eight times, six to the Celtics, is called Mr. Clutch – with indisputable correctness – while some still insist Wilt just wasn't good enough. At age sixty Wilt explained the resentment: "I was the Goliath of my time. I had too many tools. And I had too much arrogance."

In retirement, Wilt wrote two books: *Wilt: Just Like Any Other 7-Foot Black Millionaire Who Lives Next Door* and *A View From Above*. In the first, Wilt often displays the intelligence and sophistication of a man who's traveled the world and met leaders from politics, business, and entertainment as well as a legion of regular folks. Sometimes, however, he wounds himself and others by too eagerly trying to prove his personal appeal. He asserts, for example, that a man of his cultural excellence naturally finds it hard to meet black women worthy of his company. Regarding white women, they're tolerable only if good looking; it is, he explains, no easier to find a compatible ugly woman than one who's beautiful. He also proudly notes he used to tease his teammates on the Harlem Globetrotters, for whom he played one year between college and the NBA, whenever they went out with a "mullion," Wilt's term for any woman he considered unattractive. He also endlessly complains about those who disagreed he was the greatest. His second book will always be known for The Boast. I'm not going to insult him by quoting the mathematically absurd number of women he claims he slept with. Tennis champion and human rights activist Arthur Ashe responded he "felt sorry for Wilt Chamberlain." Many people did. Ultimately, though, one simply concludes that Wilt cherished mammoth achievement and unprecedented output; hot air didn't diminish his substance.

Wilt continued to immerse himself in sports, lifting weights, playing volleyball, and attending many events. I saw him at a college track meet at Berkeley in 1976. He'd competed in the shot put and high jump in the 1950's at the University of Kansas. In 1977, while living in Santa Barbara, I twice watched Wilt play for the Los Angeles team in the International Volleyball Association. The IVA had an intriguing format: four men and two women always held the court for each team in a league stocked with top players and some ex-Olympians from around the world. Wilt wasn't a forty-year-old celebrity given a pass to promote the league. He was a pro.

I last saw Wilt in person during the 1981 USA Track and Field Championships in Sacramento. He was an enormous presence all three days of competition. At the time I worked as a newspaper correspondent in the press box. Wilt periodically came in for personal chats with people he knew but was firm, even unpleasant, when telling reporters there would be no interviews. He was no more encouraging to kids seeking his autograph. And that's all right, I suppose. By 1981 Wilt Chamberlain had for thirty years been a towering target of admirers, detractors, groupies, journalists, and hangers on. He wanted to enjoy the track meet. And, despite past and subsequent claims, he was working hard to try to line up social activity for the evenings.

The second day of the meet, Wilt stood near the press box, talking to a young man anxious to please the distinguished guest. Finally, frustration in his voice, Wilt asked, "Can you arrange it?"

"Oh, yeah. Tomorrow, for sure," he replied.

"Arrange it," Wilt said.

The young man did not return the following day. As Wilt watched the meet, he spent much time having a rather loud and banal conversation with a young woman who did not, it can subtly be noted, share his dedication to exercise. In his second book he claims that virtually all his women were so beautiful "the Average Joe would have proposed marriage to them on the first date." Yet, Wilt was never married or engaged and boasted he rarely dated any woman more than a couple of weeks, and any time he got bored he simply "fired" them. I share this observation not to criticize a man I admire, but to regret the loneliness that undermined his personal life.

In the nineteen eighties and nineties, though Wilt rarely made headlines, I occasionally read that pro basketball players in action felt the buzz when he entered the arena and stopped to watch as he walked to his seat. I don't know how Shaquille O'Neal really feels about Wilt – the former claims he's much better than Russell, Wilt, and Kareem Abdul Jabbar. He isn't. But he's fundamentally as good.

So, irrespective of team records, when you talk about the best big men ever, you talk about the Big Four. I think Shaquille understands that. He surely hasn't forgotten when Wilt, dressed in street clothes, walked onto the court before a game. Both men warily studied each other, and as seven-foot-one Shaquille shook Wilt's even larger hand, the young man was looking up.

Wilt would've been seventy in August. I can't imagine he's already been gone seven years. He didn't smoke, drank little if at all, and trained his body to endure, but congestive heart failure ended his life as he slept. Sometimes that happens to people who've done everything right and should've had twenty more years. To those who knew or watched him, his personality and presence remain vivid. Bill Russell still feels Wilt Chamberlain as if they were shaking hands before tipoff. They'd reconciled long before the end, and at a memorial service the old champion spoke movingly of his comrade. And recently, with customary eloquence, he noted: "The fierceness of the competition bonded us as friends for eternity."

September 2006

Battling Kids for Rebounds

The experience was so painful and disillusioning I thought I'd never be able to write about it, but in three intervening years there's been enough healing I can finally reveal I tried a modest comeback in basketball. I never envisioned actually playing the game well, or really even playing at all. Competing in basketball against vigorous opposition demands a trim body, lively legs, cardiovascular endurance, court awareness, and great intensity. And recapturing any part of those ancient qualities would've required more time and physical and emotional commitment than I could give.

My task was going to be much simpler: I merely had to prepare myself for a cameo role before my old high school's annual alumni-varsity charity game. There was modest demand for my appearance. A number of former classmates promised donations to the school fund if I'd go out and, while unguarded – I insisted – shoot some jumpers and free throws. Even this unthreatening public display unnerved me, but when I tried to back out several electronic pledges arrived with a reminder: "It's for the kids."

Part of the determination to shove me out there resulted from my having used the alumni-wide email system to offer other 1952 babies five bucks for every basket and twenty for each cheerleader they danced with. I noted those exertions shouldn't faze them since they only weighed about three hundred pounds. Some of the now-distinguished lads were unamused, though I did eventually emphasize that few of them moved the scales as much as I, who've long carried fifty pounds more than my prep playing weight and thirty beyond my prime.

As the essential event loomed a mere three weeks ahead and three hundred miles away, I had to respond, and raced in my groaning 1990 Honda Civic to a sporting goods store to buy white high top basketball shoes and a glowing light brown ball. The shoes looked good caressed by my blue Dockers, and, dribbling, I shuffled side to side while explaining my task to a saleswoman born at least fifteen years after my high school graduation. I didn't need to make any other purchases since I already owned and regularly used gym shorts for such mundane and athletically-insufficient pursuits as calisthenics and labored semi-running on the treadmill. Since I work weekday mornings as well as Monday through Thursday nights, I'd only be available for outdoor workouts three evenings on two consecutive weekends. I didn't consider going to a gym because I knew I'd get trounced.

There was a less painful way. I'd break in with the neighborhood kids always outside playing on a portable basket. I was more than moderately concerned about the transition from waving-as-I-pass neighbor to older-than-their-parents fellow hoopster. What would they think? On a Friday evening I pressed the garage door opener and, shirtless in blue gym shorts and white socks and shoes, dribbled down my driveway onto rough asphalt of the street.

"Hi, can I shoot around with you?" I asked three youngsters.

"Sure," they said.

"You guys are getting better all the time. You play for your school's team?"

"We don't have a team for fifth-graders," said Darryl, the boy who lived across the street.

"Oh."

Without even taking a lay-up, I went straight up – perhaps three inches – for my once-dependable jump shot. This one fell about two feet short and three wide. The kids glanced at each other.

"I haven't shot in at least ten years. I averaged twenty points a game my senior year."

They didn't say anything but were doubtless impressed as my air balls got a little closer to iron each time and ultimately I began battering the rim with shots more like line drives than jumpers. I even made a couple but still felt earthbound, as if impeded by a weight vest. Actually, I was wearing a fleshy vest around the middle.

"Let's play," said a boy from down the street.

"Well, I was just planning to shoot around." And I explained why.

"Come on."

"Okay," I reluctantly said.

Darryl and I teamed against the other two. Determined to instantly assert myself, I dribbled hard to my left, stopped quickly, and cast an eighteen-foot jumper that about dented the metal backboard. At least shots like that are recipes for long rebounds, and this one I lunged for and grabbed, knocking my largest opponent aside with a foul I was already too desperate to call on myself, and went straight for the basket and, instead of putting the ball softly on the board, fired a shot that bashed the bottom of the rim, hit me in the face, and caromed out of bounds.

"Do you have asthma?" Darryl asked.

"Of course not. Why?"

"The way you're breathing."

We rapidly fell behind five-nothing in a game to fifteen goals counting by one. The big kid on the other team was almost as beefy as I was, albeit a foot shorter, and had a good touch on set shots he arched very high.

"Why is a pudgy guy five-foot-one getting set shots on you?" one might ask, and every coach would.

The physical part of the answer has already been suggested, and for a long time I felt almost as if I'd never been on a basketball court. Eventually, a modicum of court sense returned and we caught them at twelve all and I prayed I wasn't going to lose to a couple of eleven-year olds. At this point I could hear the pathological breathing my teammate had commented on and felt the consequences of every sip and puff I'd taken years before. I wanted to quit. Why was I doing this? I couldn't quit. I wasn't going to. I knew what to do. After every shot I charged the boards and got lots of rebounds, more than half offensive. I remember them most because every time I tried to put the ball back up my legs felt leaden and almost every shot underneath slammed into the bottom of the rim and either bounced back into my hands or out of bounds.

Owing primarily to my height and hundred-pound weight advantage, we won, narrowly, by the required two-goal margin. I agreed to another game, played almost as poorly in another victory, and hobbled up my driveway and inside to clean a squalling blister on each heel. My legs were already aching and next morning I struggled to climb out of bed. That would be all for this weekend. I'd be better prepared next time.

The following Friday I bandaged and taped both heels, pushed the garage door opener, and ran out to join two of the fifth graders and three pretty big and mature looking guys. Not wanting any surprises, I asked, "What grade are you in?"

"Eighth."

"You on the basketball team?"

"No, we all play baseball."

When I confess I was relieved not to have to go against even junior high school players, I feel not ashamed but a universe removed from those vigorous days in the nineteen seventies when I'd go to Sacramento State University and north Sacramento and other places around town, looking for good competition.

"Don't you guys have that rim set too high?" I commented.

"Ten feet," said Darryl.

"It's a helluva lot higher than last week."

"Yeah, just nine feet then."

A pipsqueak hoop had overpowered me a week before, and now ten feet looked like eleven. People who regularly play basketball will note even an inch variance.

This game I teamed with the fifth graders. We fell behind eight-zip, and I knew we were going to lose unless (in a conscientious way) I applied my heft to kids seventy pounds lighter and sealed off the boards. At the foot-higher target, however, I began shoving two, three, four, even five shots in a row straight into the underside of a rim I'd once known but that now might as well have been on the moon. I'd understood I wouldn't be good but hadn't imagined a debacle. Though our team won three games, you don't really win when you poorly play a game you'd once been dedicated to.

The following weekend I drove from Bakersfield to suburban Sacramento and eased into the parking lot of my old high school, still the only place I've run out of gas, in 1969. I was of course thankful not to be competing. Even though a couple of guys almost sixty had played well (and would again in subsequent alumni games), I was content in the cafeteria, eating hot dogs and hamburgers and not worrying about the outcome of a game and the probability of playing poorly and embarrassing myself.

Over in the gym everything looked like my old home except the three-point line, which is less than twenty feet in high school. Shots that distance used to go down like free throws. Now they seemed like across-the-river efforts, and almost everything I shot was short until I moved into the fifteen-foot range. My legs felt pretty good, since I didn't have to play defense or elude opponents to get my shots, and I nailed some jumpers and then walked up into the stands where I shook hands with my eighty-year-old former coach and sat back and watched vigorous young men run up and down the court, trying to convince myself I could still do it if I really wanted.

July 2007

Basketball and More in Las Vegas

As summer school ground toward conclusion in late June I was anxious to get a break from teaching and spend hours a day writing in my office at home. I wrote stories on the computer but hadn't remembered, though it happens every year this time, I also need release from solitary concentration. I'd planned plenty of activities but none were beginning for almost two weeks so found myself periodically mired in lassitude that appears when I'm bereft of out-of-home commitments. Mercifully, the NBA Summer League had begun in Las Vegas, and on a Sunday in July I filled my tank and headed east out of Bakersfield on Highway 58.

The forty-mile climb to Tehachapi is always pleasant as it reveals first hills then small mountains alive with oak trees, a soothing contrast to the dehydrated fields of Bakersfield. Alas, motorists thereafter move east toward morose Mojave and barren Barstow, gifts to many standup comedians, then the Mojave Desert, grim and dry and frighteningly hot, and into Nevada, which divine forces decreed be ninety-seven percent hideous. The geographical shortcomings of Las Vegas, though unignorable, are quickly overwhelmed by glorious gambling palaces whose location must have been inspired by forces too dark to contemplate. Why didn't they put these generators of vast wealth along a stretch of California coast, enough of which is still available to benefit the Golden State's forty million struggling residents?

Despite all, I was delighted to be there for but the second time in my life; the first came in 1971 when the community was, by comparison, a hamlet. I drove to my attractive, non-gambling motel about a mile off The Strip and committed a reasonable seventy-two bucks per night, quickly unpacked, and headed to Bellagio, the casino everyone said I had to see: it soothes and glistens and exudes fine living. Former owner Steve Wynn collected hundreds of millions worth of masterworks by Monet, Van Gogh, Picasso, and the boys, installed them in a gallery at Bellagio, and charged customers to take a look. The smiling lady selling tickets warned me Wynn's collection was gone and the current exhibition "wasn't everyone's cup of tea."

"Who's in it?"

"Andy Warhol and Roy Lichtenstein, among others."

The two most publicized icons of sixties pop art sounded worth a fifteen spot. I entered two rooms, about the size of Joe Blow's Gallery, that contained the most lifeless pieces I've seen by Warhol and Lichtenstein, and works by abstract painter Frank Stella were also substandard. No big deal. I was starving after my journey into the desert so headed across the wide hall to a café where I got a chicken sandwich, blueberry muffin, and glass of milk for a tad under twenty dollars. The food was delicious and fueled my foray through the gallery of sculptor Richard MacDonald whose whimsical statuettes of people exercising, dancing, and performing cost five and six figures, and just ask if you want to know how much the big ones go for.

I had something better: a twenty-five dollar ticket to basketball games at the University of Nevada at Las Vegas. Using my notebook as a shield against unrelenting sun, I scurried from the parking lot into Cox Pavilion, a gym with a few thousand seats in the same building as the renowned Thomas & Mack Center, which accommodates almost nineteen thousand fans and for many years was home to coach Jerry Tarkanian's Runnin' Rebels, who won more than five hundred games, a national championship, produced forty professional players, and got tagged with an astonishing number of alleged violations by the NCAA. Tarkanian said it wasn't true there any more than it had been had Long Beach State, and later would say the same at Fresno State: I'm just giving kids from the streets a chance to play ball, and maybe go to class, kids who otherwise might have nowhere to go but down. I agree with Tark. Why should coaches, university presidents, school administrators, NCAA officials, television executives, and popcorn vendors inequitably split a fortune every season while the stars, the poor kids on the court, get nothing but room, board, and three squares a day?

This late afternoon, the guys in motion were professionals, or at least those trying to be, and little Cox Pavilion was almost full of people watching Oklahoma Thunder rookies and assorted others play the Memphis Grizzlies. There was an unoccupied seat on the aisle a few rows up.

"Is this saved?" I asked a handsome young woman.

"No, it's for you," she replied.

She and two female friends were visiting from Connecticut where in the fall they'll begin their senior year at a state university.

"Were you raised in Connecticut?" I asked the one next to me. I only addressed her since I didn't want to lean over and raise my voice, which had suddenly become hoarse.

"Yes."

"I'll bet you're from an elite suburb."

She laughed and said, "Willimantic."

"Sounds like a place William F. Buckley could've lived."

"It's a pretty nice town but several years ago *60 Minutes* came and portrayed us as 'Heroin Town.'"

"It's not that way?"

"Not most places."

In the Oklahoma backcourt I noted two players on opposite sides of the wall of fortune. Shaun Livingston stepped out of high school straight into the NBA and, as a fast and aggressive six-foot-seven point guard who could penetrate defenses and create shots for teammates, seemed certain to be a star. In a February 2007 game his third season he tore up his knee with such force the leg dangled, virtually detached. YouTube warns visitors to be careful about watching the replay, and I'll never tune in again. Now, after two and a half years of strenuous rehabilitation, Livingston is armored in a heavy knee brace and trying to make one of the worst teams in the league. He isn't playing poorly but his speed and instinct to attack are gone, and he understand-ably appears apprehensive about reinjuring the knee. Conversely, his partner in the backcourt, Russell Westbrook, is one of the fastest and most athletic players in the league, last year as a rookie sprinting full court for dunks or, in the half-court offense, slicing to the basket for acrobatic layups.

When action stopped on the court, and tall young men rose from their seats and walked toward concession stands, the Connecticut ladies sometimes cooed, "Hello, there" and such, and wielded iphones to access the internet revealing how many millions of dollars the players make a year, and wouldn't that be nice. Meanwhile, the lady next to me several times left and returned with a pink beverage. Finally, I asked, "Is that wine?"

"Yes," she said.

"I hope you're twenty-one."

"In a couple of months, twenty-two. I'm partying on my vacation."

"You've mentioned seeing a lot of people who haven't taken their medications. Are you studying to be a psychiatrist?"

"No, I'm just working sixty hours a week in a clinic this summer. When the people take their meds, they're usually okay. But when they don't, they're wild."

"What are you studying?"

"I'm majoring in history."

"To be a teacher?"

"A lawyer. But after I graduate I'm going to take off a few years and kick back. Most law students start in their mid- or late-twenties."

Halftime entertainment featured some songs by Michael Jackson.

"Hard to imagine he was already fifty," I said.

"Starting to get old but too young to die."

While the Memphis Grizzlies were hammering the Thunder by what would be a twenty-nine point margin, the ladies continued their entertaining commentary. One evening they'd seen Los Angeles Lakers guard Jordan Farmar at a nightclub, and late Saturday at another spot they'd talked to some Ultimate Fighting Championship competitors celebrating their victories on the card that night at Mandalay Bay. The UFC, and mixed martial arts in general, is rapidly attracting fans intrigued to see men attack each other with punches and kicks and submission holds around the neck, wrist, elbow, knee, or ankle. There were eleven fights on Saturday's sold-out card, and pay per view topped one million viewers and fifty million dollars.

"Was Brock Lesnar there?" I asked. "He's the huge, mean-looking guy."

"They're all huge and mean looking."

"Yeah, but this guy's really big."

I'm confident Brock Lesnar wasn't there or they'd have remembered the former college wrestling champ and professional wrestling thespian who is the UFC heavyweight champ and had that night flung Vegas native Frank Mir around the ring, pouncing on him, immobilizing his head with one massive arm and bashing his face bloody with the other fist. After Mir submitted, Lesnar railed at his groggy foe, flipped off the audience with both middle fingers, made public his bedroom plans that night with his beautiful blonde wife, and insulted the beer company sponsoring the event. UFC president Dana White, who himself is sometimes prone to public tirades, pigeonholed Lesnar in a bathroom and demanded he apologize. And this Lesnar did with seeming sincerity, noting he'd never been the smartest kid on the block and had always wanted to be a fighter and that's how he settled business. He also mentioned he felt he'd given away his first fight with Mir when he was likewise dominating the smaller (two-hundred-fifty pound) man but allowed Mir to wrap three or four limbs around his ankle and leg to force a submission. Lesnar implied that Mir, who had often spoken dismissively about Lesnar's technical skills, needed first to be punished physically, then mentally.

Most who don't follow mixed martial arts probably can't identify the name Fedor Emilianenko. He ranks in his profession where Tiger Woods and Roger Federer do in theirs. He's had thirty-two fights, an enormous number in a collision sport with so many ways to lose, and but one defeat, and that on a cut sustained early in his career. He later reversed that with a technical knockout. Fedor can flatten opponents with either hand but usually wins with chokes, armbars, and other submission holds. Now Brock Lesnar has defeated a renowned submission fighter, Frank Mir, and, with strength and bombast, broken out of the specialty box mixed martial arts had been confined to, and general sports fans around the United States, and in many other countries, are starting to say – as for decades they've done with Dempsey and Tunney, Ali and Frazier, Leonard and Hearns – it's time for Fedor and Lesnar to get it on. Fedor fights for a different company but public demand and money will be the ultimate arbiters and this fight should happen.

While a globetrotting coach sitting behind us commented on the improvement in the Iranian professional basketball league, and the fair potential of Memphis' seven-foot-two Hamed Haddadi, a young man sat in front and looked back at his lady friends who were excited he'd refereed the previous game and might soon be blowing his whistle in the NBA. This was an upbeat group, and after the next game I pumped their hands.

Though the first games began at one p.m. and starting times of six or seven o'clock would be available daily starting Monday, I vowed to be restrained, watch only two per diem, and show up no earlier than a half hour before five-thirty tipoff. In a city where temperatures soar above a hundred in the morning, that meant I had to find indoor activities. Monday I drove to the theater complex attached to the Palms Casino and watched *Bruno*, starring Sacha Baron Cohen, the creative and quite outrageous star of *Borat*. Instead of an English-challenged, Kazakhstani nincompoop seeking the love of Pamela Sue Anderson and making buffoons of numerous American Southerners while so doing, Cohen this time is gay Bruno of Germany who yearns to be transformed into a heterosexual stud. He questions two painfully solemn preachers who offer counsel and evidently don't realize they're being hoodwinked. Bruno attempts to turn macho by going hunting with tough-looking men. But that night, after stripping and trying to sweet talk his way into one of their tents, he's nailed by a profane rebuke.

Before a mixed martial arts event, in a cage surrounded by fans, he ignites cheers from rednecks by denouncing gays and is outraged when his doting assistant yells from the stands that he, Bruno, is gay. Proud Bruno yells to come on down and get into the fighting cage where the men grapple with vigor, though not much skill, thrilling fans until the poignant moment the combatants look into each other's eyes and see love, and begin kissing and hugging and panting while head-clutching men and women watch in open-mouthed agony. Prior to an interview Bruno tells a Palestinian leader he has sun-damaged hair and makes silly comments about Osama bin Laden that prompt the activist to terminate the proceeding. Senator Ron Paul is even more outraged after Bruno tells him they can't start the interview now and should wait in an adjacent room where Bruno tries to seduce the good senator. Bruno also attends a swingers party, tricks a still-clothed man into emulating a variety of sexual positions, then, when the Good Samaritan has gotten naked and mounted a moaning lass,

Bruno disturbs his mentor by stroking the busy man's shoulder. Sacha Baron Cohen makes me laugh harder than any comedian in the world today, and also makes me cringe. That's why he's so funny; he must need bodyguards when he's making movies.

After a nap I drove to Thomas & Mack Center and this time opened my umbrella for the journey across sizzling asphalt. This was a special night, the debut of Blake Griffin of the Los Angeles Clippers, first overall choice in the 2009 NBA draft. Commissioner David Stern entered with a blonde lady, perhaps an administrative assistant, and two security guards covering the rear. The commissioner was undoubtedly sanguine about the league's health as he watched Griffin – six-ten, muscular, clean cut, and only twenty years old – warm up with an arsenal of dunks and soft jumpers, including the traditional (and oft-ignored) bank shot. Seconds after the game started, Griffin sped to a layup. Soon he swished a fall-away jumper and nailed a three-pointer from beyond the top of the key, giving him seven points in about a minute and fifteen seconds. He had ten points after one quarter. Thereafter he scored as he pleased on dunks, jumpers, bank shots, layups, drop-ins, and free throws, which troubled him a bit as he made four of eight. He ended his first game with twenty-seven points and twelve rebounds. Teammate Eric Gordon, a dynamic guard who excelled the second half of last season as a rookie, was powerful at the rim and scored twenty-one points. The losing Los Angeles Lakers were not the reigning champions but a summer squad led by skinny Adam Morrison who continues to strengthen his surgically-repaired knee and may earn a spot on the roster and perhaps some playing time as the ninth or tenth man.

At the final buzzer, Clippers coach Mike Dunleavy, who during regular season usually bears the expression of a man with abdominal pains, verily glided from the stands onto the floor, smiling like a child on Christmas morning, dreaming, perhaps even believing his guys can win enough games to save his job.

In the nightcap, the Kings from my hometown Sacramento lost to the Milwaukee Bucks. No one cared much about the scoreboard. What mattered was the play of the Kings first pick, and fourth overall, Tyreke Evans. This guy is nineteen-years old, six-foot-six, two hundred twenty pounds, and has the first step of a sprinter, the ball handling skills of a point guard, the physique of a wide receiver, the aggression of a fullback, and a rare ability to penetrate defenses at will. He hit eight shots but more impressively drew numerous fouls and made seventeen of nineteen free throws, presented teammates with seven assists, and snatched nine rebounds. Bet on this guy becoming a star.

"Evans'll be great right away, don't you think?" I said to the guy who sat next to me both games.

"Definitely."

"What do you do in New York City, by the way?

"I'm a poker player."

"A professional?"

"Yes."

"You out here for a tournament?"

"No, just a two-week vacation. I rarely play live poker anymore. I prefer online so I can play six hands at once."

"Isn't it a lot of pressure to earn your living that way?"

"Not too much. I was in financial services but got bored."

"How many hours a week do you work at it?"

"About twenty."

He mentioned that nightclubbing Lakers guard, Jordan Farmar, noted above, had been participating in a poker tournament.

"Is he a good player?"

"Not really. He doesn't have time to be. Poker players below professional level generally feel they know almost everything about the game. They don't. There's so much to it. It's like chess."

"How would you rate Farmar?"

"On a scale of one to a hundred, I'd give him a three. And I don't mean that derogatorily."

"What about Jerry Buss?"

He rated the Lakers owner a ten or twelve at the poker table.

Given my compulsive nature I knew not the make any bets because "one would be too many and a thousand would never be enough," as addicts chant in anonymity.

I began Tuesday, day three, my final in Las Vegas, at the Liberace Museum a few miles east of The Strip. There were many interesting photos of the young Liberace playing piano, and some of older brother George holding his violin. Every time I think about George Liberace I remember careening through a Sacramento nightclub in 1972, on the twenty-first birthday of a friend, and feeling sorry George played for peanuts at an obscure place while his brother, colorful costumes aglitter, enlivened audiences the world over. I should have realized the unfortunate thing was my drunkenness, and that George was a lucky man to be paid, even modestly, for doing what he loved.

An even stronger Liberace memory originated much earlier, around 1957 when I was five and living in Bowling Green, Kentucky. On black and white TV one afternoon there was this guy hammering the keys, theatrically raising his hand nearest the screen, smiling, exuding energy, thrilling this kindergartner with a memory almost as strong today as half century ago. That's a star. That was Liberace.

There were also separate photos of Liberace with Elvis and Michael Jackson, both about twenty and looking handsome and healthy.

"How those two let it slide," I said to two museum employees.

"But Liberace wasn't like that," said the older one.

"I know." He died of AIDS at age sixty-seven in 1987. "By the way, I've read about so many stars living in Las Vegas. Whereabouts?"

"Andre Agassi and some of the younger ones live way over on the west side," said the senior lady. "Wayne Newton, Mike Tyson, and record producer Suge Knight live near here."

She gave me directions I followed through suburban desert streets to the high walls of Casa de Shenandoah which encompass Newton's fifty acres of Arabian horses, miniature kangaroos, penguins, flamingos, swans, wallabies, dogs, cats, custom cars, and other collectibles amassed by Mr. Las Vegas during a career of thousands of shows that have transformed his once silky, almost feminine voice into a rather rough instrument that now grinds out his signature song "Danke Schon." Even though Wayne Newton Boulevard is nearby, and for many years there was a Wayne Newton Showroom at the Stardust before it was demolished, and his helicopter readily transports him to his yacht and speedboat on Lake Mead, it's perplexing a man who earns five hundred grand a week doesn't live in a place with a better climate. He must make his own.

Inside Planet Hollywood air conditioning excluded the heat but the saleslady in a gallery was hot to sell me a painting, several times declaring, "Everything here is an original and every painting today is half price. Aren't these paintings wonderful? Which one do you like?"

"This is an unusual way the canvases are folded and stapled over the frames," I said.

"Oh yes, that's how our artists do it for the gallery. Most of them live in the Southwest."

I didn't tell her that as a veteran of hundreds of art galleries my bones told me I was surrounded by reproductions cranked out by machines. And I refrained from picking up a virtual copy of Van Gogh's *Irises* and holding it next to the same painting on a smaller canvas. Either one was available for about sixty bucks, and you don't get good originals from your neighbor for that. You don't even get your frame cleaned.

Vegas is a lousy art town. The best galleries in the casinos sell overpriced lithographs and Giclées and other reproductions of work that feels more decorative than inspired, and away from The Strip the Las Vegas Art Museum has been closed since February twenty-eighth because two million people in the area can't produce the modest number of memberships and donations required to keep the place solvent. Yet, every hour enough money is burned at the craps tables to keep a much larger museum alive. The Southern Nevada Museum of Art was recently closed ten days and can only manage to stay open four days a week in summer. Bakersfield and Fresno, by comparison, have active art museums with a variety of exhibitions. What about the Guggenheim Las Vegas? No one answered the phone. The recording said send an email. Perhaps the Contemporary Arts Collective would be open after noon, as the recording said. I should've called before driving north of downtown and pounding on glass backed by curtains shutting out heat and the rest of the world.

At least basketball is abundant in Vegas, and I watched two games my last night in town before deciding to relax in the Venetian, a place where gentle clouds caress sundown blue sky painted high over canals and lovers ride in gondolas guided by young gentlemen. A cold bottle of water invigorated me before I left and eased into crawling traffic caused by crews repairing a highway to excess – The Strip.

July 2009

Violent Players and Fans

Dozens of us were honoring a retiring colleague and had been too occupied with talk and tri-tip to watch televisions mounted high on the walls of a noisy franchise restaurant. I'd only glanced at the basketball game a few times and last seen that the visiting Indiana Pacers were comfortably ahead of the Detroit Pistons with little time to play. When I next looked up I thought it was the newscast of a riot among aggrieved people in some abject place. But no, this was still the basketball show. Some Pacers had charged into the stands to battle fans in the expensive seats.

What could have caused such unhappiness in the Palace where gladiators make millions and the Romans have enough to pay not merely for tickets but also parking and hot dogs and lots of beer? That's ultimately what started this. A drunken Neanderthal threw beer on Ron Artest as he reclined in victory pose on the scorer's table after big Ben Wallace had shoved Artest in the face following a not-too-hard foul.

NBA Commissioner David Stern was correct in suspending Artest and two teammates, but he erred in banishing Artest for the rest of the season. A less severe penalty – a half-season in exile – would have sufficed. At the same time, Stern should have been aware of, and willing to act decisively in regard to, two issues that are as critical as the fighting.

First, the beer. That's easy. Remove alcohol from athletic events. Ninety percent of fans don't drink alcohol at games and would prefer not listen to inebriated slobs shout insults at their athletic and financial superiors. There'd also be another significant benefit. People wouldn't have to drive home after drinking. The posted limits on beers per customer are meaningless. A hard-drinking fan can load up at a different saloon each time or send a friend on the next beer run. And how is a beer defined? Rationally, it would be twelve ounces of brew. But lots of arenas, in a nation obsessed with supersize, offer beers two or three times larger. If you can't get through a game without a drink, stay home and watch on TV. Is David Stern going to be a tough and righteous commissioner on this issue? Revenues from alcohol sales will probably trump common sense.

The final issue is more personal. Ron Artest is a man under siege from within. Kicking him out of the league for seventy games probably will deter him from reentering the stands with his fists clenched. But it will not address the fact that Artest is yearning for help. His recent request to take a month off during the season, to promote a rap album, was not merely inappropriate; it's part of a pattern of instability that even a few years ago, when he played for the Chicago Bulls, prompted a doctor to prescribe medication. He declined to stick to that regimen.

David Stern can't force Ron Artest to do what the doctor says. But he can insist that Artest participate in counseling twice a week for a year. Authorize that action, Mr. Commissioner, and reduce the suspension to a half-season. Do that the same day you rid arenas of beverages incompatible with pure enjoyment of sports.

November 2004

Memo To David Stern

To David Stern:

Though you have faithfully and on occasion creatively served the NBA, you've done so too long and, consequently, your powers of reason have weakened not merely because of advancing age but due to your delusion that everything you do or delegate is efficient and proper. As that is demonstrably not the case, I must hereby relieve you of all authority regarding stewardship of the NBA, and install myself as the de facto administrative king of professional hoops. Your new task will be to post my player assessments on the NBA website.

In your current condition, Mr. Stern, you may not understand which provocation, of many, ultimately compelled me to hogtie you. It was your incompetent and/or cruel scheduling of the 2010 NBA Summer League games in Las Vegas. Only a moron or sadist would keep spacious Thomas & Mack Center closed Sunday night, and instead force the payers of your inflated salary, the fans, to cram ourselves into the Cox Crackerbox that's called a pavilion but in truth offers little more than a high school gym. And that is not all: we had to take our ass-busting positions an hour early in order to secure one of the few seats you made available to see John Wall, the NBA's top draft pick this year and a young man with drawing power you and your schedule makers well understood.

As eighteen thousand empty seats beckoned a few paces away, the witty public address announcer declared, "It's going to be Wall to Wall tonight, so everyone scoot over and fill empty seats."

In the large arena fans could've arrived when we wanted, acquired a good seat, and relaxed as we enjoyed the league's next major star. John Wall, a six-foot-four point guard, is renowned for authoritative dunks but will most help the Washington Wizards with the athletic but unspectacular maneuvers he exhibited Sunday. In sequence, he hit a long jump shot, showed a smooth shooting touch as he sank two free throws, drove left and pulled up to swish a jumper, turned on speed and made a layup with his right hand, and then accelerated and laid one in with his left. In my notes I wrote, "Wall is quiet and efficient." He didn't need YouTube pyrotechnics. He often passed the ball to teammates positioned to score. Late in the game he twice lofted passes to seven-foot Javale McGee for alley-oops. The Golden State Warriors rallied in the final minutes and sliced the Wizards' lead to two. Wall responded with a move that drew a foul, and confidently converted both free throws to secure victory.

The following evening, Thomas & Mack Center was open but for games with no evident allure. Before I began another sit-athon, I strolled over to the big arena and thought, "Why the hell is the Crackerbox jammed while a couple hundred people are watching here?" That must be how you want it, Mr. Stern. You generally get what you want.

You wanted the big market Los Angeles Lakers to beat the better but backwoods Sacramento Kings in the 2002 Western Conference finals, so the referees in game six whistled the Kings for innumerable phantom-fouls and kept your guys in the playoffs. Maybe that's good business. Maybe you didn't explicitly tell the referees to make calls too ridiculous to attribute to mere incompetence. So even if you didn't know what the referees were going to do, you afterward knew what they in fact had done. And you did nothing.

In the packed Crackerbox Monday night, John Wall again controlled the game with a "quiet and efficient" display of generalship, racing by defenders, throwing passes long and short to teammates who scored, hitting jumpers, and driving to draw a foul and making both free throws and then doing so again. Near the end of the first half Wall appeared to have an open lane, and the crowd roused in anticipation of a highlight dunk. Instead, as he sliced toward the basket from his right, a defender stabbed at the ball which Wall protected by changing its position, pumping it, and long jumped in for a layup.

The Wizards led the Los Angeles Clippers forty-nine to thirty at halftime and Wall already had fifteen points. I then fled the big show in a small place for a little show in the right place, and that should not have been necessary, Mr. Stern.

GTC

July 2010

Notes: Admittedly, I'm as displeased with myself as David Stern since in 2009 I hadn't had the foresight or stamina to join the hordes who stuffed Cox Pavilion to watch Steph Curry light it up.

How to Eliminate Tanking

You've seen them: fighters barely hit falling like boxes off shelves, punters fainting after delicate touches, defenders flopping as if trampled by dribbling rhinos. They're not fooling you, only the referees. And you're even more irritated by behavior of NBA teams in Philadelphia, New York, Detroit, Boston, Minnesota, Los Angeles and elsewhere at the bottom of standings. These teams aren't really fakers. They're not unequivocally tanking. Be fair or put on your sneakers: the players are competing. But their directors, having failed in player acquisition, conclude success is unreachable this season but imminent if, by accumulation of losses, they certify weaknesses and ineptitude in order to secure top picks in the draft.

The NBA must stop encouraging this farce. Rather than promising the most hapless teams more ping pong balls in the lottery, the league can eliminate all malingering by instituting this system: place one ping pong ball for each of the bottom ten teams in the glass cage, spin it, and one at a time determine the order of the draft. Will the NBA do this? Certainly not. It's too simple and fair.

January 2015

PROFESSORS

Basketball at Caltech

You're the basketball coach at Caltech and your most formidable opponents aren't opposing players but the scientific and mathematical pedigree of a school that's generated more than thirty Nobel Prize winners and accepts only students who project to play NBA ball in the classroom. Successful applicants generally score seven hundred points or more on each of the three SAT disciplines – math, reading, and writing – and register very high, though not always perfect, grades in rigorous high school classes, and demonstrate passion for independent academic endeavor in clubs, competitions, and robotics. Those who've built things, such as computers, are also favored by admissions officers who reject almost ninety percent of those trying out for the team.

As a coach you yearn for large and swift players who shoot the basketball like a laser. At Caltech, however, you know such skills are subordinate to mastery of mechanical engineering, astrophysics, computer science, and business economics management. And you understand players won't have as much time as opponents to improve basketball skills; instead, they'll frequently grapple with equations most of the night. Perhaps most daunting, you as coach inherit a tradition of formidable basketball futility: Caltech has won but five league games the last half century and lost three hundred ten straight Southern California Intercollegiate Athletic Conference contents during a twenty-five-year drought. Sometimes the team was competitive but more often overwhelmed and needed advanced math to compute opponents' baskets: a ninety-eight-point loss to Redlands in 2003 boosted the record for largest defeat; the following season La Verne beat the Beavers a hundred eight to sixteen.

You know the records but don't often think about them. You're the current coach, Oliver Eslinger, and you came to Pasadena in 2008, determined to change the program. The season before, Caltech lost games by an average of forty-one points and committed twenty-nine turnovers, a rare degree of imprecise ball-handling. In your third year the Beavers' typical margin of defeat shrank to ten points and turnovers decreased to a reasonable fourteen a game. In the final contest that season your team beat Occidental forty-six to forty-five, the first league victory in the lifetimes of your players and catalyst for a full house of three hundred students to dash onto the court.

Two years later it's noon on a cloudy Saturday and your team, preparing to play Cal Lutheran that evening, moves at half-pace through a one-hour shoot around. Players get loose and practice jumpers, layups, and dribbling. They then huddle around you at center circle, and about half the guys make you look short though you're six-one. The team next sits on the floor in a corner of the gym and watches video images on the wall as you say, "Tell me what play this is. Who's the post player? The point guard? Who're you guarding? What are they doing? We don't want them to reverse the ball here. Put pressure on them..." You then take the team back onto the court to run through plays. Some of your players are good athletes.

The 2007 documentary film *Quantum Hoops* chronicles Caltech's hardwood struggles and features an interview with your predecessor, Roy Dow, who stresses his team has more valedictorians than players with high school experience, and there's simply not enough talent to secure any league victories. I mention this after the shoot around and, sounding like a mellow professor rather than barking Bobby Knight, you tell me: "When I got here, basketball had no culture of recruiting. I inherited a team with only five guys who had played high school varsity ball. Now most of my guys have played in high school, and about half made all league.

"We work our butts off to get our brand out, to let people know our vision. We attend camps every year. Not basketball camps. Academic camps where students may be qualified to come here, and a few may also be candidates for college basketball. I know we can attract students who have a passion for basketball and academics. My goal is to keep recruiting guys who want to improve their games and win the league title and go to the NCAA Division III tournament."

If this still-distant goal is to be realized, Caltech will need more players like KC Emezie, who you describe as having an "unlimited ceiling and athleticism we haven't had. He creates his shots, and is hitting fifty percent of his threes. He didn't play much early in the season but is developing rapidly." You summon him to talk to me. Emezie is six-five, thin, soft-spoken, and a proficient dunker scoring in the mid-teens in recent games. He was born in Lagos, Nigeria and at age five moved with his family to the United States.

"How old were you when you realized you had unusual talent at science and math?" I ask.

"I was interested in learning things when I was five or six," he said. "And in middle school I discovered I was fascinated by physics, which explains so many things. For example, a basketball will roll better down a smooth surface than a rough one. But why? In physics I learned about friction and drag."

"What do you plan to do after college?"

"I may go into web development."

"Caltech hasn't won any leagues games this year but has been pretty close in four of the last five games. How do you think your team's talent matches up with other teams in the league?"

"I think we match up well with any of them."

I thank the young man and, as I request, you call over starting guard Collin Murphy, a senior. I'm intrigued he's listed as being from Wasilla, Alaska.

"You must be asked this frequently, but do you know Sarah Palin?"

"Yes," Murphy says. "I went to middle school with her daughter, Bristol. I didn't see the family as much after she became governor because they moved to Juneau. But they invited some of us to come and eat dinner in the governor's mansion."

"What's Sarah like?"

"She's cool, very friendly, and a lot different than she appeared after becoming the Republican vice presidential candidate in 2008. She moved to the right then. When she was governor she broke down some big oil companies, and she also said abortions shouldn't be determined by states' rights. A lot of Republicans in Alaska didn't like her. There are some hardcore right wingers up there."

"What was life like in Wasilla?"

"It's very small. I played outside all the time. Even in winter I'd just bundle up and go."

"When did you discover your math and science talent?"

"In first grade the teacher started sending me to the third grade class for math and fourth grade for science."

"I hear you guys don't get much sleep."

"Lots of times we sleep two or three hours. Our leading scorer, Michael Edwards, only got one the other night."

"What are your plans after college?"

"I'm a computer science and business management economics major. I'd like to be a project manager. I've been contacting firms all over the country."

"Does being from Caltech help?"

"Most places get back to me right away."

Tonight, impressing Google and Facebook is irrelevant. There's a more complex task: outscore the other team. In warm-ups it's clear Cal Lutheran has larger and more athletic players, and when the game starts it's evident the Kingmen have collectively played thousands of hours more basketball. Those so bright and certain in the classroom sometimes play basketball tentatively and throw bad passes and shoot errantly even when not pressured. They always hustle, though, and play with passion and rebound aggressively. KC Emezie, jittery at the start, makes two reverse layups and a high-arching three point shot. At halftime Caltech trails thirty-one to seventeen.

During break I estimate attendance at about a hundred fifty and see students, parents, and some professors enjoying an upbeat atmosphere. Behind me a young man says to his friends, "There's Roy Dow, the former coach," who is above noted as appearing in *Quantum Hoops*. I later learn online that the urbane Dow, crowned by a shaved head, isn't there to check on his old team; he's just coached the Cal Lutheran women to victory. Dow is greeted by several fans including a striking, mid-forties blonde woman, attired in tight blouse, miniskirt, and high boots. I remind myself not to stare as she moves to talk to others nearby and mentions people she knows who're going to various grad schools.

I'm sitting in the third row but note veterans of the gym line the upper row of bench-style bleachers and use the wall to ease their backs. I too find room at the top, and watch Cal Lutheran shoot and defend well while building leads of eighteen, twenty-one, twenty-three, twenty-five, and twenty-nine points – fifty-five to twenty-six with nine and a half minutes to play. You bench your strongest and toughest player, ardent rebounder and weightlifter Alex Hunkel from Germany, when he yanks the ball from an opponent and seems ready to tussle. You also give significant minutes to reserves who make plays and delight the crowd. The final score's unimportant. It's about the vibe.

February 2013

Notes: With mathematical precision we report that Caltech has developed a dynamic hardwood formula and won a combined thirteen conference games the last two seasons ending in 2017.

John Wooden at the Lectern

I am a peaceful man of faith and daily prayer. I do not smoke or drink or swear, and have kissed but one woman in my life, my lovely wife Nell. I cherish our children, grandchildren, and great grandchildren as well as many friends and colleagues through the decades. For me, family and faith will always be foremost, but I must tell you what you may have surmised: there's an inferno inside that compels me to blow you off the basketball court. One could not otherwise coach ten college basketball champions in twelve years, capture seven consecutive titles, win eighty-eight straight games, and complete four seasons undefeated.

There are moments when the scale of those achievements embarrasses me, and I remind myself of the times when, in a relative sense, I struggled. Our high school team won the Indiana title only once during my three years as the best player in the state. In college at Purdue, where they called me "The Indiana Rubber Man" because I dove into opponents and on the floor as others do into water, I became the first player named consensus All American three years in a row, but our team only won the national championship, by vote, my senior season in 1932.

My first year as a high school coach, our team posted an appalling record of six wins and eleven losses. Even family and faith couldn't relieve much of my pain and embarrassment. "Failure is not fatal, but failure to change may be," I would one day say. I rededicated myself, and our teams went two hundred twelve and thirty-one over the next decade. On weekends I played professional basketball for fifty dollars a game, and during a stretch of forty-six games hit a hundred thirty-four straight free throws. In person I never said it but from here I can: when's the last time you did that, buster?

World War II pulled me into the navy for three years and during this period I realized how lucky I was not to die like so many others, and particularly so since a ship I was originally scheduled to be on was attacked and several hundred perished. In that vein, a couple of decades later, I was booked on a commercial flight in the United States but had to cancel and that plane crashed and killed everyone aboard.

After the war I was playing golf one afternoon in South Bend, Indiana. On a front-nine par three about a hundred eighty yards I stroked a five iron somewhere I could not see but did notice the group ahead jumping and waving and realized I had an ace. On the back nine I hit a decent drive on a par five but thought I probably couldn't get home in two. I pulled out my brassie, which today is about like a two wood, and blasted it toward the green, and that same group started whooping again. Goodness gracious – the ball had gone in the hole for a double eagle. To this day only five people, including me, have recorded an ace and a double eagle the same day. And never again did I come close to either feat.

I was lucky. In 1948 the University of Minnesota, where I wanted to coach in the elite Big 10, tried to hire me but I didn't know since storm-battered phone lines were down between Minnesota and Indiana but functioning from Los Angeles to my home, and I agreed to coach UCLA, provided the Bruins gave me a three-year contract. After two years, the job at my alma mater Purdue opened and I said I wanted to take it. But my bosses, delighted I'd immediately transformed the Bruins with twenty-two and seven and twenty-four and seven seasons, insisted I honor the contract I asked for. I did not fret, though Nell and I were thoroughly Midwestern in style. At prestigious UCLA, which was attractive to many great athletes I knew I could recruit, championships were surely imminent.

In fact, my teams merely hovered between good and pretty good for fifteen seasons, save 1960 when we went fourteen and twelve and some said maybe Wooden just wasn't good enough. That really galled me. I'd already been tired hearing about The Baron, Adolf Rupp of Kentucky, and his greatness and four national titles. I wanted the titles. By 1962 we were back in the NCAA tournament, the first time since 1956, and made it to the Final Four but lost our first game. I was now in my early fifties and wondered if I'd ever break through.

My 1964 team had no starter taller than six-foot-five but featured a pro-caliber backcourt of Walt Hazzard and Gail Goodrich. We zone-pressed opponents and stole balls and intercepted passes and rolled into the championship game with twenty-nine wins and no losses against the much larger and favored Duke Blue Devils. I knew we had a better team. I knew we were quicker. Let's be frank: Duke was all white. Southern teams were going to have to change. I'd been coaching black players since my first collegiate job, at Indiana State in 1946-47, and refused to play anywhere I couldn't bring Clarence Walker. In 1964 our sixteen-point run against heavy-footed Duke propelled us to a ninety-eight to eight-three victory. We repeated as champions in 1965.

Meanwhile, I had recruited the finest high school basketball player in history, Lewis Alcindor of New York City, and if freshmen could've played in 1966 we'd have won then, too. Led by Lewis and other fine players in 1967, we both dominated and intimidated everyone – yes, the latter pleased me – en route to an undefeated thirty-win season. We would've been undefeated the following season but Lewis had a scratched eyeball and shot poorly during a seventy-one to sixty-nine loss to Houston and hot Elvin Hayes before fifty-two thousand fans in the Astrodome. A lot of people said Houston was too good, that Lewis was overrated and so was his coach. I may have impersonated a minister-coach before and during our rematch against Houston in the NCAA semifinals, but I felt more like General Patton storming through Europe and made darn sure our troops beat those cocky fellows as badly as possible, which was a hundred one to sixty-nine on the scoreboard and worse on the floor. We then manhandled North Carolina seventy-eight to fifty-five for the title. The following year we overwhelmed another inherently slow team, this one from my old Purdue.

I'm not going to give you too many more details. I generally sat composed on the bench, gripping a rolled up program, and in a gentlemanly but persistent way scolded the referees for not calling more fouls on the other team. Some say I often insulted referees and opposing players, but I don't remember that. In 1970 and 1971 we won our fourth and fifth straight championships – and sixth and seventh overall – led by Sidney Wicks and Curtis Rowe. Then the big red head Bill Walton, who I told to either cut his hair and shave or I'd miss him, controlled both backboards his first two seasons, undefeated in 1972 and 1973, while making his teammates better. He also converted twenty-one of twenty-two shots in the title game against Memphis State. I'm still amazed we lost at all in 1974. Good heavens, we slipped four times, the last being in the NCAA semifinals. In 1975, with a new group of starters, we stood at twenty-seven and three following our semifinal victory when I announced it would be time for me to leave after the championship game. I wish Adolph Rupp had still been coaching when we beat Kentucky ninety-two to eighty-five. What really mattered, though, was that we had done our best, and, to a lesser extent, that I got to walk off the court with a tenth net around my neck.

If you watched us play, you know before each game I'd turn to look behind our bench and wink at Nell. She was my ultimate love, and when she died of cancer in 1985 our son and daughter planned to help me want to survive. And I usually did. Whenever I felt I needed to die, I reminded myself of my many aphorisms over the years that urged people to help others and to learn and adapt and persevere. I too bore those obligations. I spoke at clinics. I gave interviews. I attended many UCLA basketball games. I walked a round of golf with Tigers Woods. I spent time with my grandkids and great grandkids. I continued to read the news and history and poetry. For a century I believe I did all right.

June 2010

Notes: Lewis Alcindor changed his name to Kareem Abdul Jabbar early in his professional career.

Adolph Rupp on Integration

Don't call me a racist. You didn't know me, and neither did those who offer one-liners about my life as basketball coach at the University of Kentucky from the Great Depression to the first Nixon administration. Times were different and so were the rules. You need that perspective in order to understand *Glory Road,* but don't expect to learn much about me because it's only a movie and primarily about Don Haskins and his 1966 team at Texas Western University. And though the Hollywood people at times insinuated I was a symbol of the Old South, I watched the whole show and especially enjoyed the finale when you see skills I used to create four national champions and inspire Kentuckians to rise in the morning and bow toward Lexington to say three Hail Rupps.

Every time my boys lagged in the big game, I challenged them to be worthy of the Kentucky Wildcats, the finest basketball players in the world. I assured them they could win. They would win. And, by implication, I'd become the greatest coach of all time. It could've happened. It should have. I was destined. I never stopped believing that. History came a little too soon. The first time five colored players started for a team in the college championship game, Texas Western ran and jumped and defended like no one we'd seen that season and beat us seventy-two to sixty-five.

Now, I hope you know upstart Coach Haskins and I weren't really involved in a battle of racial politics and social change. We were two guys who'd played college ball for legends, Haskins for Hank Iba at Oklahoma A&M and I about thirty years earlier for Phog Allen at Kansas, and we were obsessed with winning, not leading political crusades. Do you really think, as the movie implies, that as late as 1966 a sixty-five-year-old man who'd always breathed basketball could be unaware of the talent of colored players. Don't insult me. A decade earlier Bill Russell had led the University of San Francisco to sixty straight wins and two college championships and then started dominating the National Basketball Association as a Boston Celtic.

I'd also seen Wilt Chamberlain and Elgin Baylor and Oscar Robertson star in college and the pros.

I knew Negroes could help my program, and wanted them to, and anyone who says I didn't is wrong. How badly did I want? Not enough, I concede, to become a civil rights leader and take on the whole South and lots of other areas too. We played in the Southeastern Conference. Look around. Who else in our conference had colored players at the time? No one. In fact, SEC schools generally refused to schedule home games against opponents with even one Negro. I was ready to take care of that. Twice I petitioned the league to integrate. That brought fire from college presidents, athletic directors, regents, boosters, and fans. Same thing happened in 1961 after I'd told some spunky reporter that I just might integrate and go into opponents' towns and start collecting forfeit victories until they played.

In 1964 I tried to get the greatest high school player in the history of Louisville, Wesley Unseld, but the University of Louisville people told Unseld the only reason I'd wanted him was because I thought he was white. I hope you don't believe that. The following year I also visited the home of star guard Butch Beard but he later said I scared his mother with stories of hostile crowds on the road in the South. I was just trying to entertain the woman. Maybe the colored people and I just didn't understand each other. But I always had a keen eye to spot more modest white talent in the hills of Kentucky and brought those boys to Lexington and made them winners. I certainly did see the future, though. After Texas Western beat us in 1966, I knew who was going to win the next three titles: John Wooden at UCLA. He couldn't miss with that New York City kid Lew Alcindor, graceful and determined at seven-four. I had a real good boy in six-nine Dan Issel out of Illinois, but it wasn't the same.

I eventually got motivated enough to seriously counterattack, in 1969, and sign our first Negro, seven-foot Tom Payne. He left us after only two years to turn pro. In 1971, after forever avoiding our little cross-state neighbor, Western Kentucky, we had to play them in the NCAA tournament, and the long and agile Hilltoppers beat the tar out of us a hundred seven to eighty-three, and advanced to the Final Four. Next season I turned seventy, the mandatory retirement age, and was forced to leave the job I'd devoted my life to.

I'm still keeping up with basketball and think I understand today's players and am ready to return to coach guys named Shaquille, Amar'e, Kobe, LeBron , and Chauncey. I'll have them running the greatest fast breaks ever. And I'll hire my 1966 All American Pat Riley as assistant. He needs a better role than a six-four Rupp's Runt jumping center against the big boys in *Glory Road*.

January 2006

LEBRON

The Battle for LeBron James

I'm grateful for the passion and wealth focused on me since puberty and, particularly, in the delirious days since long-yearned-for free agency has given me the opportunity to bestow my interplanetary style of basketball on a new metropolis where fans will also call me King James.

The President of the United States is beseeching me to come to Chicago. The Mayor of New York City has beckoned me to that grand stage. I could list every political powerhouse and all economic and entertainment luminaries in each NBA city, but that is unnecessary. You, too, know about the frenzy. I'm in my private jet en route to Hawaii, wondering. What am I to do?

The millions who read this column will not have to wait till Independence Day to foretell the future. My thinking is thus. The Chicago Bulls promise the best pure basketball scenario: they already possess two star players, point guard Derrick Rose and center Joakim Noah, who can consistently punish opponents in the playoffs, as they recently did to my devoted but championship-unworthy teammates; the Cleveland Cavaliers prevailed in that series only because of my virtuosity. I'm confident tall and feisty Noah can control ten to twenty rebounds per playoff game, against even the finest competition, and that blooming Rose can relieve me of oppressive ball-handling duties far from the basket and generate shots for me, rather than my always having to create shots for myself and others. The Bulls' role players are already adequate, and I don't doubt they and the two stars and myself would command a title next year and relieve me of off-season angst from another playoff fanny-whipping like that recently administered by the distinguished Boston Celtics.

I must also consider the off-court enticements. Chicago is the most robust economic market outside of New York and Los Angeles, and I believe I'd become the most powerful businessman in the City of Broad Shoulders since New Yorker Al Capone stormed west and applied a full-nelson. I appreciate, as well, Oprah Winfrey's offer to let me take over her show when she soon retires to lovely Montecito. President Obama's desire to serve as my chief of staff is certainly alluring, but I've urged him to continue in his present job until, and unless, I call.

The New York Knicks are assuring me they'll get another star, but, even if it were Toronto's sleek power forward Chris Bosh, we would still be minus a third knockout artist, a deficiency that would ensure continued playoff degradation. The Knicks' vow to acquire the right guys is unpersuasive since this management group is more adept at cooking the books, tanking several straight seasons, and goosing female employees than building a dynasty.

I nevertheless consider New York a worthy suitor. I love the city's excitement and energy and its self-proclaimed status as the sports, entertainment, literary, and financial epicenter of the world. I appreciate Mayor Bloomberg's offer to maintain a suite for me in the right fist of the Statue of Liberty. I'm intrigued by Spike Lee's vow to give me his penthouse and live in a Central Park tent. I'm humbled the city wants to drop Madison and simply call our crib LeBron Square Garden.

I am also tempted by the Clippers of Los Angeles. Though their owner is a miser and buffoon, he has managed to acquire the requisite two stars, power forward Blake Griffin and smallish shooting guard Eric Gordon. In 2009 I considered Griffin the most talented rookie since I entered the league but, inevitably, the Clipper hex inflicted a leg injury that shelved the massive and once-mobile lad an entire season. Something unfortunate befalls everyone who joins that team. Wise employees have escaped. Rather than unfurl the red-flag list, I will merely cite coach Larry Brown, who would win championships at the helm of the University of Kansas and the Detroit Pistons. Imagine the void if he'd stayed with the Clips.

I'd be delighted to play for the other basketball tenants at Staples Center – the Los Angeles Lakers – but they cannot pay me a fair wage since they're capped out on superstar Kobe Bryant and seven-foot obstacles Pau Gasol and Andrew Bynum. If I went to Miami, I'm not convinced the Heat could afford another star to give Dwyane Wade and me what I need. And would Dwyane be duly deferential? Would Pat Riley's intensity compel me to gag him at critical moments?

I'm contemplating these onerous issues in Sacramento, where an air force general adroitly lands my jet on a farm near the confluence of the American and Sacramento Rivers. Kings owners Gavin and Joe Maloof arrive in a limousine and beckon me inside. Thousands of farmers, fans, and media members converge outside, urging me to join their team. They have Tyreke Evans, a young point guard who almost plays like a slightly-smaller me. They also have a series of poor records and no third option in the clutch, I remind myself as the limo pushes through humanity. It stops, and the Maloofs exit from opposite doors in back. Governor Arnold Schwarzenegger bounds from the driver's seat.

"LeBron," they in unison shout. "Come to Sacramento and the Capitol is yours."

May 2010

Dan Gilbert Condemns

As a rich and righteous man I must try to soothe you after that evil and narcissistic creature bitterly disappointed us with his deceitful and degrading behavior. Indeed, he has betrayed you and me and all of Cleveland and northeast Ohio in despicable and cowardly ways that dwarf the traitorous acts of Benedict Arnold. This creature devastated his city and his team, which I own, and his fans, who pay me millions every year, certifying he's a heartless beast. And of course he's a quitter. He quit in four of the six games during our playoff loss to the Boston Celtics this spring. Watch the tapes. They prove he's a lout and a loser. Only my magnanimous nature compelled me to offer him a guaranteed hundred twenty-five million dollars to play the next six years for my Cavaliers. I'm not bitter the value of my franchise, which had increased by a hundred million dollars on his coattails, probably plummeted a quarter billion bucks when he stabbed us in the back and declared he was going to sign with the Miami Heat. Let me guarantee you right here on this official team website, in even larger type than the heap big type I've been using in this compassionate letter, that my bold Cavaliers will win an NBA title much sooner than the satanic Miami Heat and the creature and his two lapdog stars, Dwyane Wade and Chris Bosh. His bad karma will infect all of south Florida and his team will be pitiful losers. Their tragedy will only cease when the cowardly quitter betrays another team and another community and takes himself straight to hell. For us in glorious Cleveland, that is where LeBron James already dwells.

July 2010

LeBron Visits Beloved Cleveland

Evidently a beast I shall ever remain. I have concluded thus in the days since my virtuoso return to Cleveland, where on a typically-frigid northern Ohio night I serenaded my former teammates and, by extension, the fans who used to cheer me but now only boo and curse, with thirty-eight points including a delicious twenty-four in a third quarter, composed by Mozart, during which I also verbally reminded some Cavaliers, in a manly way, just who I am and they are not.

Before you don your crucifix and label me a trash-talking bully who is clueless about himself in particular and life in general, as many professional moralizers have done, please grant me a few words of explanation. Several months ago, when I announced on a special television program that I would be leaving Cleveland after a lifetime in the area and seven splendid years leading an otherwise nonde-script group of Cavaliers into the international limelight, the owner of the franchise and many others in the area, and more than a few elsewhere, called me many unpleasant names and burned me in effigy and threatened my family and me, and one very brave sportswriter went on air and said my family and I probably would not be safe living in my native Akron. How would you feel, if you'd merely decided to move from your hometown to a prettier place in order to work with more talented people? Indeed, I'm not callous about the human heart, and know you'd be wounded and angry, and, like me, would take names while yearning for an opportunity to counterstrike. In most professions you wouldn't get that chance. In basketball you would.

In Cleveland the squalling fans, whom I still love and respect, generated much unpleasantness in the days leading to my appearance with the Miami Heat, and security in the arena had to be manifestly increased. On game night there were many T-shirts and placards of profundity, among them LeBum, Benedict Arnold, Quitness, Betrayed, and Lyin' King. When I entered the arena I was denounced, every time I touched the ball I was reviled, every moment there I felt the blistering eyes of jilted lovers. And with utmost clarity I understood how fortunate I'd been to end this marriage.

December 2010

Dallas Does James

This thing is over and you know it so don't try to ruin my coronation. We're up one game zip and by fifteen points with seven minutes left and our speed, quickness, and athleticism are overwhelming the timid Dallas Mavericks. Look at the seven-foot German, Dirk Nowitzki. He's afraid of us and so are his creaky teammates Jason Kidd, Jason Terry, and Shawn Marion. Tyson Chandler's tall and young but a career underachiever and J. J. Barea, five-foot-ten, at most, never will be a big-time player. Terry gets hot on jumpers a little while, and Kidd and Marion score to slice our lead to four, but I'm not really worried. Did you see me crush the Boston Celtics and the Chicago Bulls in previous playoff rounds? I'll own this fourth quarter. Nowitzki hits a jumper and I miss two three-pointers before he hits a left-hand layup and a three-pointer to put those guys up by three before we tie it. Now I'm sure we'll win. We're at home. The Mavericks will choke. Nowitzki can't get to the basket, not all the way, and again uses his left hand to kiss the ball off the board. It's disgusting, a non-athlete tying the series at one.

Three days later we storm into Dallas and win game three by two points and know we'll get at least one of the next two in their house. With ten minutes left we're in control by nine and sissy Nowitzki is sniffling and complaining about a sinus infection. He's only scored eleven points and won't do much in the crunch. I'm confident of that but he keeps scoring, ten down the stretch, including a layup with fourteen seconds to play, and grabs five rebounds in the quarter while I can't figure out that stifling Dallas zone defense and am reluctant to shoot and frequently miss when I do, and this series is even.

Before game five, following the shootaround, Dwyane Wade and I send little Dirk a message: as cameras roll we giggle and sniffle while pulling our shirts up over our noses. That'll shake him up and keep us relaxed. And it sort of works. I get a triple double, seventeen points along with ten rebounds and assists. But how do the critics respond? They call my triple-double weak and irrelevant. Folks, there's no such thing as a bad triple-double. Dirk Nowitzki doesn't get one though he does score twenty-nine points, including eight in the fourth quarter, and our bombardier opponents nail thirteen three-pointers to our eight, a fifteen-point advantage. Pipsqueak Barea and ancient Kidd combine for seven of ten from downtown. God must love them. Meanwhile, I score but two in the fourth and have a late-game sequence of missed jumper, offensive charge, turnover, and missed jumper as we lose and trail two games to three.

None of that's going to matter. We're going home to South Beach where the Miami Heat are devastating and I'm ready to play two historic games that'll win us the title. Nowitzki starts bricking jumpers and hits only one of twelve before half yet we still trail by two. The second half can be brilliant but Dallas keeps throwing in radar-guided threes, eleven for the game to our seven, more than the victory margin that I often try to erase with hot-potato passes instead of drives to the rim. Sometimes I'd rather anyone shoot but me. I don't know why that is but don't care because next year I'll definitely get my first ring.

June 2011

Hires Basketball Guru

Humbly I accept your inspired proposal to serve as personal basketball coach and psychotherapist, and agree that vigorous corrective action must at once be undertaken lest you become not a celebrated King James but a reviled and even laughable figure on the American cultural landscape. Do not further fret. Your utterly generous offer of a ten million a year plus a free South Beach penthouse, chauffeur, and social considerations is sufficient, and I shall with haste board your private jet taxiing now in front of my home.

In a few hours I land in your tropical bailiwick and review my new blueprint, "Regimen for LeBron," in back of the limo driven by black-uniformed Pat Riley who eases by the opening iron door and down into the garage beneath your secret subterranean gymnasium. I doubt anyone else knows you're here. Even those brought in to berate and battle you will arrive blindfolded.

I know you're shocked by your first combatant, Dirk Nowitzki, the stellar German gunner who's staring at you and doubtless remembering you considered him inferior but who trounced you in crunch time, dozens of points to zero, to highlight the Dallas Mavericks' four games to two face slap of the not-as-wonderful-as-self-proclaimed Miami Heat. Don't worry. Dirk is not here to continue the drubbings. He's yelling in strident German, though, thankfully, not with a throaty Austrian accent, and the translator, ever-dutiful Pat Riley, is thus rebuking you, like millions of others, for not establishing a formidable low-post game.

But Dirk's not a killer in the low post, either, you protest. True, but he's four inches taller and one of the greatest long shooters in history. We'll deal with that during other sessions. Now Dirk, through Rottweiler Riley, is accusing you of liking to pick on smaller players and, when they push back, becoming meekly content to cast off usually-errant twenty-five-footers, which are decidedly outside your operational range. It's time to learn the basics of interior destruction.

Dwight Howard sprints onto the court, brandishing a frame much larger and more muscular than yours, ignores your feeble hello, and takes up an aggressive defensive position underneath the basket. Dirk orders you to pound Howard with your back and buns, and for the next two hours, with but two brief respites, you're from both sides drilled to spin rapidly right and left toward the baseline. At first you have several shots blocked, by the finest inside defender in the world, and then you clank quite a few, but, blessedly, you eventually become an enraged but still-focused warrior, not thumping your chest in the faces of weaker men, but scowling at and pushing and outmaneuvering the baddest of big man as you swish baseline jumpers or drive past Howard for strong layups and thunderous drunks. After an extended break, lasting a full three minutes, you do the same things in reverse, spinning right or left to the inside, and either create space for right-hand hooks or short jumpers or lanes to the rim. And an elated Nowitzki, forgetting his native tongue, announces in English that your teammates will be open in scoring position, rather than in the irrelevant outlying stations of the finals when you repeatedly unleashed paranoid passes rather than do what you're now working on and are manifestly qualified to continue. Dirk and Dwight embrace you and vow to work with you the rest of the week, and periodically throughout the summer, though they stress you can also hire other stalwarts as sparring partners. Indeed, I've already booked Tyson Chandler and Andrew Bynum, and am determined to train you to be resourceful and aggressive inside against bigger men.

The following week you plant hands on hips and grimace as Ray Allen glides onto the court and eases around the arc, pointing at the basket. You're going to shoot twice as many three pointers as ever, he promises. In practice. And you're going to shoot fewer in games. You and Ray then start releasing long jumpers, his soft, smooth, and well-targeted, and yours hard and ominous, like the trajectory of a shot put. I've read lots of quotes of you bragging about how big and strong you are and how nobody would dare attack you, Ray says. Don't try to be a defensive end or the heavyweight champ, he continues. You're packing ten extra pounds, most of them in your shoulders, and that's limiting your flexibility when your arms are extended above your head, in other words when you most need touch as a jump shooter. Trust me, he insists, you'll never be a good long-range shooter as long as you have that much muscle mass nor will you be a dependable medium-range shooter under stress or when tired, both problems you often experienced against Dallas. And that emphasizes another concern: your stamina is also diminished because of extra weight. How many weak shots are you going to cast in the fourth quarter? Trim down, keep your energy up, take fewer three pointers, don't think you're me when a few long ones do drop, says Ray, and put the ball on the floor so you can get inside or to the foul line. When defenders close your lane, pull up for the midrange jumpers I guarantee you'll nail Thank you for promising to double the number of practice jump shots.

Since your ball handling, passing, and rebounding are generally solid even in defeat – you had nineteen rebounds in your triple-double in the closeout loss to Boston in game six last year and another triple-double in game five last week against Dallas – I've determined that post moves and jump shots are the only mandatory physical additions to your off-season regimen. Regarding mental adjustments, we have much work, but you have a healthy mind that's problematic only when you become intoxicated by your fame and celebrity, which began too soon. I'd originally planned to assign you several weeks of part-time work in a McDonald's but decided that experience might damage what we must confess is a rather fragile spirit. So don't worry. You'll be selling clothes at a cool shop in a South Beach mall, and after what will be only minutes of embarrassment you'll relax and start relating again to people as equals, and they'll like you for it and next season will root for you as you alternately pound finals opponents inside and nail them with jump shots and, as a new man of the masses, hoist a trophy fans consider theirs too.

June 2011

LeBron Released

I'm not angry or bitter many called me loser and coward when I left my hometown. I'm in overdrive and have been since late game six when, facing execution by the San Antonio Spurs, I unleashed in ways only I can, firing inside, outside, everywhere, assisting teammates, swarming opponents, drilling sixteen points in a fourth quarter to force overtime and then push Miami Heat into the ultimate duel, game seven against San Antonio Spurs.

Who's going to stop me? I never asked that two years ago and played timidly against Dallas, and howlers again set upon me. But let's not dwell. Let's remember winning my first championship last year, against Oklahoma City and Kevin Durant, and celebrate game seven 2013. I won't brag. Don't believe in that. I knew my off-season work made me the most confident as well as best player on any floor, and seized the game, scoring thirty-seven points and demanding twelve rebounds. I hit half my threes and all free throws and passed and stole some too, guiding my team to a second straight title. If I'd done less, they'd be calling me names. Right now I imagine it's just King James.

June 2013

Curing Dan Gilbert

As a psychiatrist, a man of medicine and healing, I am both legally and emotionally required to guard the privacy of my patients, and am not ignoring sacred duty here by discussing my long-term treatment of Dan Gilbert, founder of giant mortgage lenders, builder of businesses and employer of thousands in downtown Detroit, and, most significantly, owner of the Cleveland Cavaliers and, until hours ago, an obsessive and quite dangerous enemy of the basketball player LeBron James.

When Gilbert, after four years of rigorous therapy, suddenly ceased loathing LeBron, he in writing authorized me to share our therapeutic experiences, believing other troubled people could learn how to overcome anxiety and hatred. I attempted to dissuade Dan Gilbert from undertaking this noble but masochistic effort but, like all self-made billionaires, he insisted on his way, and said we must review the painful past.

"You just took down your letter to LeBron from the team website," I said.

"Yes, everyone remembers the venom, but some have forgotten that the spontaneously-conceived prose came from a devastated man. Let's review the highlights. When LeBron announced he was leaving my Cavaliers, after seven Herculean seasons, to play for the more gifted Miami Heat, I at once demoted him to a 'former hero' who has 'deserted' us, leaving us starving in a psychic foxhole, after a 'several-day, narcissistic, self-promotional buildup,' and that the fans, to whom I addressed my feelings, 'don't deserve this…cowardly betrayal.' They 'deserve so much more.' Indeed, 'I personally guarantee that the Cavaliers will win an NBA championship before the self-titled former king wins one.' None of us deserved his 'shameful display of selfishness and betrayal, but we must realize 'some people think they should go to heaven but not have to die to get there.'"

I met Dan Gilbert later that dark day in 2010, having been summoned by police who responded to the 911 call, from a distraught woman, about a man threatening to harm himself and LeBron James and assorted others. Gilbert was writhing on his back in the carpeted living room of a still-secret mansion.

"In the name of God, do something," his family and staff urged me.

From my medicine bag I at once retrieved a syringe laden with Happy Serum and plunged the needle into the largest vein of a Dan Gilbert arm. Within minutes he stopped moving and merely whispered, "He's ruined me, he's ruined us every one." In my forthright medical opinion, had I not interceded and followed up with cutting edge therapy, Gilbert would have been forever locked in a vortex of rage and bound to destroy himself.

Responding at once, I ordered the installation of hundreds of baskets seven-feet high in all the palaces and offices of Dan Gilbert. Perhaps naively, I expected the hyper-dunking Gilbert, the new king of the boards, to feel less angry. Instead, he daily screamed a multitude of epithets, many of which I refuse to quote, but can politely note a few, "In your face, bitch" and "Down you lying throat" and "Up your arrogant ass." I had hoped to wean my patient from all medications within a fortnight but since living without sedation pushed Gilbert to the precipice of insanity, I prescribed twenty milligrams of Mellow daily, and explained, "Dan, your money is meaningless in this matter. The doctors of Elvis and Michael Jackson should be in jail. You will receive this amount of medication every day the rest of your life, if you want it, and it is quite therapeutic at this level. But you will never, at least from my pen, receive a single milligram more of this or any other medication."

Dan Gilbert assured me he too was aghast at the doctor shopping of Elvis and Jackson and, more so, at the drug-dealing mentality of their unscrupulous physicians. I appreciated that in Gilbert I had a patient of high intelligence and a reasonably strong, albeit seriously damaged, emotional makeup, and who was ready for the next therapeutic phase. I hired, with Gilbert's money, a crack Hollywood editorial team to assemble many hours of footage of LeBron James missing dunks, layups, short jumpers, medium jumpers, three-pointers, and getting shots blocked and throwing balls away and dribbling them off his knees and getting blown by on defense and getting dunked on and committing foolish fouls and scowling and shouting and gesticulating and daily slumping off the court after his hundredth straight loss.

At times Dan Gilbert undercut his treatment by sitting in a baseline seat when the Cavaliers played the Heat and watching LeBron pillage his team. My medical staff and I were always on hand and ready with emergency measures and insisted on an immediate return to therapy, which I augmented with new LeBron-face punching bags, heavy bags, dart boards, and video games all of which Gilbert attacked with glee, growling at moments of triumph.

The horror of LeBron being in the 2011 NBA finals dissipated when I sensed Dallas getting hot in the series and decided not to further, and secretly, medicate Dan Gilbert, and was thrilled as he when a rather timid LeBron and his Heat crumbled. In 2012, despite my offer to lower all Gilbert's rims to six-feet and accompany him to the world's most beautiful places without televisions, he demanded to watch the Heat play the Oklahoma City Thunder for the title. It was a mistake, and as LeBron, Dwyane Wade, Chris Bosh, and company moved toward victory, and demolition of Gilbert's promise to first bring home championship hardware, the distraught Cavs owner had to be straight-jacketed and issued two hefty syringes of Happy Serum and shown a dozen hours of LeBron Bloopers. "Yeah," he said, "he's a bum who contributed little to the victory." In 2013 we believed the San Antonio Spurs were better and began celebrating in the second half of game six when LeBron appeared defeated. Appallingly, our departed king unleashed scoring and leadership reminiscent of Michael Jordan and Bill Russell, and I reached for my medicine bag but held off as I noted that Dan Gilbert was not hysterical, merely crying in a dignified way, and that he also did when LeBron hoisted his second trophy after game seven. Gilbert, though no doubt tempted, did not misbehave during the 2014 finals as the Spurs devoured the Heat. He only said, "LeBron choked again. Wish we had Tim Duncan and Manu Ginobelli."

Then he returned to his seven-foot rims and special LeBron films and punching bags and video games and was having a great time when the phone rang. It was one of LeBron's representatives. Would he be willing to discuss bringing LeBron home to Cleveland? To his knees

Dan Gilbert dropped and shouted, "Hallelujah."

July 2014

At the Summit

Two championships aren't nearly enough. I know Bill Russell rebounded, shot blocked, and emotionally guided the Celtics to eleven titles in thirteen years. But that was half a century ago. Today, facing more great athletes, Russell would probably only lead four or five champions. I'm a historian but more concerned about recent guys like Tim Duncan. He has five titles, so do Kobe Bryant and Magic Johnson. Michael Jordan owns six, same as Kareem Abdul Jabbar. I've got to get at least four, like Shaquille O'Neal. Everyone senses that. If I fail, then I'll be judged as merely one of the handful of greatest players ever. That's inadequate and not who I believe myself to be.

If that sounds selfish, remember I've always been a team player, a passer, a facilitator, a general on and off the floor. I'm about winning. That's why I'm writing this in my hotel room the night before we play Golden State in game five of the 2015 NBA Finals. It's two-two, and if we can win the series without injured all stars Kevin Love and Kyrie Irving, people will remember this as one of the greatest achievements in the annals of sports, and I'll be the one credited. Don't call me egocentric. In my place, you'd want the same. I logged forty-seven minutes a game the first three. Try that on an NBA court accelerated by a twenty-four-second shot clock.

In game one, though we still had Kyrie till near the end, I had to shoot from everywhere and pass and rebound and play defense all night, scoring forty-four points, grabbing eight rebounds, and mainlining six assists. We could have won, and should have. I missed a shot at the end of regulation. It's on me we stumbled into overtime and got blown out. Fine, bring on game two. I was in a zone, seeing the court better than others, moving big and fast like only I can, cleaning the boards sixteen times, and threading eleven assists. I made only eleven of thirty-five shots but canned fourteen free throws and totaled thirty-nine points of our ninety-five that beat the Warriors by two in another overtime. We were gassing with a slender seven-man rotation but got our mandatory win at Golden State.

Back in Cleveland, the city that loved me till it hated me when I left and now loves me more, I was both frenzied and calm. We needed the third game. We may be few but we're big, Tristan Thompson, Timofey Mozgov, and I, and the Warriors have struggled to handle us. Tristan vacuumed thirteen rounds, I consumed twelve and generated eight assists and forty points, and our new hero, scrappy Matthew Dellevedova, who played only nine minutes in game one behind Kyrie, dove on loose balls like an enraged linebacker and also hit seven shots and totaled twenty points, helping us topple the Warriors by five in blessed regulation. I knew what people said: LeBron's in a hoops place no one's entered. I loved it but told an interviewer after the game I didn't know if I could keep posting monster numbers: my hundred twenty-three points is most in the first three games of the finals. Add my twelve rebounds and eight assists and dramatic alley-oops and blocks and frowning intensity, and I was pretty damn tired.

Don't conclude I'm discrediting the Warriors in game four. They made a master switch, benching passive seven-footer Andrew Bogut and replacing him with six-six tiger Andre Iguodala who outscored me twenty-two to twenty, and that can't happen if we're to win. He also defended me well, along with a host of helpers who forced me to pass the ball to teammates less likely to score, and the Warriors kicked butt, shooting forty-seven percent from the field to our thirty-three. Not pretty. Our three guards hit an atrocious seven of thirty-five. That's twenty percent, folks. And I shot poorly, too.

What's going to happen in game five Sunday night? I'm going to keep saying I'm confident in my guys. I've got to say and think that and I do. Look at the series. It's tied but maybe we need to rest our guys three or four minutes more a game. On the other hand, when I'm not on the court we tend to get trounced. I love the challenge but also hate it. I'd rather have a deep, healthy team like the Warriors. Nevertheless, if Thompson and Mosgov keep hammering the backboard, and our guards can hit some shots, as they've sometimes done, and if the Warriors billion dollar backcourt of Stephen Curry and Klay Thompson doesn't ignite, and if I can resume filling the basket as I did the first three games, and if my head quits throbbing after being cut by the camera I fell and hit last night, we may be able to win the next game. And if we do, then maybe we can somehow win a fourth game.

June 2015

Wilt Calls LeBron

WC – LeBron, this is Wilt. I want to tell you I know how you feel.

LJ – How can this be Wilt?

WC – Listen to my voice.

LJ – Okay.

WC – I've been reading the news, some of the blogs, listening to garbage people are saying after you guys lost to the Warriors in six games, but I had it worse than you. I was a seven-three Goliath. Be thankful you're only six-eight and not automatically the bad guy.

LJ – People are still calling me a loser.

WC – Not the majority.

LJ – It wasn't the majority with you, either. But I know similar comments always bothered you.

WC – Right, it galls me when guys who can't play ball rip those who can. I played fourteen years and won "only" two NBA championships. Several times we lost close games in the conference or NBA finals. Look, I credit the Celtics. Bill Russell, Sam Jones, and John Havlicek and their guys were usually the best. But when I had great teammates, in 1967 and 1972, we were overwhelming, too.

LJ – That's how it worked for me in Miami. Without Dwayne Wade and Chris Bosh, I still wouldn't have any rings. People don't understand how difficult it is to win a championship. You need luck as well as talent. Look at my team this year. After Kyrie and Kevin fell, who did I really have? Some solid pros going against several Warrior standouts and ten healthy guys good enough to start on most NBA teams. Yet, people are saying I'm only two and four in the finals, and a failure. I know you wanted more titles, and so do I, but sometimes the other guys simply have too much.

WC – I played a hundred and forty-two games against Bill Russell and the Celtics. He won eighty-four and I won fifty-eight. Does that make a loser? I averaged twenty-nine points and twenty-nine rebounds in those games. People dismiss that and say all I cared about was my statistics. I cared about winning.

LJ - That's what it's about. I contributed what I could: thirty-six points, thirteen rebounds, and nine assists a game. Who else in basketball history could've done that? Maybe you and Michael Jordan.

WC – That's about it.

June 2015

The Underdog

The Warriors burned a lot of gas down the 2016 stretch to win seventy-three games, besting Jordan's ninety-six Bulls by one, and looked beat in the conference finals, trailing Oklahoma City, and Kevin Durant and Michael Westbrook, three games to one. They came back, though, winning three in a row, and then smacked us in the first two games at Golden State. I thought I might've scared them with my sky-high right-hand alley-oop slam in our game three victory, but the Warriors took the fourth game and held a three to one advantage never overcome in the NBA finals. See, LeBron's gonna be two and five on the big stage, I continued to hear. Were these words spoken to me or simply sounds in my head? Both, probably. At worst I'd be able to tell myself: two titles and six straight trips to the finals. But maybe we could still win. Let's move to game five in Oakland where Kyrie Irving smoked the Warriors backcourt, nailing seventeen of twenty-four from the field, amassing forty-one points, same as I got. I also contributed sixteen rebounds and seven assists, and that feels great any time, especially during a fifteen-point victory in an elimination game. Now we were going back home, and the Warriors still needed only one more game, of two, and most money, real and emotional, rode on them. In the first quarter we ambushed and outscored them by twenty points, and won by fourteen, and I again dropped forty-one on the defending champs.

Game seven loomed at their place in Oakland. So what? I'll be frank. They'd be going against LeBron James and Kyrie Irving and company, who've blitzed them twice in a row, and the first time I played in a finals game seven, in 2013, you know what I did to San Antonio. Can the Warriors really match that? My guys and I were confident and played high-level ball. So did Draymond Green, who shot three-pointers like Steph Curry, swishing six of eight. The first forty-six minutes of the game resulted in a tie and a Warriors fast break that promised to yield a layup and the lead. Steph Curry from left of the lane bounced a pass to streaking Andre Iguodala who with his right hand laid the ball on the glass, and as it flowed some foot and a half above the rim I sprinted at the target, planted my left leg, and soared to right-hand pound the ball against the glass and into the hands of my teammate J.R. Smith. With fifty-five seconds left, and the game knotted at eighty-nine, Kyrie skied over Curry to release and make a three-pointer. Golden State didn't score again, and Cleveland had its first championship since the 1964 NFL title game when mathematician Frank Ryan threw three touchdown passes to Gary Collins and Jim Brown rushed for more than a hundred yards in a twenty-seven zip victory over the Baltimore Colts.

Our city by the lake celebrated. We'd love to hold another victory parade this year. To do so, we'll face about the same Warriors team plus Kevin Durant, the second best player in the world. Let's say he and I play about the same. No, I've got to have an edge, if not in points then in rebounding and assists. And Kyrie Irving must play at least a little better than Steph Curry, who wasn't completely healthy last time. And Kevin Love's got to play even with Draymond Green, one of the best all-around performers in the league, a vocal man who scores inside and out and rebounds and blocks shots and assists teammates. That's their top three against ours. But now their former second or third guy, Klay Thompson, is their fourth, and our J.R. Smith, though capable, cannot match Thompson in a best of seven series. At center we have the edge with Tristan Thompson, a powerful rebounder, against anyone the Warriors play in the middle. I believe our substitutes are a little better than theirs but won't swear to that. I can't guarantee victory, either, just a superlative effort against an one of the finest teams in history.

May 2017

Ominous Game One

Shortly after Golden State disemboweled Cleveland one hundred thirteen to ninety-one in the first game of the NBA finals, Dan Gilbert stood at half court of the Coliseum Arena in Oakland, alternately raging and weeping, and pulled a cell phone from his pants pocket and said, "Please, LeBron, come talk to me right away."

"Okay, relax."

In a couple of minutes LeBron emerged from the dressing room, stepped to center court, and pointed at security guards to escort Gilbert and him toward an exit leading to a small room. LeBron closed the door, and the summit meeting began.

"We've gotta do something," Gilbert said.

"I just scored twenty-eight points, ripped fifteen rebounds, and passed for eight assists."

"Yes, but you also had eight turnovers, and your all-world counterpart, Kevin Durant, scorched you and your teammates with thirty-eight points, many scored while our defenders parted the sea like Moses and gave him uncontested dunks. He's quite good enough even when guarded, LeBron. You guys have to tighten up. The Warriors certainly played excellent defense, that's why our Cavs only hit thirty-five percent from the field. We need reinforcements immediately."

"Easy, Dan. Last year we got way down but came back."

"I'm sure you, as a basketball scientist, understand there was something overwhelming and grim about our loss tonight. We simply can't win beat this team in a seven game series. I therefore intend to act. I'd suit up myself but at age fifty-five and only five-foot-six, I'm probably not the solution. I've therefore resolved to bring in Karl-Anthony Towns for game two and beyond."

"You know that's not possible. The rosters are set, and Minnesota would never part with Towns. In a couple of years, or whenever the hour glass drains my strength, Towns is likely to be the best player in the world."

"I'm not talking about getting him full-time, just for this series.

If we have a prolific scorer and rebounder at center, I think we can beat the Warriors."

"I know neither (commissioner) Adam Silver nor the Warriors will agree," said James

"I'm going to offer them three billion, half my fortune."

"Don't be foolish. We had twenty turnovers tonight to their four. That's why they got twenty more shots and twice as many assists. If we handle the ball properly and play much better defense, we'll have a chance in game two."

June 2017

Diabolical Game Two

Into the funereal locker room of the Cleveland Cavaliers charged Dan Gilbert, shouting, "Don't worry, men. I'll never blame you. They're just too damn good."

"Dan, I won't tolerate defeatist statements in my hoops sanctum," said coach Tyronn Lue. "I must ask you to leave."

"Not until I finish what I came to say. I hope you guys appreciate I'm relieving you of responsibility for the outcome of this series."

"We were down two-zip to the Warriors last season before we rallied," said LeBron. "That's when you were by far the best player on the court."

"You're suggesting that's no longer true?" LeBron frowned.

"Suggesting, no. I'm outright stating that Kevin Durant is the best player in this series to date. You're only a bit behind him after two games, but you'd have to dominate in order for us to win, and no one who's ever lived can overwhelm Durant the way he's playing now."

"We're going home to Cleveland and that's where we bushwhack them," said James.

"Gentlemen, after game one LeBron persuasively told me if you got more shots and had fewer turnovers tonight, we'd have a chance. Well, in a turnabout from the opener, we had less than half as many turnovers as the Warriors and took a hundred shots, eleven more than our greedy opponents. Yet we still lost by nineteen. LeBron played great, attacking the basket from the start and scoring twenty-nine points and compiling eleven rebounds and fourteen assists. Kevin Love scored twenty-seven. Kyrie Irving played fairly well. That's the point. You corrected the errors but the dike sprung a leak elsewhere: they got fifty-four points on threes, thirty more than us. In game one, they had a long-range edge of only three points. Durant and Steph Curry killed us from downtown and so did Klay Thompson and Draymond Green."

"We'll seal off the perimeter like we did in the first game," said Lue.

"When they shredded us inside," Gilbert said.

LeBron charged Gilbert, tossed him over his shoulder, and carried him out of the locker room. Returning, he said, "If we win game three, it's still on. If we don't, it's over, though we'll behave like champions on the Titanic."

June 2017

Mr. Clutch

After game three, in the executive compartment of my limousine, I leaned back in the seat, closed my eyes, and thought, "Lord, I'm playing like few men ever have, and the hot air analysts are already saying I choked or disappeared or at least became mortal in the fourth quarter, though few mentioned I'd toiled forty-six minutes and burned much energy not only scoring thirty-nine points, clutching eleven rebounds, and lasering nine assists, but guarding my suddenly-faultless counterpart, Mr. Kevin Durant."

Now, I'll tell you as soon as anyone, and with more authority, that Durant is one of a handful of greatest players in history. It would be absurd not to acknowledge that and equally irresponsible to fail to mention that in 2012 my Miami Heat became NBA champions after winning games two through five to vanquish the Oklahoma City Thunder featuring Kevin Durant. And what happened last season in the 2016 Western Conference finals when the Thunder led Golden State three games to one? The Thunder lost game five, led game six by eight points after three quarters but was outscored thirty-three to eighteen in the fourth, and for the evening Durant hit a frigid ten of thirty-one from the field. After the Warriors won the deciding seventh game, sharpshooting Durant had totaled forty-two percent for the series and less than three of ten beyond the arc.

Tonight, fueled by four prodigies, the fresher Warriors scored eleven straight points in the final three minutes to nip us by five. They have us in a three-zip stranglehold, and the coronation of Kevin Durant has begun. Am I privately bitter about this? Certainly. My formula for each team change has been to join two stars, and Durant has bested me by one. That's why he's the new king and I'm merely the upscale serf.

Do I hear a knock on the window to my right? I turn a tired head to see an elderly man smiling. I wave go away.

"LeBron. It's Jerry West. Please let me in."

"Jerry West," I say through glass, and open the door, and he eases onto the seat next to me.

"I'd like to talk to you."

"Sure," I say, "but is it okay since you advise the Warriors?"

"They'll never know."

"With all these people watching us?"

"I won't be giving away any secrets. I'm here for history."

"I always think of you as Mr. Clutch."

"I did hit quite a few game-winning shots but guess the nickname's a little ironic since I played in nine NBA finals and my team won only once."

"I can relate. It looks like I'll soon be three for eight."

"LeBron, I want you to know what the bigmouths either don't or pretend they don't. When you lost, you lost to better teams. It was the same during my career. Bill Russell and the Celtics were simply too good, except for 1969 when I teamed with Wilt and Elgin Baylor and we definitely had the best team."

"You had a great series against them, I know."

"Fifty-three points in game one and forty-one in game two, both wins for us. The series went seven games. We had home court advantage but the damn Celtics jumped on us early and led by fifteen after three quarters. Wilt hurt his leg midway through the fourth and the coach wouldn't let him back in. We still made a run. I got forty-two points, thirteen rebounds, and twelve assists but Boston beat us by two."

"That would blow me away."

"I had to keep trying. In the early seventies we played the Knicks in the finals three times in four years, and finally got a title in 1972. That's the year we won thirty-three in a row. The other two seasons, the Knicks played too well. Real players know the most talented teams almost always win. Tonight, you and Kyrie Irving made as many incredible plays as you possibly could. It's fundamental. You're going to need more horses against our Warriors."

"How can we get them? Jerry?"

"LeBron, wake up," said one of my buddies, shaking me.

June 2017

88

Game Four Diary

I'm a genial public figure accessible to all who thrive on traditional and social media but must warn unborn readers that future lawyers I've already hired will sue if you steal or otherwise come into possession of these words and reveal them even a day earlier than fifty years after my earthly passing. The sentiments below belong only to readers sometime in the twenty-second century and beyond.

Thank goodness we began game four like famished lions armed with laser-guided missiles and scored a finals record forty-nine points in the first quarter and eighty-six at the half, teaching the Warriors they were fortunate to trail by only eighteen. Thank heavens Kyrie Irving, slicing and twisting and banking, assailed interior defenses better than almost anyone who's played the game. Thank the gods of emotional control that Kevin Love and J.R. Smith made a combined eleven of seventeen from three-point range. Thank you Tristan Thompson for waking up and contributing ten rebounds and five assists, and props to coach Tyronn Lue for the first time giving you enough minutes to do so. The Warriors can't beat us when we outshoot them fifty-three to forty-five percent from the floor while avoiding problems with turnovers and fouls. They can't stop us when I crown my triple-double with thirty-one points. They can't survive if we continue to play like this. And it's not impossible we can.

Still on the precipice we're preparing to go to Golden State and win game five and return to Cleveland and prevail here and, like last season, invade the Warriors den and again defeat them in the title game. Don't tell me that sequence is a fantasy. I believe it's a dream we can realize though I here acknowledge it's unlikely, and have indirectly admitted as much by saying perhaps too often the Warriors are a great team. That assessment, however, means only I've conceded a point but not the war.

Imagine if we'd lost game four and legions said LeBron's now been swept twice in the finals and no one who's been thusly dominated deserves to rival Michael Jordan. I'm sick of being compared to him, yet there must be conversations about our relative achievements or I'll never lessen the noise of his chanting troops, who are forever on the march.

June 2017

How to Win Next Year

Some fool behind me just lit up, and I spin to say, "Put that damn thing out."

The old man blows smoke in my face and says, "I always enjoy a cigar when I win. That's my prerogative in Boston and everywhere else."

"Fifty years ago. Besides, you haven't won anything tonight."

"I see how we're gonna win next year so am celebrating a little early."

I point to the court and say, "Have you been watching? LeBron and Kyrie are on fire but still trail the Warriors by eleven at half."

"They're the best now but they're also lucky. Early in the second quarter Cleveland took a forty-one to thirty-three lead on LeBron's dunk and he got whacked across the forehead by Durant, who should've picked up his third foul. That would've sent him to the bench. Instead, Durant soon hits a three and so does Curry, and the Cavaliers start making turnovers they otherwise wouldn't have, and Curry and Durant and Draymond Green keep scoring, and Andre Iguodala dunks a couple of times and all of a sudden the Warriors lead by seventeen. Cleveland's happy to be as close as it is."

"Maybe the Cavs'll get hot in the second half."

"They probably will but it won't be enough. Look at Klay Thompson, there's a three, and a Durant jumper, and another Thompson three, and two more dunks and two threes by Iguodala, and a three and a dunk by Durant, and another dunk by Iguodala, who's not even a starter, and a three by Curry, and I don't care how many layups and jams LeBron has or how often Smith hits threes, this things's over, one twenty-nine to one twenty, and the Warriors hoist the trophy."

"They're too damn good."

"For these Cavaliers."

"And way too good for your Celtics, who Cleveland destroyed in the conference finals."

"Don't call them my Celtics. They're Danny Ainge's Celtics."

"Then who're you going to make champions next year?"

"Red Auerbach's team with Bill Russell, John Havlicek, and Sam Jones – the greatest winners in the history of sports."

"Even if they were available, I don't think they'd be enough in today's NBA against this champion."

"I disagree but won't risk it, anyway. We'll add LeBron to the mix."

"You can't get him."

"I won't have to. Russ, Havlicek, and Jones will sign with the Cavs for the minimum."

"Why would hall of famers play for relative peanuts?"

"They want another title, and they want to be young again."

"What about you?"

"I'll be the red-haired coach and general manager."

June 2017

The Warrior

Wearing only blue and gold gym shorts while solo-piloting a luxury helicopter, LeBron James quite late last night landed, slightly off target, in the swimming pool of Dan Gilbert, and butterfly-stroked to steps he marched up and then, shaking off water like a massive poodle, told alarmed security guards, "Gentlemen, put away your firearms at once, King James is here."

The four men complied.

"Please tell the owner I'm here and to receive me at the front door."

One guard called the mansion. Shortly, he nodded, and LeBron walked toward destiny.

"What the hell, LeBron?" Gilbert said, dashing outside in his boxer shorts.

"I can't sleep, I'll never be able to sleep until this Golden State nightmare is resolved."

"Don't worry. We'll get you some more help this offseason."

"Who? We know we're not getting the guy I need most, Karl Anthony-Towns."

"What if I bring in Paul George."

"I might stay if you don't have to move Kyrie Irving or Kevin Love."

"What do you mean, you 'might stay?'"

"I mean I won't tolerate an annual trouncing by the too-talented brats from Golden State."

"What's the alternative?"

"I'll probably take my talents to the Bay Area."

"That's absurd. You're under contract to me next season."

"A contract that'll soon be voided because of some devious fine print my attorneys just discovered. Furthermore, as a fellow financial guru, you should know the Warriors' numbers make devastating sense. Haven't you studied their salaries?"

"I haven't had any reason to."

"I'll explain everything. Only three key Warriors are signed for next season – Kevin Durant, Klay Thompson, and Draymond Green.

They'll earn about sixty-two million. Steph Curry'll get a max deal of about forty million. That totals a hundred two million only exceeds the salary cap a little. The Warriors could still pay me a decent wage, and we'd indisputably be the greatest team ever."

"That's grotesquely excessive."

"So's being a billionaire, Dan."

"You guys would be fighting each other for minutes and shots. It would be hell on earth."

"On the contrary, we'd relieve each other's responsibilities. I'd only have to play about thirty minutes a night and score twenty points. The whole experience would be sublime. I see Draymond Green, a bullish Mr. Everything, playing center between dashing Durant and myself at forwards. Combine that front line with the magical backcourt of Curry and Thompson, and we might not lose more than five games all season."

"You're the selfish, vile person who abandoned us for Miami in 2010."

"I'd brought you plenty of success before my first departure, blessed Miami with two titles and four conference crowns, and have taken this team to three straight finals and one title. I'll be thirty-three next season and want to lighten my burden and prolong my career while adding a minimum of five more championships. If I do otherwise historians will forever shout about lost chances that weren't really chances but executions."

"Cleveland will hate you forever."

"Cleveland, unlike you, will forever appreciate my contributions."

Dan Gilbert lowered his head and butted LeBron in the abdomen. The cager countered by enveloping his assailant around the waist and handing him upside down to the security guards who complied when told, "Toss him in the pool, but don't hit the chopper."

June 2017

The General Manager

Appearing at Quicken Loans headquarters in Detroit, LeBron waves to security guards who tell him to pass right on but please give them some autographs when he leaves.

"You got it," he says, heading into long halls before he rides an elevator high to another hall leading to Dan Gilbert's private suite he enters walking fast.

"Do you have an appointment, sir?" asks the secretary.

"I don't need one," he says, stepping to a closed office door he hammers twice and opens.

"Gilbert, stand up when I enter a room."

"I am standing. And what the hell's the idea entering my office in that manner."

"I'm here to say you should've told me face to face before you forced out general manager David Griffin."

"I own the damn team and pay your salary and everyone else's."

"The fans pay our salaries, and I regret too much of their money sticks to your pockets."

"Get to the point."

"Effective immediately, I'm taking over as general manager of this franchise and shall have uninhibited power to make any and all personnel moves I deem necessary. And you're to stay the hell out of my business."

"It's my business. Furthermore, we've done everything imaginable to fulfill your egomaniacal demands to keep building this roster. You couldn't have done as well as my staff, which has taken over for Griffin."

Standing in front of the massive desk, LeBron points a big finger at Dan Gilbert and says, "Not so, and certainly not now that I realize how devious and clever the Warriors really are. For the second draft in a row they've bought a second round pick. Last year they got clever guard Patrick McCaw who helped them during the season and playoffs, and now they've drafted athletic forward Jordan Bell, who shoots a high percentage and rebounds and blocks shots, and has made the bastards even better. And what have you and your lackeys done? Nothing."

"We made some calls about Jimmy Butler."

"And you couldn't get it done because you'd already decapitated the front office. I could've gotten Jimmy Butler before Chicago undersold him to Minnesota."

"How? We didn't have a first round pick. Would you have traded Kevin Love?"

"Yes. With three elite African athletes – Kyrie Irving, Butler, and myself – we'd have had a better chance to beat the Warriors next year."

"Okay, wise guy, I authorize you to go get Paul George. Who do you suppose the Pacers want?"

"They want more than they'll get. We'll offer Love."

"He's the guy you wanted and demanded."

"And now I want and demand to get rid of him."

"Fine, LeBron. Do it. But we'll need even more."

"That's why you should've been buying second round picks."

"I might have if you'd suggested it. But you were miles behind the Warriors' brain trust."

"I'm only now assuming absolute command of this ship."

"That prerogative is still mine, LeBron, but I hereby grant you more managerial power than your predecessor had."

"Carmelo Anthony and Dwyane Wade can help us, and we can afford them after the Knicks and Bulls buy them out. I'll call some people to get their asses moving."

"So you're telling me we'll soon have Paul George, Carmelo, and Dwyane?"

"Once I finish painting championship dreams."

"This GM deal is good only if you sign a long term contract here."

"You didn't say anything about that."

"I'm saying it now."

"The only way we can compete next year is if I, as architect, use my authority and persuasive powers."

"At least have the decency to sign a contract, will you?"

"Let's concentrate on 2018. I may still join the Lakers the following year."

"Even with you, they wouldn't have nearly the talent to win the title in 2019."

"Depends on how many stars I bring with me. They've already got about sixty million in cap space next year and can create more."

"Beat the Warriors next year and you won't be tempted to take your aging body to an underendowed team."

"If we don't beat Golden State, and I can't fashion a Laker powerhouse, then I just may go to San Antonio or Minnesota."

June 2017

PHIL JACKSON

Convincing Phil about Bynum

This confession is written under shield of anonymity as I am by considerable measure the wealthiest man in Los Angeles and intend to remain uncontroversial and obscure. I don't sit courtside at Lakers games, have never met Jack Nicholson, and only once dined with the team's cheerleaders, at the behest of a friend of Jerry Buss, the chemist who fled his laboratory to invest in real estate, acquired the Lakers, and immediately altered elements to transform them into Showtime winners of five titles in the nineteen eighties.

The friend revealed Jerry Buss had been despondent for a year since he asked, urged, ordered, and ultimately pled with coach Phil Jackson to play his seven-foot prodigy, Andrew Bynum, and Jackson raised hands glittering with nine championship rings and said, "Don't interfere or I'll leave and you'll again be out of the playoffs."

Though that claim is no more certain than Jackson's conviction he was the only coach who could've steered the Chicago Bulls of Michael Jordan and Scottie Pippin to six titles, Buss, let us concede, was intimidated. Several years ago he'd coaxed Jackson to abandon his Montana ranch and lead the Lakers who, despite the athleticism of Shaquille O'Neal and Kobe Bryant, had not sniffed a championship since the demise of Showtime. Jackson at once guided the team to three NBA crowns before Bryant's ultimatum – them or me – forced Shaquille and Phil out. The Lakers promptly plummeted to a ghastly thirty-four and forty-eight record, and Buss entreated his comely daughter, Jeanie, Jackson's companion and team vice president of business, to bring her man back. That she did, but Phil insisted on royal prerogatives.

In his first post-exile season the Lakers improved to a sub-Showtime but encouraging forty-five and thirty-seven mark. That turnaround, and the fact Andrew Bynum had begun the 2005-06 season at age seventeen, youngest in NBA history, allowed Jackson to pigeonhole the long-armed lad, limiting him to seven minutes a game and a miserly eighty-two shots for the season, but one a game. Pressure to play Bynum erupted early last season as the athletic center abused opponents with some double-figure outputs in points and rebounds and thereby convinced almost everyone, Phil Jackson being the most disturbing exception, that he was on the cusp of stardom, at least, and more likely superstardom.

The Lakers were performing well enough to suggest a return to eminence but an avalanche of injuries undermined them and they finished a desultory forty-two and forty. So, on a team with a critical need for manpower, why did Phil Jackson limit to twenty-two minutes a game a nineteen-year old with a huge and lively body who averaged eight points and six rebounds and blocked many shots? With adequate opportunity he'd have produced twice as much and pushed the Lakers to ten more victories. Jerry Buss ordered general manager Mitch Kupchak to force Jackson to play Bynum appropriately in the upcoming playoff series against the Phoenix Suns, a high-scoring group of greyhounds. Jackson pretended Kupchak was mute, halved Bynum's already-miniscule minutes and told reporters "not really" when asked if he'd thought of using his big guy to challenge the Suns near the basket. As a result, the Lakers were hammered with four losses while posting a solitary win.

Vice president of personnel Jim Buss, son of Jerry and brother of Jeanie, long an advocate of Bynum, was the next soldier sent to battle Stonewall Jackson. After the Phoenix debacle, he warned the coach, "Either Andrew gets big minutes next year or you'll be back in Montana from whence you came." Despite a failing back and two hip replacements, Jackson is only an inch or two shorter than his six-foot-eight playing height as a subordinate on the cerebral New York Knicks of the early seventies, and he delivered a leveraged, NBA-style elbow to what he termed the "impudent mouth" of Jim Buss, dropping him to a knee and bloodying his lips. Jeanie Buss, ever an ally of her beau, said that while Jim probably deserved the whack it might really be better for the Lakers if Bynum were given a chance to multiply his contributions. Jackson restrained his elbow but told Jeanie that several Lakers cheerleaders had been beckoning and his back would strengthen if she again broached the subject.

Jackson's arrogance, matched only by that of Kobe Bryant, was reinforced when the latter sneered the Lakers should have traded Bynum for someone of value, and that he, Bryant, no longer wanted to play for such a disgraceful team and demanded a trade. Jerry Buss was desperate. If he lost his box office star, and his next attraction was nailed to the pine, the Lakers would free fall while the owner forfeited scores of millions at the gate, hundreds of millions in team value, and nearly that many social opportunities since, quoting Willie Nelson, "Money makes women horny."

Unwilling to capitulate, the inspired Buss paid me a modest eight-figure fee and said do whatever's necessary. I would have anyway. Posing as a Hollywood agent, I approached Phil Jackson after a preseason practice last summer in Hawaii and told him I had a fifty million dollar offer from a noted director and producer to make a film about his life. The producer wanted Jackson to come at once to his exotic mansion only ten minutes away by helicopter. Jackson gingerly climbed in and we were soon greeted by hula dancers bestowing kisses and wreaths. Inside the residence, which I own but rarely use, Jackson's hand was pumped by a fine (and therefore obscure) stage actor whose appearance prompted the coach to exclaim: "Steven Spielberg."

"Greetings, Phil," said the thespian.

Sensing that the child of the sixties, the reader and thinker of the seventies and eighties, and the Zen Master of the nineties had become rigid and tense due to a chronic lack of sedation, we offered him some special iced tea. He sipped the first glass, chugged the second, and drained the pitcher before I could offer him more.

"Do you have any Cream, Jimi Hendrix, something like that?" he asked.

On the theater screen promptly lowered from the ceiling, we displayed what he asked for as well as vintage songs by Led Zeppelin, The Who, The Doors, Janis Joplin, Bob Dylan, and the final movement of Tchaikovsky's Violin Concerto played by Yitzhak Pearlman. As these creative thunderbolts were landing, I casually and without looking at him offered Jackson a glowing joint of the stuff he'd been drinking – Kona Gold. Though I'm sure he'd been abstemious for years, he took the reefer as if at Woodstock and soon sighed the most creative thinking he'd ever done was while loaded. At that I touched my left ear and Andrew Bynum, accompanied by Beethoven's "Ode to Joy," consumed the screen, snaring rebounds, soaring to block shots, scoring inside with soft hooks, and far from the hoop devouring space with one giant dribble before sailing two feet over the rim to slam on startled opponents.

"During practice today, I'd resolved to build our team around Andrew," Phil said. "Isn't this a marvelous coincidence?"

January 2008

Notes: Shortly after I wrote this story, Andrew Bynum dislocated his kneecap and was sidelined more than half the season.

Memo to Jackson

To Coach Phil Jackson,

I am concerned about the roughneck Boston Celtics coming to town Thursday to try to take our NBA title from last year. When I say "our," I'm not presuming to be a player or insider like many fans who refer to their favorite teams as "we," despite never having scored a point, grabbed a rebound, or coached how to do so. My reference is nevertheless appropriate because quite late last night I trounced Lakers owner Jerry Buss in an ultimate stakes poker game that left him the alternative of going to debtor's prison or handing over the Lakers. He chose the latter, and I reduced his pain by promising to let him retain current access to assorted young and healthy admirers.

I hope you do not consider me naive, as a mere erstwhile fan, for telling you, the unprecedented owner of ten championship rings, a fundamental truth regarding our showdown with the Celtics. If you try to battle those brutes on the boards solely or primarily with slender and at times tender Pau Gasol and Lamar Odom, the Boston strong boys will thrash our troops much like they did in 2008 when the Celtics won the NBA crown four games to two. The forgoing certainty compels me to speak frankly to you in private. However, if I must again discuss this, I shall do so in front of the international media. The issue is unequivocal: we cannot win unless Andrew Bynum, injured and unavailable the last time, plays significant minutes and is given critical responsibilities.

Do not tell me he often gets into foul trouble. You often use that as an excuse to pigeonhole him for the rest of games while Gasol and Odom handle the big-guy duties. That duo has sufficed against outmanned teams from Oklahoma City, Utah, and Phoenix but would again be manhandled by the Celtics. I also don't want to hear that Bynum isn't healthy. In 2008 he was seriously injured and out for the season. Now he is merely tweaked. Though he'll need minor surgery after this series, he's currently running and jumping well and needs only playing time to give us the force we need.

We must not depend on Kobe Bryant to singlehandedly defeat an opponent laden with bullies and future hall of famers. That will not happen no matter how well Kobe plays. Also, keep in mind, Phil, that the physicality of Bynum makes Odom and Gasol more confident and effective. I am not asserting that young Bynum, still only twenty-two years old, will be the series MVP. I am simply telling you that in order for the MVP (Kobe) to come from our (winning) team, Bynum must be allowed to be Bynum. If I sense you're not giving him that chance, I may spontaneously appoint a new coach, sending you on an ignominious stroll to the showers.

GTC

June 2010

Notes: Bynum continued to suffer one debilitating injury per year and his athleticism and career were destroyed during his youth. In 2011-2012, at age twenty-four, he for the last time played in reasonable health for sixty games, and left us a glimpse of the hall of fame player he would have become, averaging nineteen points, twelve rebounds, and two blocks a game.

Jittery Jackson

My opponents are desperate to believe I'm no longer the cool and confident dude who invariably beat them. They're howling it's my fault I inherited a New York Knicks team lacking the talent to win many games last year. I don't care. So what if a growing chorus of blabbermouths say Phil Jackson won eleven titles simply because he had Michael Jordan and Scottie Pippin, Shaquille O'Neal and Kobe Bryant? Lots of coaches could've done the same with those guys, they contend. Now Jackson's going to suffer.

I disagree but don't have time to debate. I'm not the coach, anyway. I'm the man responsible for determining who puts on a Knicks uniform. And I've just made my first pivotal pick. I've taken Kristaps Porzingis, extremely long and lean at seven-foot-three, with the fourth pick in the draft. If he becomes a star, I'll get credit. If he struggles and is only average, I'll be further portrayed as the rich kid who for twenty years floated on the family fortune but later floundered on his own.

To the privacy of my diary, to be published twenty years hence, I hereby admit I'm acutely nervous as the Knicks and Kristaps Porzingis begin play against the San Antonio Spurs in the Las Vegas Summer League. This isn't the real season and not as many people will be watching, but quite a few will tune in or read about what several thousand are ready to watch now. No one's going to see me looking jittery as I feel. I'm ensconced in a luxury box this morning equipped with one-way windows, and I'm smoking joints, I'm inhaling hash, I'm blasting a big bong, and I'm tuned to the creative aspects of basketball and telepathically sending messages to Kristaps: stay calm, be confident, remember you're the biggest and best man on the floor.

I think he hears me. I know he does. He controls the opening tap by a foot and in the first quarter strokes two free throws like an elite shooting guard and blocks a shot inside and banks in a jumper from the left side and swats another shot and takes a seat about halfway through the quarter and doesn't return until four-eighteen remain in the half and hits two more smooth free throws and, with exceptional dexterity, catches an intended alley-oop four feet in front of the rim, controlling the ball and converting a soft jumper.

During halftime and beyond I put on headphones and let Mozart lead me to heaven where Kristaps tries a three-pointer, drawing a foul, and hits two of three free throws, giving him ten points. Soon he gets another respite he doesn't need. In the fourth quarter he again improvises and, off balance fifteen feet from the rim, lunges into the lane, almost straight away, and banks the ball in. Yes, I shout, slapping the window with both hands.

We win the game but that doesn't matter. Kristaps Porzingis, still more than a fortnight from his twentieth birthday, has played like a future all star. I am not, however, so stoned or emotionally intoxicated that I fail to write some serious concerns: Kristaps is quite weak, relative to bruising big men in the NBA, and has rebounds ripped form his hands when, indeed, he deigns to attempt to rebound. Most rebounds seem to signal him to stand and watch. I'm going to retrieve from mothballs my old Knicks uniform and, though I'm a bit stiff, pound young Kristaps during intensive rebounding tutorials.

July 2015

Phil Pursues Porzingis

I set up a large white board in my office and arm myself with markers black, blue, and red as I prepare for my ten a.m. exit interview with Kristaps Porzingis, talented but still immature at age twenty-one. I'm going to lecture and test the lad about the intricacies of the triangle offense as well as the psychic responsibilities of the best player on a team destined to win NBA titles, which I own in unequalled abundance. It's already two minutes past the appointed hour so I plan to sentence Kristaps to a few dozen pushups and squat jumps when he arrives. I won't tolerate tardiness from anyone. At ten-ten I tell my secretary to call him. There's no answer. He must be on his way. He better be here soon or what'll I do? I'll lecture his skinny ass, which, like the rest of his frame, still lacks the musculature of a champion. By ten-thirty, the presumptuous punk is aggravating my stomach.

"Keep calling," I order my secretary. "No, give me the damn phone."

After listening to a robotic voice, I leave this message, "Porzingis, you're to be in my office in ten minutes or else."

I feel it. I could wait until fall. The callow kid is jilting me in public. A few days later I learn he's skedaddled to his native Latvia and told everyone he's unhappy with "confusion from top to bottom" in the Knicks organization. He might as well have slapped me at center court of Madison Square Garden, where as a player I won a ring decades before his birth. He was either unborn or in diapers during the epic years I guided the Bulls and Lakers to the summit of athletic achievement. And this delinquent stands me up? He'll pay, by Jove.

"Book me on the next flight to Riga, Latvia," I shout to my secretary. "Yes, sir."

I wish this fine young lady stood seven-foot-three and blocked NBA shots and drilled jumpers from downtown. I'd sign her the day I cut Kristaps and trade Carmelo Anthony to the Albany Patroons.

Soon I'm flying high in first class on a public flight, eating marijuana brownies I've cleverly brought on board, and telling fellow travelers, "My protégé Porzingis has invited me to visit his native land. Reports of discord are absolute rubbish. Please post and tweet that so our Knicks fans can relax."

Making the connecting flight in a European city I'm too loaded to recognize, I finish my brownies and wobble off the plane in Riga. Don't worry. I've done my homework. I know where Kristaps Porzingis lives. And the limousine I've hired, driven by an elderly man who speaks no English, takes me straight – I dare not say where – to the mansion of the man I made rich by drafting him fourth in the league two years ago.

I don't knock. Why bother? Cocky Kristaps wouldn't answer the door any more than he answered his phone. I grab the knob but it's locked. Shall I kick the door in? I was a rugged bastard, six-foot-eight and two hundred twenty pounds during my pro career, and am only a tad shorter now and quite a bit heavier and stronger despite the aches of aging. But no, I don't want to terrify Kristaps or destroy his property. You know he'd complain about my confused leadership. I walk around the big place and am encountered by a beefy security guard.

"Phil Jackson to see Kristaps Porzingis," I pronounce.

He whips out handcuffs and I kick him in the gonads, crumpling the rube, and run to the back of the residence and look into a window revealing the long lean one reclining on a sofa and reading what I assume are comic books. I know he didn't study the tracts by Plato and Socrates I gave him during his rookie season. I pound the window, breaking it unintentionally, I assure you, and shout, "Porzingis, open the goddamn door and bury your insolence."

He instead uses his cell phone to activate an alarm that summons the recovering security guard and two more who envelop and grind me into the concrete patio before they pick me up to face Porzingis who's wearing a fancy scarf inside a silk shirt tucked into lengthy leather pants that cover the tops of his sneakers.

"What the hell do you want, Jackson?"

"That's Mr. Jackson or Coach Jackson."

"You're no longer a coach and, given your petulant behavior, I have reservations about calling you mister."

"Okay, call me Phil."

"The police will be here shortly."

"Please, let's talk like basketball professionals."

"Very well. All the players consider your triangle offense to be a Model T in the jet-propelled NBA."

"Michael Jordan and Scottie Pippin won six titles using it, and Shaquille O'Neal, Kobe Bryant, and others won five more, all with yours truly orchestrating the victories."

"We're tired of your fixation on the past. You've been with the Knicks three seasons and I two. And where are we? Presently, we're at fifty-one loses and facing lengthy reconstruction."

"That's why you should be in the United States, studying the nuances of the triangle, which can take many years to comprehend."

"It's elementary, Phil. I'll simply cite much-publicized information about which you cannot be ignorant. Players around the league say our plays are easy to predict and defend. We shoot more low-production shots – non-threes and non-layups – than everyone else, and, consequently, our shots are much too often tightly contested. We need to spread things out."

"Perhaps I should appoint you player-coach, Mr. Porzingis."

"That appears to be necessary. Your age and emotional distance from the players is ruining our team chemistry. Also, your public diatribes against Carmelo Anthony not only insulted him, they insulted me. He's a gentleman and still a high-scoring small forward, which we certainly need. I'm also worried about your draft selections."

"I picked you."

"Yes, but far too many of your personnel decisions aren't working out. A championship executive must draft, trade, and sign free agents shrewdly – rather than loading the roster with expensive, once-distinguished players now close to retirement – and he must bring the team together by respecting and adapting to their skills, and refraining from insults."

I hear sirens and soon see several police officers sprint toward me. They say something to Porzingis, in Latvian, I assume, and he responds.

"You aren't going to have them arrest me, are you?"

"No, I told them to take you to the airport and ban you from the country for a decade."

May 2017

Dolan Summons Jackson

James Dolan, aspiring rock star, eternal inheritor of wealth, and proud owner of the New York Knicks, summoned coach Phil Jackson to his office late last night.

"Please sit down," said short and plump Dolan. "I'm not going to temporize, Phil. The Knicks need a change."

"I don't think you have to sell the team, Jim. Despite your many years of incompetence and abrasive behavior, I think your popularity is growing, and that's primarily because of my skillful handling of the franchise while you've prudently hidden behind my broad shoulders."

"That's not what I mean, Phil. You're the problem."

"I'm the generalissimo of an unprecedented eleven championships teams as well as perfector of the triangle, the most sublime offensive scheme in the history of sports."

"It's just not working. Look at your record during three full seasons: eighty and a hundred sixty-six. Most high school coaches could've come in and delivered that."

"A number of the players haven't performed as expected."

"True. And that's your responsibility. You're the one who signed creaky Carmelo Anthony to a five-year, no-trade contract for a hundred twenty-four million dollars."

"I've been trying to get rid of him."

"Publicly insulting him hasn't worked, has it?"

"He should've been prideful enough to walk through the door I held open. He just wanted the money."

Dolan pointed at Jackson and said, "Many people think you took this job for the money, that you didn't do your work and even snoozed during the pre-draft workout of a college star."

"That shows my perspicacity, Jim. I instantly determined the kid didn't have the stuff of a champion, so I tuned him out."

"You snored pretty damn loud, according to my reports."

"That's just wheezing through my nose broken while contributing to the Knicks last championship. In 1973, Jim. Look at my record since then, and look at the Knicks'."

"Your coaching exploits, enhanced by numerous superstars, are at this point widely viewed as irrelevant. Besides, you were hired to choose the right coach and select the proper players. Look at the enormous contract – seventy-two million for four years – you gave a rather enfeebled Joakim Noah."

"Last year he averaged nine rebounds in only twenty-two minutes. That's one of the best per minute performances in the league."

"He only played in about half the games, and his defensive skills have evaporated. Don't bother trying to refute the analytics."

"Analytics, the overpraised pastime of nerds who can neither play nor coach."

Exhaling, Dolan said, "You've made yourself an anachronism, Phil. You're still kidding yourself that three-point bombardments aren't a mathematically sound strategy."

"Michael didn't shoot that many threes."

"Neither did Galileo. Bring your head into the present and future and understand how insane it was to try to trade Kristaps Porzingis, the foundation of this franchise."

"He needed to be thrown into the water for discipline and at the same time used as bait to see if we could attract a couple of whales and future picks."

"When you did that, people knew you'd lost control of yourself, Phil. It's sad to see you in such a debilitated state."

"I didn't really want to trade Porzingis, that's why I asked too much. I'm the guy who selected him, and well understand he's one of the finest players in the league, a young man who can shoot, rebound, and block shots. Despite some moves that didn't work out, I've indisputably built the foundation of a winner: Porzingis and rebounding machine Willy Hernangomez and my latest pick, Frank Ntilikina, form an explosive triad. We're ready to start moving up."

"I hope so, Phil, but in the future the Knicks will be under new leadership."

"I've already said there's no reason for you to leave, Jim."

"I'm not leaving. You are."

June 2017

KOBE

Einstein Calculates Kobe

More than a century it's been since he riveted the world with the rarely-understood revelation that energy equals mass times the speed of light squared, and he's grown quite tired of scientific pipsqueaks and others caterwauling that Einstein didn't do much in the laboratory after age twenty-five. He didn't need to. He was and remains a dashing bohemian with great hair who's synonymous with genius.

He should, however, reveal that he's recently resolved to reestablish himself as the world's most incisive thinker. He could've done so during World War II by helping to develop the atomic bomb but demurred because he abhorred violence and instead urged President Roosevelt to enlist others to build doomsday so the Germans could not. The destruction that followed still appalls him, and he believes anything he does in science will be misused so he's switching to sports, basketball, specifically, and planning to manifestly improve the Los Angeles Lakers who have won but one of nine games.

Don't blame Kobe Bryant for shooting too much. Blame those who haven't redirected him. Blame Einstein if he and the Lakers don't change because the wizard has just taken over as coach and general manager, and Kobe Bryant's entering his laboratory now.

"Kobe, my dear fellow, henceforth you won't be shooting twenty-five times a game, you'll be doing so about a dozen."

"Look, Professor Einstein, I don't tell you how to do physics, you don't tell me how to play basketball, a sport I know as well as you do science."

"That I doubt, Kobe, since you and your enablers are proceeding in a most unscientific manner, and this I'll explain in a way that perhaps even Jim Buss will understand. You, through the first nine games this season, are shooting a lamentable thirty-seven percent from the field. No team wins many games shooting that way."

"Yeah, but look at the guys I'm playing with. I gotta shoot because they can't."

"Quite wrong you are, Kobe. Here, let me step to the board and, with dusty chalk, prove the correctness of my position. Look, while you're hitting less than four of ten shots, your teammates, collectively, are shooting a fine forty-seven percent. That's a winning percentage. So, unless you believe your presence on the court is about shooting compulsively while more accurate teammates gaze – and I'm confident you don't really feel that way – then you'll understand my mandate for a redistribution of shots. Here, using quite elementary math, is what we'll do with those ten or twelve extra attempts: give two more apiece to Ed Davis, Carlos Boozer, Jordan Hill, Wesley Johnson, and Jeremy Lin. These men are respectively converting sixty-eight, fifty-one, forty-six, forty-four, and forty-four percent of their field goal attempts."

"I'm the hall of famer with the rings."

"That's wonderful for history but, right now, your rings are in their noses and that will either stop or you'll be sitting next to me on the bench."

"I'm not sitting next to you."

"Very well, sit at the end of the bench, if you choose. But I think you're underestimating my respect for your game, your complete game, Kobe. Rather than continuing to average a mere three or four assists a game, in our new offense you'll be an unstoppable distributor, a tall and muscular passing guard who compiles about eight assists. That's at least eight more points a game for us. I know you can do that. And I'm sure your already commendable five rebounds a game can be pushed to seven or so and provide us a couple more possessions a game."

"Maybe."

"It will make our team ten to fifteen points better a game. And you, Kobe, will receive much of the credit."

"What about you?"

"I just want a mathematically sound team. I don't care about seeing my face on a Sunset Boulevard billboard."

"Excuse me, Coach Einstein, but aren't you, shall we say, a bit of a socializer."

"No more than most celebrities."

November 2014

Coaching Kobe Bryant

Lakers coach Byron Scott called last night and asked, "What do you think I should wear to my meeting with Kobe Bryant tomorrow morning?"

"Something authoritative," I said.

"I recently bought a tailor-fitted General Patton uniform including pearl-handle pistols."

"Perhaps something with an athletic motif."

"I may have the right outfit in mothballs."

"Can I sit in on the meeting?"

"If you promise not to write about it."

"Okay."

I didn't take my notebook to the Lakers' training facility but attached a small recording device inside my upper left thigh. A security officer patted me down and noted, "Man, you need more exercise."

"Soon as my hamstring heals."

"Go sit a few rows up." I chose a great seat in the center.

Byron Scott, basketball tucked between his right arm and hip, stood at midcourt, attired not as a soldier or executive but in the Showtime Lakers jersey and short shorts he displayed during the magic eighties.

Kobe entered, dribbling. He wore the preposterously-baggy gym shorts now in vogue and a Mickey Mouse tank top. "A little one on one, Coach?"

"I'm certainly fit enough for it," Scott said, "but I'm not here to put unneeded stress on your aging body."

"I feel like a youngster, looking at you."

"I'm wearing this legendary uniform to remind you it represents championship basketball, team basketball, that led to five world titles."

"I've also led teams to five titles."

"That's the problem."

"I beg your pardon."

"Kobe, basketball is a team game and even the immortal Kareem

Abdul Jabbar, who's almost a foot taller than you and shot more than ten percent better from the field, understood he had to pass the torch to Magic Johnson, and this Kareem did when he was a few years younger than you are today."

"Fine, Coach, I'd be happy to defer to the young Magic Johnson. Is he on the team?"

"Your impertinence is another issue, along with the ball hogging I've just alluded to."

"Who do you want me to pass the ball to, D'Angelo Russell? He looks like a freshman in high school and would rather dribble than breathe."

"He's a very talented lad and will be our floor leader for the next generation. The ball will be in his hands more than yours, Kobe."

"I hadn't realized I was such a failure and he so eminent."

"You're one of the greatest players ever, but you're also thirty-seven and have played damn little the last two seasons because of three devastating injuries. Your body's breaking down and, let me assure you, your role on this team has dramatically changed."

"Not if I get back in my groove."

"Kobe, I simply won't tolerate anyone on my team shooting more than twenty times a game and hitting only thirty-seven percent, your total last year. You won't be shooting even ten times a game if you hit thirty-seven percent. That's a losing percentage, and you're far too knowledgeable to be unaware of that."

"I'm the leader of the Lakers."

"Emotionally and intellectually, you certainly are. I expect you to be a positive coach on the floor, not a ball-stopping drill sergeant, and help young, athletic Jordan Clarkson, who's physically similar to you, grow into an elite shooting guard."

"All he's got to do is watch me play the position."

"He won't have many opportunities for that since your primary position will be small forward."

"At forward I lose the size and strength advantages I have at guard."

"But you still have the edge in speed and quickness over most forwards. Furthermore, I see you as a point forward, a passer, a scorer, a rebounder, a defensive stopper, a diverse player par excellence who accelerates our return to glory."

"I can't refute that assessment."

"I also want you to make sure that young Julius Randle gets the ball inside where he can use his bulk, cleverness, and soft hands to score and draw fouls. Then his mid-range opportunities will increase, and he'll be competitively in tune to convert."

"Coach, I probably would've made these same points."

"I know you would've. And that's how it's going to the media."

Byron Scott pointed at me and said, "Right."

"Sir, yes sir."

September 2015

Kobe Decides

Rather than enjoying the athletic brilliance of this NBA season, I've been obsessing about the excessive and inaccurate field goal shooting of Kobe Bryant, and the Lakers acceptance of this spectacle, even more than critical subjects I've recently studied and written about: Israel's ongoing expansion of illegal settlements in the West Bank and suppression of Palestinian rights, the barbaric behavior of ISIS, the perils of alcoholism, and the presidential campaign clotted by candidates who, with rare exceptions, thrill voters with promises to start more wars. I'll continue to spend ninety-seven percent of my writing time on such substantive matters but must, for the first time in two months, comment on the sad state of the former virtuosos of professional basketball, the Los Angeles Lakers.

A brief review is helpful. Kobe Bryant, as a high school senior in 1996, was acquired in a trade crafted by Jerry West and soon became a star and then a superstar and ultimately one of the top handful of hoopsters in history, and the best shooting guard other than the prince of players, Michael Jordan. Kobe hit long jumpers, short jumpers, he spun, he cross-dribbled, he drove, he dunked, he drew fouls, he hit forty-five percent from the field and eighty-four from the foul line, he passed and rebounded, he played good defense, he exhorted teammates and also browbeat them, and for almost a generation played a special and exciting style of basketball. Excepting Shaquille O'Neal, he was the best player on his first three NBA championship teams with the Lakers and undisputed leader on the fourth and fifth. His record is remarkable and will remain so despite his difficulties in recent years and in particular during this season.

In April 2013 Bryant tore an Achilles tendon in his left heel and toiled to rehab but broke a bone in his left leg late that year and again pushed himself to return but in early 2015 again sustained a serious injury, this time tearing a torn rotator cuff, and in the fall came back a much slower and less explosive basketball player who has trouble making shots and is hitting an anemic thirty-one percent from the floor, and an embarrassing nineteen percent on three-point shots. I'm surprised that a proud and unusually intense player like Bryant would refuse to stop shooting from long range and instead pass and rebound more and help develop his three talented young teammates: Jordan Clarkson, Julius Randle, and D'Angelo Russell. I'm also disappointed that coach Byron Scott hasn't either ordered Bryant to stop shooting so much or benched him. Instead, Scott stated that benching Bryant isn't an option and neither, apparently, is compelling him to alter his style to fit his current athletic abilities. It's clear the Lakers believe that letting Bryant stubbornly pursue past greatness will ensure the team continues to flounder – they have two wins in sixteen games – and thereby finish in the bottom three in the league and retain a first round lottery pick they would otherwise lose.

Generally, when former superstars decline they either continue to play well, albeit on a modified basis, like Michael Jordan and Tim Duncan, or they quietly retire. I can think of no one of Kobe Bryant's stature who has so fiercely refused to acknowledge either the effects of aging or the need to fashion a game that blends with reality. Anyone who loves basketball must be cringing at what's happening. Though Bryant may improve a little, since he's still recovering from injuries, I sense his struggles will continue until the season mercifully ends.

Wait – I need a break, let me scan Kobe's statistics and relax while thinking about the great years.

I see big news online: Kobe has just announced this season will be his last. I'm instantly relieved. And Kobe's exhilarated at the press conference following another loss, and four of twenty shooting: he smiles as he talks about how hard he's always worked and he did everything possible to get his skills back but he couldn't so he's com-fortable moving on to what comes next, and most fans must be happy that in this final clutch situation Kobe Bryant made a perfect pass.

November 2015

STERLING SILVER

Donald Sterling Speaks

Ladies and gentlemen, it's time you heard my voice in person rather than through the concealed tape recorder of a courtesan. I must tell you I'm shocked you're so angry with me. Some of you are even pretending to be surprised. How is that? For years I've made unflattering remarks about blacks, saying they "attract vermin," for example, and though some of my comments were reported they never caused such a firestorm. Neither did my loss of a three million dollar housing discrimination lawsuit, the biggest ever. So I don't get it. Can't you tell from the tape? I'm a tired and emotionally exhausted old man who was being strip searched and clawed by a gold-digging former mistress. Repeatedly I told her I didn't want to fight, I was tired of fighting, I just wanted to quit arguing and that I loved everybody including blacks. All I said was I didn't want her to embarrass me by bringing them to my Los Angeles Clippers basketball games or having her photos with them published in the social media. Okay, maybe I see why that upset some people. Like Charles Barkley said, I only paid about twelve million for the team, and the sweat of many black men have helped boost the value to seven hundred million. I wish I'd looked at it that way. But why are all of you are so outraged? There's a lot bigger issue than hot air from bigoted old Donald Sterling. It's called privacy, privacy in your own goddamn house. That's right, Big Brother's everywhere. And I want you to buckle your seatbelts because when I press this button we're going to start hearing tapes secretly and illegally recorded in your homes. I'm appalled, frankly, by many things you've said.

April 2014

Donald Sterling v. Adam Silver

I have been ringside for many of the most compelling fights in history – Plessy v. Ferguson, Roe v. Wade, and Ali v. Frazier I and III, to cite only four – but I've never felt such tension, excitement and, yes, bloodlust. How could one be otherwise affected? Two powerhouse lawyers, champions of the Constitution, titans of basketball and commerce, and sexy celebrities, as well, are minutes from trying to maintain their sublime prerogatives while knowing one will as the other hurtles into ignominy.

Tension between the two men had tightened during their first televised negotiation when Donald Sterling said he was neither going to disappear nor waste money winning in court. Adam Silver said he wouldn't have to, and at once accepted a challenge by the Los Angeles Clippers' owner to adjudicate matters in the most manly way imaginable. But what would that be? Sterling initially demanded a duel, and even proposed firing the pistol of Aaron Burr while the NBA commissioner aimed Alexander Hamilton's. Silver said only cowards need weapons. Fine, countered Sterling, let's wrestle or fight in the octagon of mixed martial arts. Silver examined Sterling's massive gut, which, though aesthetically displeasing, would be an asset on the mat, and stated they would put up their dukes, sell tickets (ringside fifty grand), and let the winner determine whether Donald Sterling is a racist who should be forever banished from professional basketball and forced to sell his team.

Their second negotiation was barely less contentious. Sterling demanded the title bout be fought bare-knuckled, as it sometimes was back in the days of supreme champion John L. Sullivan. Silver countered that Sullivan had avoided, and thereby degraded, every opponent of African descent and was a poor model for Sterling to emulate. The commissioner then called for sixteen ounce gloves. Sterling said no larger than eight or they'd at once settle matters in whatever manner he deemed expedient. Undaunted, Silver said he'd feed Sterling both eights for sixteen total. Neither man, despite boasts of being primed for fifteen three-minute rounds, wanted an interminable tussle and agreed to fight three one-minute blasts. Octogenarian Sterling privately told aides that Silver, three decades fresher, was an imbecile not to prolong matters. Silver assured his staff the shorter struggle would allow him to punch ceaselessly and keep Sterling in a shell from which he couldn't land a lucky haymaker.

Blessedly, all the rancor and posturing have ended, and Donald Sterling, accompanied by special assistant V. Stiviano and the team's cheerleaders and clad in a red and blue robe emblazoned Los Angeles Clippers, first steps through the ropes of a ring at center court of packed Staples Center. Everyone boos, and Mrs. Sterling stands and fires a loaded beer cup her husband ducks. Two minutes later Adam Silver, surrounded by white-uniformed Clippers and bobbing and weaving, bounces into the ring and delights the audience with his ebony robe and commitment to rectitude. Sterling shouts that he pays every ingrate there, stomps across the ring, and shoves his opponent. Forget the niceties of introduction, Silver declares, let's get it on. The ring is cleared save for the two combatants and referee Magic Johnson, who's just entered as the nondescript decoy dashes away. Sterling says, I'm not worried, Magic, you're a wonderful man except you're promiscuous. V. Stiviano clasps Sterling's face and gives final exhortations and a lengthy French kiss. Doc Rivers puts his hands on Silver's shoulders and says, this is for liberty. Pencils poised, judges Jesse Jackson and Al Sharpton, wearing yarmulkes, await the bell. Bareheaded Magic is also enfranchised.

And the warriors race to ring center where without cease or concession to defense they flail each other with a malicious mixture of left hooks and right crosses and uppercuts from either hand, and smashes from both elbows, and butts aimed at eyes, noses, and mouths, and at the end of round one each fighter bears crimson from eyebrows to bellybutton, and fans stand and roar profanities and other inspired insults. V. Stiviano guides her wobbly man back to his stool and smears his cuts with the arcane elements of corner medicine. Doc Rivers applies a mysterious, pine-tar-like substance to Silver's ripped areas. Magic Johnson and two eminent plastic surgeons examine the fighters, agree they're unfit for battle, and motion to resume firing.

Donald Sterling, bearing eighty years of revelry and breathing like a coke fiend, takes two tentative steps and beckons young and slender Adam Silver to attack. Sterling covers his head and retreats to the ropes, pretending to be brilliant Ali v. lumbering Foreman, and is clobbered, and slides into a corner, his own, incidentally, where Silver, who hadn't fought much until training for this war, fires a twenty-four-punch volley, a dozen hooks from each hand, and Sterling collapses to his knees. As Magic begins to count, V. Stiviano vaults into the ring and floors Silver with a mighty right uppercut to the solar plexus, then jackhammer jabs Magic on a suddenly red nose, knocking him on his keister, and in five sudden seconds counts out the referee and the commissioner before lifting Donald Sterling and pushing him back against the ropes around the top of which she hooks his arms, stabilizing him upright and victorious albeit unconscious.

May 2014

New Owner of Clippers

Hi, I'm V. Stiviano and so proud to attend my first press conference as new owner of the Los Angeles Clippers. I'm only a little nervous since I'm a confident and dedicated young woman determined and ready to lead the Clippers to many championships, and I'll make it happen fast. Look how little I had just a few years ago: a pretty face, a hot body, and hunger. When I met Donald Sterling at a Super Bowl I tingled because of that bulge in his pocket. An ambitious girl's got to be aware of stuff like that. Even though Donald's fifty years older, I told him he was the most charming and fascinating man I'd ever met, and he believed me or acted like he did. He sure loved the way I stroked him and gave me four cars that totaled a half million and almost two million to buy a duplex.

A less motivated woman would've been satisfied. Not me. I decided to go for more. Donald may have been losing interest. He'd been complaining about me and hinting he had other girls. Those bitches weren't going to get my man. I got his attention posing with famous blacks like Magic Johnson and Matt Kemp, and then waited for him to erupt.

He sold the team to a large group of modest investors I headed, and when Adam Silver and the owners tried to block me I unleashed my team of professional girls around the country, many of whom now own a slice of the Clippers, and they released devastating tapes of some things those guys said, things so revolting I won't repeat them, unless I have to. It doesn't matter some of the owners were drunk or talking in their sleep. If they hadn't been thinking it, they wouldn't have said it. I'll be muzzling myself at bedtime, just in case.

May 2014

Chasing DeAndre Jordan

We knew we might be too late so I opened full throttle on Steve Ballmer's private jet Wednesday afternoon. Our reports, confirmed by U.S. military satellites, proved that Mavericks owner Mark Cuban and ace recruiter and forward Chandler Parsons had already arrived in Houston in a piper cub, not as obscurely as they'd hoped, and in an old Volkswagen were driving fast toward the mansion of DeAndre Jordan, the best rebounder and interior defender on the planet and perhaps, at least temporarily, the most changeable as well. Was he going to sign with Dallas as he'd recently promised? Or did he really want to forget Dallas and stay in Los Angeles as he more recently confided? Or would he lurch back toward Dallas? Cuban and Parsons clearly hoped for the latter, and we feared precisely that.

I know I'll have to pay a fine – that is Steve Ballmer will have to pay my fine – since I illegally broke the sound barrier, shattering some windows and pounding millions of eardrums as we, coincidentally, crossed over Dallas en route to Houston where Ballmer ordered me to ignore airport landing instructions and force the plane down between the interminable arrivals of two giant passenger jets. That I did, before airport police arrived, and our team – Ballmer, coach Doc Rivers, Chris Paul, Blake Griffin, J.J. Redick, and Paul Pierce – hopped aboard a helicopter I piloted toward Castillo de DeAndre Jordan. We got there quite rapidly but Cuban's Volkswagen was already there. As blades still whirled we dashed from the chopper, and I'm glad we didn't knock since Jordan, pen in hand at the dining room table, and Mark Cuban drooling at his side, prepared to stroke his signature onto four years of imprisonment in Dallas.

"Wait," shouted husky Ballmer, who sprinted behind Cuban, locked forearms around his neck, and choked him until his tongue shot from his mouth and he passed out, and Ballmer shoved him under the table. J.J. Redick and Paul Pierce bound and gagged Chandler Parsons, who'd been sitting nearby, and tossed him into a closet. "Cuban hasn't a fraction of my money, DeAndre. Everyone knows about Microsoft.

What was the name of Cuban's company? You don't know. No one knows or cares. It was third tier."

"DeAndre, I had no idea you considered me icy and resented that I frequently slapped hands with three other guys on the court and ignored you," said point guard and team commandant Chris Paul. "I assure you, I was just giving you the space your transcendent talent deserves. Henceforth, I'll make my respect entirely clear. I'll chauffeur you to and from all home games throughout the upcoming season. And, remember this, despite your rather limited offensive skills, I'll make you our number one option, demoting Blake to second and myself to third. Under these conditions, I believe you can begin to score like Wilt Chamberlain and Shaquille O'Neal, and your abysmal free throw shooting, like theirs, won't matter. What do you think?"

"I'm encouraged," Jordan said. He motioned for his butler to drag away groggy Cuban. "Just throw him in with Parsons. If he starts babbling, push this dishtowel in his pie hole."

"DeAndre," said Doc Rivers, "this urgent meeting is about considerably more than playing basketball. It's about guiding a team. As you know, I may have bumbled in the potential closeout game six against the Houston Rockets in the playoffs, and it's possible, though not certain, that I've lost the right stuff I once clearly had when I coached the Boston Celtics to the NBA championship. That was several years ago, however, and I'd be more comfortable making you our head coach – the first NBA player-coach in two generations – and also serving as your appointments secretary and publicist. Does that sound congenial?"

"It's not uncongenial."

"DeAndre," said Blake Griffin, "I've been appearing in entirely too many commercials, getting too much publicity, and making more money than I care to. I've already notified my agents that all my cinematic offers should be forwarded to you. I made about forty million last year from endorsements, so this should sweeten your portfolio."

"I'll take that into consideration. What have you to say?" asked Jordan, nodding at Redick and Pierce.

"Go Clippers," they shouted.

"Here it is DeAndre, a maximum deal, twenty-two million a year for four years, plus all that other stuff, which will be far greater," said Steve Ballmer.

"I'll have my attorneys take a look, and we'll get back to you."

"We'd feel more comfortable if you signed now, if it wouldn't be too much trouble."

July 2015

Odom to the Hoop

It's late in a Los Angeles Clippers game early in Lamar Odom's rookie year but the young man, who just turned twenty, is given the mandate of an all star: take the ball to the basket every play. To facilitate this, coach Chris Ford tells the team's older players to clear the right side so Lamar – six-ten, acrobatic, and a skilled ball handler – can drive and fake and twist to get inside for layups or draw fouls. Lamar's in no way reluctant to assume this responsibility. He's in a zone, making plays and giving the Golden States Warriors, who appeared destined to win, more than they can manage. Ultimately, penetrating again, he banks in another left-handed layup from the right side, the winning shot, and a small crowd at the Staples Center stands to cheer. They've witnessed something splendid and likely understand, as I do, that Lamar Odom will distinguish himself for a long time.

* * *

A year or two thereafter I wasn't alarmed when I heard Lamar had tested positive for marijuana. I'm not advocating anyone smoke pot or drink alcohol or take any other recreational drug. I'm advocating don't do it. But the hysteria about pot is baffling considering the devastation caused by alcohol and nicotine, society's two beloved legal, and lethal, drugs. Drinkers, informed people know, generally cause many more problems than pot smokers. What did strike me about Lamar was how vulnerable he seemed as he asked his teammates and friends to forgive him. He was in distress and, according to later reports, smoking far more pot than anyone should. He may have been sedating himself to treat undiagnosed depression or a nervous disorder.

Then began a series of personal tragedies – relatives and close friends died, some prematurely, and his infant son succumbed to SIDS – that would wobble the strongest of souls, and Lamar Odom is perhaps a bit more delicate than most. Despite this he generally averaged about fifteen points, eight rebounds, and four assists a game, and played a key role coming off the bench for two Lakers championship teams. He'd joined the Clippers' big brother several seasons earlier, after a stop in Miami.

Many of us in fandom, despite lacking the perspective of people who knew Lamar well, should have suspected he had more problems than declining athletic skills when he played for the Dallas Mavericks, during the 2011-2012 season, and not only performed poorly but without conviction. He returned to the Clippers, where he'd started fourteen seasons earlier, and after one final mediocre year was out of the league. His personal difficulties became soap operatic when he married one of the Kardashians, Khloe, and opened his life on reality television, an inhospitable place for the sensitive. According to online gossip Odom and Khloe fought a lot and Lamar frequently visited other women and took cocaine, a drug about which there can be no compromise: one puff can stop a heart or rupture a blood vessel in the brain. On YouTube I recently watched a short video of Lamar from last summer. He appeared either intoxicated or hungover and, unlike the friend and teammate who was universally liked, even loved, he berated a reporter about how everyone had been mistreating him. Others can debate that point.

What's certain is that on an October 2015 weekend Lamar Odom began a binge that included cocaine and alcohol, and on Saturday phoned a place called the Love Ranch about an hour drive from Las Vegas. He asked them to come and pick him up. When a man's got a drug problem and lots of money, door to door service is an option. He arrived at the Love Ranch and hired two prostitutes who, for more than thirty-seven grand apiece, over the next three days gave him all the attention and cognac and herbal sexual enhancers and food one can imagine, and by Tuesday morning Lamar Odom was about dead, unresponsive in bed as strange fluids oozed from his nose and mouth. An ambulance was called and a woman stated Lamar had been using the substances above – but no cocaine after his arrival Saturday, of course, since the Love Ranch absolutely prohibits everything illegal.

Authorities may examine that issue but at this stage it's irrelevant to Lamar Odom, who's no longer unconscious or on life support and can sit up and talk a little to Khloe, who said she loves Lamar, and he indicated he loves her, too, and if that's true then he may have her help during what doctors say could be a lengthy recovery. Once he's out of physical danger, Lamar and his companions and doctors need to determine why a man who has so much in life retreated to a whorehouse where people watched him rot while raking in seventy-five grand for three days labor.

October 2015

NEWSWORTHY

Point Guard Mania

Damn it, Kyrie Irving, I'd planned to focus my comments on rookie point guards but now you and your advisors have upset everyone by announcing you want to leave Cleveland so you can be king of a franchise. Please note you began your career as the team's only prodigy, and in three seasons the Cavaliers respectively won twenty-one, twenty-four, and thirty-three games and failed to qualify to the playoffs. Three years ago LeBron James, whose 2010 departure pulverized the community's self-image, returned to regain the status of a hero and, with you as his essential costar, thrice led the team to more than fifty regular season victories and a berth in the NBA finals, and, during the second of those battles with the Golden State Warriors, the Cavaliers became the only team to recover from a three games to one death sentence and win the title, the historic moment coming as you rose above Stephen Curry and nailed a three-pointer. Furthermore, you took more shots than LeBron last season, when you averaged a personal record twenty-five points, as well as in the recent playoffs when you again played like an agile magician and made yourself a legend.

Those of us on the outside must assume that either playing with, and occupying the same space as, LeBron James causes you emotional pain or that you're appalled by the ouster of general manager David Griffin and ensuing personnel chaos, which resulted in the team getting older and sinking further behind the Warriors. You can't be pleased by the team's front office, so let's assume that's part of your discomfort. Do you also find playing with LeBron so unappealing? More likely, you sense he'll depart after the 2018 season and leave you contractually obligated to play another year on a team more resembling your first three in Cleveland than the three most recent. You're earning about twenty million a season. If the Cavaliers can't get fair return on a trade, you may have to continue your creative play near the shores of Lake Erie.

Now, in random order, I dash to stellar point guards Markelle

Fultz, Lonzo Ball, De'Aaron Fox, and Dennis Smith, picks one, two, five, and nine in the 2017 draft. I'm a tad obsessive but even allowing for structural imperfection I'm justified in protesting the situation facing Fox in Sacramento. Rather than announce that this speedy young man – who toasted Ball and UCLA for thirty-nine points in Kentucky's Sweet Sixteen victory – is the most promising player the Kings have drafted since DeMarcus Cousins in 2010 and a guaranteed starter, Vlade Divac, in a relapse to self-contradictory behavior, jacked up fifty-seven million dollars for a three-year contract, two fully guaranteed, for journeyman point guard George Hill and declared Hill would mentor Fox. For much less the Kings could have hired an assistant coach, and tutor, who wouldn't have counted against the salary cap or gobbled developmental minutes of a rookie who must play. Hill is a solid veteran and this isn't criticism of him. He's simply been brought to the wrong team and given an inappropriate task. For twenty million bucks this season, he couldn't have been expected to decline the misguided generosity of Divacs. At some point De'Aaron Fox will transcend Hill's level of play. But when? After forty games, one season, or two seasons? If Fox has to sit and watch George Hill play point guard for long, he'll probably begin planning his escape from Sacramento.

In contrast to the Kings, who haven't been to the playoffs in eleven seasons and generally lose more than sixty percent of their games, the historically excellent Los Angeles Lakers and Dallas Mavericks have already anointed Lonzo Ball and Dennis Smith as their floor generals. Magic Johnson, the ultimate point guard, virtually elevated Ball into the hall of fame, saying he hoped the long, lean passing wizard won't break all his records. Coach Rick Carlisle indicated that strong and athletic Smith would be a key to the team's resurgence. The Kings in effect said slender but slick Fox shouldn't be put under too much pressure, that he can't be a starter at age nineteen, he might wilt. Don't worry, Fox will be twenty in December, when Lonzo Ball and Dennis Smith are already establishing themselves as stars. Anticipate comparable progress from gifted Markelle Fultz as he enhances the future of the Philadelphia 76ers.

Expect the Sacramento Kings to moan and make excuses why their most talented athlete isn't playing many minutes. I hope I'm wrong.

July 2017

Rodman Goes Nuclear

I never claimed to be a diplomat but still resent Senator John McCain and others saying I don't have a great intellect. I must be pretty damn smart or I couldn't have gotten into North Korea several times, I forget how many, and had fun personal visits with President Kim Jong Un, who's very humble and a good guy, and he let me be the first to hold his baby daughter. You should've seen how happy he was.

I admit I got drunk a lot during one of my visits and sang happy birthday to the Dear Leader at a basketball game and cussed out reporters who questioned why Kenneth Bae had been sentenced to fifteen years in prison.

"Do you understand what he did?" I asked.

They didn't know Bae had planned to preach some religious stuff in the country, but he still got out and I hope you know he thanked me for publicizing his case. Now college student Otto Warmbier has been released after more than a year in jail for trying to steal a political banner that said, "Let's arm ourselves strongly with Kim Jong Il's patriotism!" You can't disrespect the late Dear Leader any more than you can insult his son. It's too bad Otto's in a coma and about to die. That's not cool.

I plan to do some great things this trip in North Korea. Remember, Kim loves basketball and oldies rock and roll like The Doors and Jimi Hendrix. Sure, he loves power, too, but he's got a lot of responsibility for a kid only thirty-three and wants to please his father and grandfather, who I've sorta met in the museum where they're frozen under glass. They're still impressive dudes but they did some bad stuff and I've told Kim he can be better. I also understand, unlike most Americans, that Kim Jong Un and North Korea only need nuclear weapons because they're a small country and have to deter the United States from attacking them.

I haven't seen my friend for life yet because I've been busy watching their women's basketball team practice, talking to a lady tall as me, and visiting the birthplace of his grandfather, Kim Il Sung. I know Kim's also waiting to see if I start drinking again. He doesn't want to have to make excuses for not seeing me if I'm overdoing it. This time I won't. I went into rehab after getting back last time "just to sort things out. I'm not an alcoholic. An alcoholic drinks seven days a week. I don't... I don't hurt nobody, I don't have no DUIs, nothing like that."

Once Kim Jong Un hears I'm okay I know he'll want to see me. I know he gets as big a kick being with me as I do hanging with him. I'm thankful for this visit and would like to thank my sponsors, the hip people at PotCoin, who're trying to make it easy for pot smokers to safely pay sellers online.

June 2017

Odds on Jimmer Fredette

Today I start writing gingerly to avoid being called a "hater" by YouTube fanatics whose ancestral pride is wounded by anyone who believes Jimmer Fredette was drafted too high by the Sacramento Kings and will not be a star in the NBA. I shall therefore stress Jimmer is already a one-name phenomenon, charismatic on and off the court, a certain marketing powerhouse, a dynamic seller of season tickets in a struggling market, the reigning college player of the year, an excellent outside shooter, a good ball handler, a decent passer, a muscular athlete who likes to work on his body as well as his basketball game, a clean liver, the boyfriend of a pretty blonde, and a nice young man.

Those attributes would have justified a mid-first-round selection, something in the thirteen to seventeen range, in the NBA draft last week. But the Kings held the seventh pick and the opportunity to select a more gifted athlete and natural point guard, Kemba Walker or Brandon Knight, or a small forward who can score and rebound, Kawhi Leonard. Instead, the Kings confounded most observers by trading down in the draft and, rather than getting someone better in secondary part of the deal, actually diminished themselves by in effect swapping point guard Beno Udrit, who has continued to improve and last year season hit an impressive fifty percent of his field goals, for a player two and a half years older, John Salmons, whose game was clearly eroding in 2011 as he made but forty-one and a half percent of his shots. Salmons also must be paid about twenty-five million dollars over the next three years.

The best way to clarify what the Kings have wrought is to lay out four scenarios:

First, let's be optimistic and say that Jimmer Fredette plays as well as any reasonable person can project. That likely means he's never an all star but consistently punishes defenses with long-range bombing, penetrates them with quick fakes and dribbles, creates space as he bounces defenders off his muscular frame and, wherever he is, fires scoring passes to teammates, particularly fellow guard Tyreke Evans and the massive and skillful DeMarcus Cousins. In this world Jimmer averages about fifteen points and six assists per game, and most fans and pundits don't harrumph too loudly about Kemba Walker and Brandon Knight being only a little better at point guard, which shoot-on-contact Jimmer didn't really play at BYU.

Odds – Forty percent.

The second projection has Jimmer playing like recently-departed Beno Udrit, scoring about thirteen points a game, though shooting less accurately from the field than the more prudent Beno, and averaging four assists a game, as he did in college. Jimmer's an asset, he's in the rotation as the sixth or seventh man, but, like Beno, he's lacking as a starter. Fans in Sacramento grimace and declare they always knew Walker and Knight, who often speed by Jimmer, would be much better players.

Odds – Forty percent.

Isaiah Thomas, the Kings' second pick in the second round, is at least four inches shorter than six-foot-two Jimmer but jet quick, boxer strong, and an experienced dissector of defenses. If Jimmer looks like he's moving in mud against NBA competition and is comfortable only when launching from twenty-five feet, he may become the fourth guard and watch from the pine as Thomas sets up Tyreke Evans and Marcus Thorton, a physical six-foot-four player who last season emerged as a formidable scorer.

Odds – Fifteen percent.

Joe and Gavin Maloof, the gambling impresarios who own the financially-challenged Kings and just had to relinquish controlling interest of the Palms casino in Las Vegas, know they're rolling the dice on this pick. They fantasize that Jimmer evokes John Stockton and Steve Nash as he attracts thousands of new fans and inspires a tidal wave of Sacramentans to buy the Maloofs a new arena. That would make Jimmer a savior as well as a hall of famer.

Odds – Five percent.

June 2011

Notes: I'm tempted to go back and revise downward my already-restrained projections of Jimmer Fredette's future in the NBA, but I'm leaving the observations in real time and rebuking myself for not offering stronger odds than fifteen percent that relatively short and slow Jimmer would be a fourth guard in the big leagues. In five seasons he played in only two hundred thirty-five games, averaged six points per, and from the floor hit forty-one percent, a paltry total for a guy whose value is based on precise shooting. The final NBA ignominy for Jimmer occurred in 2016 when the Knicks signed him to a ten-day contract during which interim head coach Kurt Rambis publicly groaned about the guard's inadequate defense during practice. Jimmer returned to the D-League, where he'd been starring, and that fall joined the Shanghai Sharks, owned by towering hall of famer Yao Ming. Guarded by players much less rapid and robust than those in the NBA, Jimmer flourished, averaging thirty-seven points and amassing seventy-three in one game. The kid has found a fit.

The Jeremy Lin Comet

July two years ago I drove from the hot Central Valley into infernal Las Vegas, host of NBA summer league action featuring prodigies John Wall and DeMarcus Cousins, both from the University of Kentucky star factory that loses lottery picks every season and promptly replaces them. Wall, a point guard, delighted overflow crowds with athleticism and floor generalship, scoring on jumpers and layups and distributing accurate passes. Cousins, early in the ten-day session, grabbed rebounds in traffic and alternately converted soft jumpers and bullish inside moves.

While fans previewed these destined pro stars, it's unlikely anyone predicted – or even considered – that Jeremy Lin would someday become an NBA force. I made this cursory assessment: he's pretty good to qualify for the NBA summer league but played at Harvard, which produces more presidents than pro hoopsters, and he's Asian American so probably not athletic by pro standards. People who say they then perceived more in the nondescript play of Lin must produce written documentation.

No Asian American had played in the NBA; few have even started for top college teams. The Golden State Warriors, for whom Jeremy Lin rarely appeared last season, discerned no future and cut him. The Houston Rockets released him before this season. Lin thus began a low-rent tour of the Developmental League. He was discouraged but accustomed to rejection. In 2006 he'd guided Palo Alto High School to the state championship and earned California player of the year honors. Generally, a six-foot-three floor leader with comparable credentials and straight A academics receives numerous Division I scholarship offers. Jeremy Lin's phone never rang. Coaches said privately what some now publicly concede: he didn't look physical enough and resembled a walk-on. In fact, at Harvard he starred individually, enhanced the play of teammates, and lifted his team to a rare NCAA tournament appearance.

NBA indifference lingered until a couple of weeks ago when Mike

D'Antoni, coach of the expensively-constructed but losing New York Knicks, was being ushered toward the gangplank and in desperation told bench-bound Jeremy Lin to take the floor at hallowed Madison Square Garden and try to ignite a lethargic team. D'Antoni had not foreseen – or he'd have acted sooner – that Lin would instantly launch himself and the Knicks into a vortex called Linsanity. He seemed a step or two quicker than everyone else, zipping by defenders for layups, swishing jumpers, and assisting with chest and bounce passes and alley-oops.

The struggling Knicks won one, two, three, four, five, six, seven games in a row, and Lin became the first player in league history to amass at least twenty points and seven assists in each of his first four career starts. On an electric Friday night in the Garden he bombarded the Los Angeles Lakers with thirty-eight points. Now talk radio buzzes, the blogosphere hums, tabloids blare, TV celebrates, magazine covers project his likeness, advertisers scramble with contracts, and fans obsess. Jeremy Lin's a wanted man.

February 2012

Notes: Linsanity quickly cooled into something rational and sustainable, for a man who stresses he's not "freakishly athletic," and Jeremy Lin produced a journeyman fourteen points and six assists for the Knicks in 2012, and the following season moved to Houston where he played comparably for two years, then to the Lakers and the Hornets, for whom he scored and assisted a little less, and in 2016 he joined the woeful Booklyn Nets, signing a three-year contract for thirty-six million dollars, and generated fourteen points and five assists while only playing twenty-four minutes a game. He's a tough and aggressive player who'll provide some entertainment and efficiency while the Nets recover from catastrophic trades that have denuded the franchise of lottery picks. Meanwhile, Lin donated a million dollars to Harvard to help renovate ancient Lavietes Pavilion, where he played for the Crimson.

Okafor on the Boards

I don't go to Las Vegas for scorched earth or gambling traps. I go for the NBA Summer League where imminent pro stars perform. On Friday, following a three hundred mile drive from Bakersfield, I watched two games, and on Saturday, after two hours of sightseeing, observed three more in crowded, Lakers-crazed Thomas & Mack Center, thereby totaling five contests in little more than a day. I suppose some Herculean scouts and journalists devour four games ten straight days. But they're on salary. For a half million a year, or a lot less, I'd stay night and day. Lacking that incentive I decided to take Sunday off, do a little more driving around the outskirts, and then visit friends who took me to a Chinese buffet. I couldn't refuse to enter the restaurant they'd chosen. And I declined to confess my concern: I can't stop eating anything I like and at buffets they don't make you stop. After three plates of entrees and one of desserts, a bulging stomach compelled me to retreat to my hotel room for a nap. Usually, I can sleep an hour in the afternoons but not this day. The air conditioner blew too cold and I was bored and an inner voice kept reminding me: Jahlil Okafor's playing tonight for the 76ers against the Celtics; don't squander this opportunity to see the guy who led Duke to a national championship as a freshman and who'll soon be a pro stalwart; get out of bed and over to the gym.

The Lakers didn't play Sunday, and this seven-thirty game would unfold before a sparse and more relaxed audience. When the 76ers entered I scanned both revolving layup lines for Okafor and then, worriedly, looked more carefully.

"Where's Jahlil Okafor?" asked a young woman, glancing at my pen and notebook.

"I don't know," I said.

"Are you a scout?"

"No."

"There he is," said her friend, pointing to Okafor clad in casual gray sweat pants and a white sports shirt and standing several feet behind the 76ers' basket with three teammates who also would not be playing.

"Why isn't he out there?" another woman asked.

I was honored she thought I might know but had to consider a moment before saying, "It's just a team decision. He played yesterday. They know he's going to make the team and need to check out some of the other guys."

If I ever meet Jahlil Okafor I'll mention this event but won't chide him because he'd rather have been on the court. He had clearly enjoyed himself against the Lakers the day before. During that game I wrote and drew a box around: "Okafor already one of best players in league." This opinion was forged by the young man's ability to use his large frame – six-eleven and two-seventy – to establish position underneath and deploy a variety of spins and drop steps and plain old power basketball moves to get shots close to the basket. That's where he belongs. I also wrote and boxed: "Too many twelve to fifteen (foot) jumpers." Okafor doesn't have a smooth shooting stroke yet – and may never develop one – so his free throws and intermediate-range jumpers come out heavy and fast. He also needs to adjust to large and athletic pro athletes who'd blocked a number of his shots a week earlier in the Salt Lake City league. A few days later the Knicks would swat five of his shots, three by Kristaps Porzingis. That's not particularly worrisome because Okafor has the tools to shoot more rapidly, fake defenders, and move to open areas. He'll also be a force on the boards, grabbing rebounds with either huge hand or clutching the ball with both. There's an online photo of Okafor holding a baseball, which looks like a golf ball in a normal-size hand. Since we were in Las Vegas, I should have made a large bet that the rookie will average ten or more rebounds next season. He accumulated eleven with nineteen points and three blocks during the close loss to the Lakers.

There's something else about Jahlil Okafor: he exudes gentleman-liness as he regularly extends his hands to help fallen teammates and even opponents. Part of his sensitivity may have developed because his mother died when he was nine. His father and aunt raised him in Chicago. Okafor told *Chicago* magazine, "My deepest fear is losing someone else close to me. That's something I think about way more than I should."

July 2015

Notes: Jahlil Okafor probably is a nice, dependable fellow but in his rookie year he in a span of days argued with a motorist he tried to punch and who exited his car, pointing a pistol at Okafor's head; he cursed and swung on those outside a bar who he said had cursed and swung on him; he was ticketed for driving a hundred eight miles an hour on the Ben Franklin Bridge, a velocity and venue that would've delighted the kite-flying patriot. On the court Okafor reminded me I should've written he's "already one of the best (young) players in the league." And he was, shooting fifty-one percent from the field while averaging seventeen points and seven rebounds. I'm lucky not to have wagered he'd get ten rebounds a game, though I emphasize he has the size, strength, and athleticism to get at least that many.

His most formidable opponent during his second season, when off-court troubles seemed to vanish, was teammate Joel Embid, an oft-injured prodigy who missed his first two seasons and played only thirty-one games as a rookie before injuring his left knee. He scored twenty and grabbed eight a game in twenty-five minutes. That's the pace of a hall of famer. If Embid's healthy, he'll start, and in this era of small-ball the 76ers probably won't try to resurrect the twin towers. Embid's minutes will always have to be limited to protect his twice-broken right foot as well as his knees. That means Jahlil Okafor, who played seven minutes a game less than as a rookie, will be a substitute who probably can't get out of town until his contract expires in two years, when he'll be ready for prime play at age twenty-three. He needs a team that needs him to be more than health insurance for the main man.

The Point of Emmanuel Mudiay

Emmanuel Mudiay was born in Zaire after it was the colonial Belgian Congo and just before it became the Democratic Republic of the Congo, and as a child lived there during the First Congo War and the Second Congo War but don't be distracted by names. This is the essence: he was born into a region where fighting, disease and starvation killed more than five million people, and his father died, too, and his mother struggled to feed the family on vegetables she grew and they eventually escaped to the United States where Emmanuel started playing basketball and while still in his early years of high school became one of the best point guards in the nation and in his senior year stood a sturdy six-five and played the game with speed and quickness and exceptional court vision and declined a scholarship offer to play for legendary coach Larry Brown at SMU and instead signed for more than a million dollars to play professionally in China. He was injured there but did perform well in twelve games and, though he slid from a projected first or second pick in the 2015 draft, was still chosen at number seven by the Denver Nuggets in what may prove to be a heist. I didn't need long to make that assessment after arriving late in the first half of a Las Vegas Summer League game between the Nuggets and Sacramento Kings who, incidentally, held the sixth pick used to acquire seven-foot center Willie Cauley-Stein of Kentucky.

Mudiay introduced himself on a drive to the basket, absorbing defensive contact and muscling up a shot that was goaltended for two points he made three after hitting his free throw and putting the Nuggets up by eight. In the third quarter he demonstrated how to dismantle opponents: he drove to his right, instantly determined he was blocked from the basket, and fired a pass cross court to the wing and watched a teammate hit a jumper; next he dribbled down the middle and passed for another assist; his jumper late in the quarter increased the Nuggets lead to seventeen. The Kings weren't playing poorly, they were getting the Mudiay massage.

In the fourth quarter Mudiay hit a jumper, converted a fast break dunk, and, on a portentous play, drove to his right, saw an opportunity most guards wouldn't, and fired a pass into the left corner to set up a three-pointer and a lead of twenty-four. He completed the evening with two more free throws and a driving shot to total nineteen points and ten assists in the lopsided win.

Here's what forthright scouts will tell their teams. Don't get too close to Emmanuel Mudiay or he'll drive by you for pull-up jumpers, layups, dunks, or precision passes to open teammates. Better lie back defensively and let him take long jumpers, which he still shoots inconsistently, and try to force him to make plays from outside. That will sometimes succeed, but Mudiay will usually speed or power by first defenders en route to becoming a star.

July 2015

Notes: My observations remind me of a breathless fan who's read scouting reports that Emanuel Mudiay can't consistently shoot outside but erases the memory after seeing the athletic point guard drain a few jumpers. In two real-world NBA seasons Mudiay has hit a frosty thirty-seven percent from the floor and misfired himself out of a starting job. A back injury sidelined him for eleven games in the second half of the 2017 season but even when healthy he registered numerous did-not-plays as veteran Jameer Nelson provided steadier shooting and passing. Mudiay pleased coaches and teammates by working hard during and after practice and that ethic may offer hope: in his final five games of the season he averaged twelve points, hitting more than forty-five percent of his shots, and five assists. This sample is too brief to use for long-term projections. Overall, one fears he may be an errant-shooting Ricky Rubio who lacks the Spaniard's mastery of ball handling and passing. Coach Clark orders Emanuel Mudiay to shoot several hundred daily jumpers this summer.

Ready for Bismack Biyombo

I was going to start this article by cleverly comparing, in some still undetermined way, the Prussian master of shifting alliances to maintain peace, Chancellor Otto von Bismarck, to his contemporary basketball namesake, Bismarck Biyombo. Only when studying some scouting reports did I note, for the first time in four years of reading his name, that the cager is in fact Bismack without an r between the a and c. Other than the issue of spelling I think I've had and continue to have a good understanding of what Bismack Biyombo can do for a team in the NBA: he can be similar to Ben Wallace, a great rebounder and shot blocker and defender and the tough core of a very good team.

That did not happen in Charlotte. Not many good things are likely to happen on the Bobcats' hardwood unless cigar-smoking owner Michael Jordan sends himself backward in a time machine and takes the court. Then Jordan the genius will exert himself. Jordan the owner should not be expected to equal the nonpareil player, and Bismack Biyombo should not have been expected to enter the NBA at age nineteen, youngest in the league in the fall of 2011, and rapidly overcome his limited basketball experience which began, quite belatedly, at the age of sixteen.

He irritated his bosses by turning the ball over too much, dropping passes despite having enormous hands, and failing to finish near the basket as often as expected. All right, those were the demerits when he was aged nineteen through twenty-two, a basketball baby who should have received credit for rebounding at a rate that would result in ten or more if he'd played the minutes of a starter. With more time he would've also blocked two or three shots and scored about ten points a game. This isn't mad science. For his career Bismack Biyombo has played merely twenty-one minutes a game yet averaged six rebounds and a block and a half an outing.

Losing teams, in particular, love to publicly complain about what their players can't do. Biyombo can't shoot outside and made only five shots beyond the paint during the 2013-2014 season. So what? He doesn't take many long shots and during his career has precisely no three-point attempts. His game is underneath, blocking shots, changing shots, changing the way people feel when considering shots, getting rebounds, dunking, alley-ooping, and getting offensive rebounds for put-backs or offensive resets. Two years ago, when Charlotte acquired Al Jefferson, a fine all around center, I understood Biyombo would no longer be starting two-thirds of the games and would indeed rarely start. A better player then held the starting center position.

Charlotte recently deemed itself too talented for Bismack Biyombo and did not offer him a contract after the 2015 season ended. In other words, he was fired. Toronto was delighted to sign him for two years at about three million dollars per, a pittance in the NBA of today, and he is slated, depending on which reports you trust, to either back up center Jonas Valanciunas or take over at power forward for less-athletic incumbents. Though I'm clearly rooting for Biyombo, I concede he'll never have the offensive skills of Valanciunas. In that case, perhaps he can earn starting minutes playing next to the big Lithuanian. I commend the Raptors. Basketball authorities are rash in counting out a player who won't be twenty-three for a month, who stands a muscular six-nine, boasts an astonishing seven-seven wingspan, and leaps like an Olympic high jumper. His basketball journey has now taken him from the Congo to Yemen to Spain to Charlotte and around the NBA, and now to the beautiful international city of Toronto. I doubt the Raptors will worry about what Bismack Biyombo cannot do or that he was drafted too high in 2011 after punishing U.S. juniors in an international game or that some of those taken after him – Klay Thompson, Kawhi Leonard, Nikola Vucevic, and Brandon Knight – are already distinguished. Forget all that. Just focus on twelve rebounds, two blocks, ten points, and a field goal percentage of fifty-five percent. If those projections are too low, I apologize to young Mr. Biyombo.

July 2015

Notes: Damn, I guess I'm like the general manager who won't admit he's wrong, but my delusion continues because in 2016, for Toronto, Biyombo averaged eight rebounds, a hefty total for one playing only twenty-two minutes a game. He also shot fifty-four percent from the floor. In a playoff game he grabbed twenty-six rebounds, the best post-season total in more than thirty years. Next he signed a four-year contract for seventy-two million with Orlando but produced slightly less impressive results under time constraints now standard. I concede above-mentioned teammate Nikola Vucevic is a better player, at least statistically, since he scores a lot more than Biyombo and has become almost as good defensively and on the boards. It's possible Biyombo's intensity unconsciously waned a bit after he became rich, and certain he needs more playing time to charge his engines and determine if he can become a dominant defender and rebounder. Let's ask Ben Wallace to decide how many minutes he plays.

SHORT STORY

Therapy

The basketball bounced long into Jimmy Barton's strong hands, and he dribbled straight at the player who'd shot and was now backpedaling, and as he passed half-court Jimmy planted his right foot and drove left but instantly cross-dribbled, twisting the defender onto the floor, and glided in for a layup. Haggin, the center, ran up waving long arms to harass the player trying to inbound, and the pass was lofted slightly too much and Jimmy Barton grabbed it as if he were the intended receiver, took one dribble, and went straight up for a jumper that almost blew out the net.

"Time out," yelled the opposing coach, who grabbed the inbound passer's arm when he reached the huddle.

"I didn't see him, Coach."

"You've gotta know where he is all the time."

Detected or not Jimmy Barton controlled every space he entered while scoring thirty-one points, six more than his average, and his El Lago High School team won by thirteen to stay unbeaten in league play.

At the party that night friends congratulated Jimmy as he sat on a sofa with his girlfriend, Karla, who held one hand and stroked his leg with her other soft one.

"Smitty, give me a beer, will yuh."

"You don't need it, Jimmy," she said.

He'd only drunk alcohol twice, vomiting each time, and was determined to learn to handle beers like most guys.

"Here you go," said Smith, a defensive tackle who during his off season had already become a drinking expert.

Jimmy grimaced after each sip, and said, "I can't imagine anyone loving this shit," and struggled a half hour to drink two cans of bitter beer before it started going down like water. When Karla objected, he asked one of his friends to take her home. She should have relaxed. Jimmy didn't heave but woke up next morning with a foul mouth and head.

"Jimmy, what's the matter with you?" said his mother.

"Nothing. It's Saturday."

"It's noon."

"Get the hell outta here."

"You wouldn't talk to me like that if your father were here."

Jimmy was glad his father was gone, living in another city with a new wife and their two infants. The old man would've ruined his dreams. He'd certainly screwed up the old ones, frequently commenting, "You spend so much time shooting that damn ball, and you'll never make a dime at it."

"I could make pros."

"You're not gonna make pros. Do your homework."

* * *

"Get in their faces," Jimmy screamed at teammates during the section title game against Central High. He was the only El Lago player comfortable with fast city ball. In summers he'd tried to take teammates downtown to play pickup games but they didn't like driving by drug dealers and hookers, and feared leaving their sleek cars in parking lots, and above all they didn't like the trash talk, which could be stopped if you attacked on offense and defense. But the suburban guys wouldn't do it. All night Central High hounded El Lago and, despite thirty-three points by Jimmy, rumbled to victory.

"Don't worry," El Lago fans told Jimmy. "You'll be playing at the next level."

In a few weeks Jimmy had stopped brooding about basketball. It no longer mattered. He'd gotten drunk at another party and Karla caught him necking with a cheerleader out by the pool. He apologized, and later sobbed when he learned she'd starting going with some guy from the debating team who laid her the first date. Everyone knew. It had taken Jimmy several months.

"Snap out of it, Jimmy," said his coach. "You've got scholarships to consider."

"I'm only playing for a major program. Why aren't they calling? I torched that punk from Central High, and everyone wants him."

"They like his athleticism. We're talking about a guard who touches the rim with his head."

"I'm better."

"Prove everyone wrong. Play JC ball a couple of years, then try to get an offer from an upper level D-1 team. But remember, you're not going to play anywhere unless you get back in the classroom. And get your ass back in the gym."

Jimmy wanted a break. Instead of going to school in the mornings, he now went to the houses of new friends and smoked pot and laughed and ate junk food and listened to loud music. He didn't drink in the mornings, though. That would have been a crash. He just needed good green weed. As spring afternoons warmed up he floated out to parks among trees and bushes along the river and drank cold beers before switching back to weed. He was proud how rapidly he'd mastered this new and creative way of living, and he and the other guys disapproved of those sitting like hams in classrooms.

"Jimmy, I'm worried about you," said his mother.

He stared at the window.

"You're pale and sniffling so much. Do you have an allergy? What have you been doing?"

"I'm not doing anything."

"You certainly aren't. The school keeps calling me about your absences. Listen, Jimmy, I got another call."

"From who?"

"Doesn't matter. I got a call and I know what you're doing."

"Then why'd you ask?"

"I wanted you to tell me."

He was still staring at the window.

"Your father will be here tonight, Jimmy."

"Well, I won't."

"Yes, you will. I took your car keys."

"No problem, I'll call my buddies."

"Your father wants to see you."

That night he said, "Jimmy, I hope you remember what I told you."

"Yeah, basketball's bad."

"It's fine, but insignificant compared to studying."

"Jimmy doesn't even play basketball anymore."

"That shows," said his father. "And here you are, not even graduated from high school."

"He's not going to graduate unless he finishes his U.S government class and a couple of others."

"I don't need to graduate."

"Jesus Christ, Jimmy, in America only future bums and convicts fail to graduate," said his father. "And high school's far less than the absolute minimum. You've got to be disciplined and learn to do something to support yourself."

Jimmy did not understand bourgeois talk. Only the senior prom mattered. He had to convince Evelyn to be his date, and that was easy. She'd had a crush on him for years.

On prom night he wore a rented white tux, borrowed his mother's black Cadillac, handed Evelyn a bright and fragrant bouquet, respectfully greeted her parents, opened the car door for her, got in the other side, reached for the floor, pulled up an open beer, and said: "You want one, too?"

Evelyn reluctantly took a sip of his, and they moved on to meet three other couples at a French restaurant. One of the girls had studied French four years and translated the menu and ordered for everyone. When she finished, Jimmy gallantly said, "And four bottles of champagne, the best."

"Certainly, Monsieur – in three years," said the waiter.

One of the guys later pulled out a flask and passed it around. Jimmy didn't like whiskey, and urged everyone to eat up so they could party.

Driving to the dance Jimmy drank three beers then filled his pockets and Evelyn's purse with several cans and put an arm around her and escorted her into the community center ballroom decorated with wreaths and banners and filled with attractive couples who looked so mature. Jimmy chose a seat where he could watch Karla, her thick brown hair shining way down her back.

While Jimmy drank, the soulful band played for a group of primarily stiff and repetitious dancers who, when they loosened up, danced even worse. Eventually, Jimmy tried some slow moves on the floor, putting his arms around Evelyn's neck, hugging her as he looked for Karla, who seemed unaware he was in the room. Late that night Jimmy went over to her table and said, "Madam, may I please have the next dance?"

"No, thank you."

"Come on, just one."

"No means no, Barton," said the debater.

"Shut your mouth, punk."

"Jimmy, go sit down," Karla said.

"I don't wanna sit. I wanna dance with you."

The debater stood up fast and Jimmy punched him in the nose.

Security guards rushed in and grabbed Jimmy and were going to call the police but Jimmy and his buddies convinced them he'd only acted to defend himself. And perhaps he had.

Karla ministered to and kissed her new boyfriend before helping him up and leading him away.

* * *

A few weeks later Jimmy's father was sitting next to Jimmy's former coach and across from Jimmy and his mother.

"Jimmy, this is the most humiliating experience of my life," his father said.

"One of my worst, too," said the coach. "You have so much promise. It just burns me you threw away scholarship offers. But don't give up. I've already talked to the coach at City College. If you take classes this summer and get your diploma, he thinks you can earn a starting spot. He wants to see you the first day of school."

"Yeah, but I don't want to see him."

"You'd better be interested, at least in school, or you'll be living on the goddamn streets," said his father.

"That's right, Jimmy," said his mother.

"Don't worry, I'm not leaving."

"Jimmy, and your mother agrees with me on this, you won't be permitted to live here and do nothing, to drink and God knows what else. You've either got to go to school or get a job. In fact, we may require you to do both."

"They're right, Jimmy," said the coach. "And will you please get back in the gym?"

Jimmy wanted a longer vacation from basketball but agreed to go to summer school. The first day – two three-hour classes – he listened and took notes and wrote down assignments, and at home after dinner he tried to read the books but could not concentrate. A half-hour into the second day Jimmy rose from his desk, walked to his car, opened the ash tray, plucked a perfectly rolled joint, put it in his mouth and lit it and inhaled pungent smoke quickly sedating his brain but also prompting him to stare in the rearview mirror at red eyes above darkening circles on a very pale face. Imagine if Karla saw him. He'd want her to understand he wasn't always ugly. He wouldn't be when he was no longer loaded. But he wouldn't want to be unloaded long.

"Jimmy, I have wonderful news," his mother said shortly before registration deadline. "I called a counselor at City College, and you don't have to be a high school graduate to go to a community college. All you need to be is eighteen. And in two years, when you get your AA degree, you can go straight to a university. Isn't that great?"

Jimmy never saw the coach at City College but lasted three weeks before he stopped attending classes. He decided he did not need them, and began studying on his own in the library where he went every morning. Now he read literature and history from a list he'd compiled and was sure he learned more than by listening to the babble of self-impressed teachers. This routine also enabled him to smoke a joint of good stuff before school and, when required, take a few quick puffs in an obscure spot in the big library. He had to be careful, though. People were always looking mean at him.

"Jimmy, your father and I want to see your report card."

"I don't have it."

"Where is it?"

"It doesn't exist."

"Then you'll have to get a job."

"I'm not taking some menial job."

"Either get a job or move out now."

"What if no one'll hire me?"

"Your father's already taken care of that."

Within a week Jimmy was loading trucks in the warehouse of a building contractor and driving the material to construction sites all over California. He was amazed how heavy everything was in construction and disgusted his sweat was not pure like a basketball player's but the rancid sweat of a pack mule. Jimmy longed for weekends when he could hole up in his recently-rented studio at the rear of a house in the bad part of town and watch football and basketball games, turning off the sound and letting images of vigor shine on him as he ate big bowls of sliced peaches and bananas with sugar and milk while sucking hot weed that deadened his feelings and opened his mind and closed him in. He never considered leaving at night until he'd cooled his throat with a six pack. That picked him up and got him in the shower at nine p.m. His fellow material handler, Hightower, was expecting him this Saturday night.

"Jimmy, have a tequila sunrise," said Hightower.

"No thanks. I don't drink alcohol, only beer."

"There'll be lots of babes at the party."

He didn't reply.

"You can't keep thinking about that chick, Jimmy."

"I'm gonna get her back."

"Let's go."

Some guy's parents were out of town, and their beautiful home and its large backyard were full of young people passing bottles and joints as they listened to window-rattling music.

"Over there," said Hightower. He tugged Jimmy's elbow and led him to two slender blondes wearing jeans and bright tank tops. "My friend and I can't believe how beautiful you are. Are you models?"

"We've done some at the mall," said the shorter girl.

"I gotta get over there more often. Wanna dance?"

Hightower took the shorter girl's hand and eased her to a place where several couples swayed.

"So, what do you do?" Jimmy said.

"I go to City College."

"I used to."

"What did you study?"

"I studied there independently. I don't need school."

"What're you doing now?"

"I'm a material handler."

She glanced into the night.

"You wanna smoke a joint?" Jimmy asked.

"No thanks."

He mumbled "cool" and walked to the far corner of the yard, behind a huge oleander bush, and started taking big hits.

* * *

"Listen to me, Son," Jimmy's father said, "you must quit smoking pot."

"I've quit lots of times."

"You're addicted."

"When I don't smoke, I get down and hyper, and I'm awake all night."

"You need discipline."

"What Jimmy needs is a psychiatrist," said his mother.

At the clinic he answered several pages of intrusive questions and then was taken into a cold room where he waited a long time before Dr. Blanchard entered and introduced himself and said, "Let's see, on your chart you indicate there's a family history of depression. Your parents?"

"Not them."

"Brother and sisters?"

"I don't have any. My father's sister definitely isn't right."

"Has she had professional treatment?"

"Yeah."

"How long?"

"Forever."

"Depression?"

"And alcoholism."

The doctor wrote fast on clipboard in his lap.

"And that woman's mother, my grandmother, was crazy most of her life."

"We don't use words like that anymore, Jimmy. She was ill. Was she ever hospitalized?"

"Often. And her brother was worse."

"What was he like?"

"He used to go around looking in windows, and eventually shot himself in his neighbor's yard."

"Do you own a gun, Jimmy?"

"No."

"Do you have access to one?"

"Everyone does."

"Have you ever thought of suicide?"

"No. But I can't take this forever."

"There's relief, Jimmy. I promise you modern medicine offers many psychopharmacological wonders. We'll start you on elavil, an antidepressant. Take fifty milligrams a day for a week, then a hundred for a week, then we'll maintain you at a hundred fifty a day.

"Beyond that, there are reactive reasons, factors in your environment, that also account for the way you are, and I think we should meet once a week for a half hour."

"How much does that cost?"

"Don't worry. Your parents are taking care of it."

"What do you want to talk about?"

"What's most important is what you want to talk about."

"I still miss my girlfriend."

"Is she out of town?"

"No. She broke up with me."

How long has it been?"

"Three years."

"And you still want to be with her?"

"Yes."

"Do you ever talk to her?"

"I try sometimes but she always hangs up or slams the door."

"Jimmy, a therapist has to be very careful giving advice, but it's my professional duty to tell you that you must stay away from her."

"I'm not going to hurt her."

"Are you sure?"

"Yes."

"Beyond your personal feelings, you have to concern yourself with legal matters. Has she gotten a restraining order?"

"No, but her husband threatened to."

"Jimmy, in cases like this, when so much time has elapsed, you need to accept you're feeling bad for reasons other than an ex-girlfriend. Have you had any girlfriends since?"

"No."

"How often do you date?"

"Sometimes."

"How long do these relationships last?"

"Usually just one time."

"Why?"

* * *

Jimmy didn't think he'd ever taken anything as strong as elavil, except when he'd dropped LSD. Though he wasn't actually hallucinating now, his vision was blurred and his skin clammy, and he couldn't let anyone look into his eyes. Symptoms worsened as dosages were increased to therapeutic levels, and his depression remained, so he resumed smoking pot and drinking, and his face bloated and looked spooky.

"You've got to be patient, Jimmy," said the doctor.

"I've already been on this stuff too long."

"We can give you something else."

Jimmy tried doxepin for several months, then triavil, and a torrent of other medications with strange names and wicked side effects until, following three years of treatment, the doctor announced: "Let's throw everything out – you aren't keeping old medications around, are you, Jimmy?"

"No."

"Good. We'll put you on the most promising psychotropic medications I've ever seen."

Prozac gave him headaches, stomachaches and cramps, and did not ease his mind nor did other new and popular medications. Jimmy hoped basketball would help. He bought a pair each of gym shorts, tube socks, and the latest basketball shoes, and went to the YMCA and shot air balls his first three practice shots and was the last guy chosen for a five-on-five full-court game. Then the ball began pounding the floor, wood screeched rubber soles, walls echoed grunts, the ball battered the rim and whistled nets, and everything was familiar and stimulating but a couple of minutes into the game Jimmy was gasping and not looking when the ball smacked the side of his face.

"Heads up, fatso," yelled a teammate.

A few minutes later, not having shot but having committed several turnovers and permitted his man to score often, Jimmy raised his hand for relief from the sidelines.

* * *

"Are you still smoking pot, Jimmy?" the doctor asked.

"Yes."

"That's a big part of the problem."

"I couldn't survive without it."

"Are you serious?"

"I've been going to the medical library and reading the *Comprehensive Textbook of Psychiatry* and lots of other books."

"That's fine, Jimmy, but you're a layman."

"And I'm talking in lay terms. My brain's making chemicals that might as well be acid."

"I understand, Jimmy."

"What do we do?"

"There's another promising medication. I want you to give it a try and write down what you think."

Jimmy got the new stuff at the pharmacy and went back to his filthy room at the rear of a house in the bad part of town and spent the rest of the day cleaning his place. A guy can be clean in a dirty place, but Karla wouldn't understand. She wouldn't have to because Jimmy's place was immaculate. He felt proud looking at the framed picture of himself, arm around Karla after a big game, and put on his gym shorts and tube socks and basketball shoes, and turned on the air conditioner and pounded the ball on the old tile floor.

FOOTBALL

KICKOFF

The Rogers Brothers: Triumph and Tragedy

Twenty-seven years ago this month I went to Norte Del Rio High School in north Sacramento and interviewed a sprinter named Roy Mosley who'd just won two races at a large invitational meet. As a visiting correspondent I received lots of attention from kids wanting to learn what I was doing and some, after watching me shoot a few jump shots on an outdoor court, asked about basketball, too. At that point a young fellow my size – six-foot-one – came up, offered me his hand, and said, "Hi, I'm Donald Rogers. Keep an eye on me. I'm only a sophomore and I'm already dunking and I just averaged twenty-four points a game on the junior varsity."

"That's damn good," I said. "I play a lot of ball. Here's my phone number. Give me a call." The most surprising point here is that during the four years I covered high school sports, as well as some events at higher levels, that was the only time I gave my phone number to one of the athletes. It simply never occurred to me, except with Donald Rogers. He was a charming guy people instinctively liked and trusted. I really didn't expect a phone call from even a confident kid a decade younger but I certainly attuned myself to the athletic exploits of Rogers. Over the next two autumns, he played quarterback, hurling the football seventy yards or running like a halfback, and as a defensive back he sped to break up passes and flatten ball carriers.

During basketball season Donald Rogers was indeed a dunker as well as an outside shooter and a driver, rebounder, and defender. He was a winner, and he was exciting. The highlight of some two hundred basketball games I covered came in January 1980, Donald's senior year. Right now I'm looking at the yellowing newspaper clip from that game. My opening sentence announces: "The Rogers brothers were unleashed on Jesuit Tuesday night and the Marauders are probably still flinching." At this point, they probably enjoy the memory of playing against two great athletes.

I'd arrived a little earlier than usual so I could watch a good chunk of the junior varsity game featuring Donald's sophomore brother, six-foot-six Reggie. As I approached the scorer's table, people shouted, "Hey, Reggie got twenty-four points in the first quarter, and scored the team's first thirty-three points."

Reggie Rogers cooled off a bit in the third quarter but poured in sixteen points in the final and finished with fifty-nine and a victory. Next, in the main event, Donald scored thirty-six. It was an exhila-rating evening. But one thing troubled me: why wasn't Reggie Rogers playing varsity, where he belonged? I asked the Norte coach who said during preseason varsity practice Reggie had demanded to be sent down to the JVs. Something in his makeup compelled him to avoid the appropriate athletic challenges and, instead, dominate much smaller and weaker players.

Next came track season, and if you're familiar with Olympic decathlon champions Jim Thorpe, Bruce Jenner, and Dan O'Brien then you have a good image of what Donald Rogers was like. He could sprint, he could hurdle, from basketball you knew he could've high jumped and long jumped, and based on his hard tackling in football he clearly had the strength to put the shot and hurl the discuss and javelin.

"If Donald decided to dedicate himself to the decathlon, I guarantee you he'd be a gold medal contender," I said to a guy I often played basketball with at Norte Del Rio during the summer.

"Have you ever seen Donald play baseball?" he asked.

"No, why, is he pretty good?"

"Oh, baseball's by far his best sport. You should see him hit."

I never got to see Donald swing a bat. After his senior year, in the summer of 1980, he was busy preparing for the sport he'd chosen – football. UCLA had only deemed one prep athlete in the Sacramento area capable of playing at its level: that guy was Donald. They told him to start lifting weights; his strength had theretofore been natural. I called him a few times that summer and asked if he wanted to play some hoops at his alma mater. He always came.

At the time I was in my prime, worked out two hours a day, weighed one hundred ninety pounds, and usually held up pretty well on the court. Donald, at this stage, weighed about two hundred but the exact total isn't nearly as important as the quality of the weight; he wielded the weight of a superior athlete. And as I battled him for rebounds I well remember thinking I'd never been on the court with a guy so strong and was fortunate we weren't playing football.

The sporting nation would soon learn about Donald Rogers. At UCLA he played safety a lot as a freshman and started as a sophomore and as a junior in the 1983 Rose Bowl he commanded attention by leveling the University of Michigan quarterback and separating his shoulder. It was a clean hit. That was the way Donald played. His 1984 Rose Bowl performance was supreme; he made plays all over the field and intercepted two passes and ran one back deep into opposition territory. There was no doubt: Donald Rogers, All American, was going to be a first round draft choice. The Cleveland Browns were fortunate to get him, and he made the all rookie defensive team in 1984 and performed even better the following season.

Every year I'd been planning to call Donald during the off season. I'd last done so in the summer of 1981 after his freshman year at UCLA. He'd greeted me enthusiastically, and we talked about how coaches push players hard, even when they're recovering from injuries. He noted that his teammate, All American safety Kenny Easley, was one of the nicest people he'd ever met. And when I asked if he thought he could play in the NFL, he softly assessed some of the aforementioned physical and competitive attributes that made him confident of succeeding at the highest level. I wrote a feature article, one of my last as a newspaper correspondent. Confounded by stylistic restrictions in the trade, I tried some other things: loading trucks and delivering construction material, publishing a monthly tabloid, and doing a little public relations work. I also received a modest inheritance and began writing a biographical novel, *Hitler Here*.

In 1986, boosted by the patrimony, I was ready to build something I'd always wanted: a personal basketball gym. My neighborhood, like almost all places in north Sacramento, was rundown. Paint peeled from numerous houses. Many lawns sat unmown. Old cars rotted all around. But in bad neighborhoods prices are low and I'd paid thirty-nine grand the year before for a small two bedroom house on a big lot right down the street from Norte Del Rio. I collected bids for the foundation, walls, roof, and myriad other things you need in construction, and for twenty grand I was going to be able to build a half-court gym much larger than my house attached to it. As the walls went up, I thought: now it's about time to call Donald Rogers; maybe he'll get a kick out of this. I'll wait just a little longer, though. I can't invite a pro to play in an unfinished gym.

On this June day the workers had just gone home, and I'd stacked wood scraps and other refuse in the backyard, and come inside to guzzle water and watch some news. Flicking the TV on, I heard the end of a story: "And Donald Rogers is dead at age twenty-three."

What the hell do you mean, I asked the screen? This has to be a mistake. I hurried to the phone and called the old newspaper office and heard: "We've been reading some of your articles. Yeah, it's true. They think it's a cocaine overdose."

That's what it was. The night before, following his bachelor party, Donald and several friends visited some clubs and somewhere in there he received a fatal wedding present: a large quantity of high grade cocaine. In the morning his mother was alarmed by his staying so long in the bathroom with the water running. Running water hides many things. Eventually, Donald was found unconscious and rushed by ambulance to a nearby emergency center then to a larger facility. Later, doctors said "his death had been assured." If they or the police knew whether the cocaine had been snorted or smoked, they didn't say. Ultimately, it didn't matter.

A couple thousand people attended his funeral in the building where the Sacramento Kings played. I usually don't attend funerals but I went, too. Two ladies were playing solemn spirituals on pianos. Jesse Jackson delivered the eulogy. Donald's college and pro coaches offered genuine tributes. His fiancé was inconsolable. College teammate Kenny Easley served as one of the pallbearers. Afterward, one of the ushers said to go on and walk by the open casket. I didn't go near it. I wanted to remember only the vibrant Donald Rogers.

Reggie Rogers was naturally devastated by the death of his older brother. We'll never know how Reggie's life would have unfolded if this hadn't happened. We're only sure he also chose football, and became an All American defensive end at the University of Washington, where he was arrested for drunk driving. In 1987 the Detroit Lions drafted him in the first round, and soon he was arrested for assaulting his girlfriend, sued by two former agents, and distraught because his sister Jackie disappeared for several days. Tragedy struck again in October 1988 when he drunkenly ran a red light and broadsided a car, killing three teenagers. He also broke his neck in the collision. Later he spent about a year in jail. Then his NFL comeback failed. In all, he'd played poorly for three teams and was considered a less than vigorous worker.

At first I thought it was bad news, at least for one writing an article, that little information about Reggie has appeared on the internet since 1992. But I realize that may be a good sign. He must not be getting into trouble. I could go back into north Sac and find out what he's doing. I'm in town a few times a year. But I'm going to leave the present alone. In this story I prefer the past, the days when Donald Rogers roamed the gridiron and dominated the hardwood and burned up the track. Those were the good days when he and others were alive and happy.

April 2005

A Book about the Rogers Family

Early in 2007 I received an email from freelance writer Sean Harvey, who'd read my article about Donald Rogers and asked to interview me. Of course, I told him. I'd be delighted to reminisce about a man as memorable for personal appeal as his athletic resume. After exchanging a number of online messages, Harvey and I talked by phone for about an hour. I was impressed his book – *One Moment Changes Everything* – would also cover the lives of Donald's notably talented younger brother and sister, Reggie and Jackie, and would as well deal with vital medical issues that are often bemoaned but rarely examined or understood.

The conversation with Sean Harvey transported me back to the late seventies, when I was a sports correspondent in my twenties, and Donald Rogers, a decade younger, was becoming a prep sports legend in the Sacramento area. Harvey had played basketball against Donald in high school and I'd done so in pick-up games during summers in the gym at Norte Del Rio, his high school in malnourished north

Sacramento. We agreed: never had we been on the court with anyone having Donald's combination of speed, strength, and coordination.

In the Rogers family, physical superiority proved a genetic guarantee. Reggie grew to six-foot-six, five inches taller than Donald, and was sought by major universities for his mobility in football and rim-rattling style on the basketball court. Long-armed Jackie dominated softball games with seventy-mph fastballs but was courted by top college basketball programs eager to capitalize on her six-foot-two frame and deft shooting touch. Many boys also followed, smitten by her by her beauty and sophistication.

The glory years had begun. At UCLA Donald commanded two Rose Bowls, intercepting a record three passes and flattening any opponent with the ball. In 1984 the Cleveland Browns rewarded him with a first round selection and, for that era, a generous contract. Donald immediately bought a house for his mother, Loretha, and new cars for Reggie and Jackie as well as his stepfather, Joe Henry Rogers, who had separated from his wife. Donald didn't know his biological father, and Loretha never commented on his identity.

Reggie received a basketball scholarship to the University of Washington and performed well on that team but, dissatisfied with playing time, accepted Donald's advice to play football for the Huskies. Fleet and muscular at two hundred seventy pounds, Reggie promptly sacked quarterbacks and trapped running backs for losses to establish himself as a future first round pick. By her graduation from Grant High School in 1983 – underfunded Norte Del Rio had closed a year earlier – Jackie was the finest female basketball player in Northern California and, from many offers, chose Oregon State University tucked in the small community of Corvallis.

The future of the Rogers family seemed unassailable. In his book, however, Sean Harvey notes that in her final year of high school Jackie had seemed "listless and lacked enthusiasm" and her mood was "flat." Then, after only one year at Oregon State, she ominously and without explanation resigned her scholarship and returned to her mother's house in north Sacramento. That wasn't in the headlines. Neither was it that Joe Henry Rogers had often been drunk when he attended basketball games at Norte and embarrassed his sons. He subsequently had three DUIs and served four months in jail.

Even if more people had known, they wouldn't have worried. Donald Rogers, an immediate standout in the NFL, would take care of everyone. His presence always promised good things.

That's why Leslie Nelson wanted to spend her life with him. They'd met at UCLA and were going to be married on June twenty-eighth, 1986. During the preceding week Donald had flown from Cleveland to Seattle, driven eight hundred miles from there to Sacramento with Reggie so they could be together, jetted back to Cleveland, then hustled to Los Angeles where he finished work on the final class needed for his economics degree, and on Thursday June twenty-sixth hurried up to Sacramento for his bachelor's party. It was a subdued gathering, Donald and Reggie and about twenty friends drinking a little and eating a lot in a suite at the Hilton Hotel in suburban Sacramento. Donald, exhausted, slipped out without saying goodbye. He wanted to be rested for the wedding rehearsal Friday night in Oakland. And he'd told Browns teammate Hanford Dixon that he wanted to ride to Oakland with him so they could talk about something important.

Friday morning Donald got up and came downstairs to have breakfast. His mother and Jackie were there. So was Terry Bolar, a bejeweled "runner" for a pair of agents illegally courting Reggie, who was asleep at the Hilton. The phone rang in the Rogers home. It was Paul Warfield, a retired hall of fame receiver then a Browns executive who assisted players in finishing their degrees.

"He was great – typical Donald," Warfield said.

Donald returned upstairs to take a shower. At about 10 a.m., Harvey writes, a "primal scream ripped the morning air, a piercing sound that others reported feeling within their houses several doors away – an agonizing release that caused the neighbors to cringe… the kind of sound you never forget." Donald pounded his bedroom walls and yelled, "Ma, call for help – quick!"

The man who had inspired so many soon fell into a coma. Paramedics arrived. A drug overdose was suspected. College basketball star Len Bias died about a week before, and Donald had called his mother and cried. What was going on? To this day, more than twenty years later, no one has said he ever saw Donald Rogers use drugs. The notion was shocking but true. And after several hours struggling to save him, doctors that afternoon, the day before his wedding, pronounced Donald Lavert Rogers dead at age twenty-three.

Loretha had a heart attack and the family again called 911. After partially recovering, she frequently went to her son's grave and for hours prayed and talked to him and declared he would protect her. Reggie returned to the University of Washington where journalists presumed to be district attorneys, interrogating the bereaved young man about his and Donald's behavior. "In 2007," Harvey notes, "no sports information director would tolerate the same litany of questions hurled forth..."

To pay family bills that mushroomed when Donald's assets ceased arriving, Reggie, through Terry Bolar, accepted money from mafia-infected agents Norby Walters and Lloyd Bloom. Despite his problems Reggie made All American in the fall of 1986 and the following spring the Detroit Lions drafted him in the first round. But football could not have been his primary concern. "Walls were closing in on Reggie: lawsuits, anonymous phone calls warning him not to testify against Walters and Bloom, Loretha's worsening heart trouble," Harvey explains. "Battling minor injuries, Reggie was splitting time at defensive end when, to everyone's dismay, the NFL Players Association voted to go on strike." During this unwanted free time, Reggie started serious drinking.

Then Jackie, who'd been indolent and depressed since leaving Oregon State three years earlier, came to Detroit for a visit, borrowed her brother's truck, and disappeared. "Frantic" Reggie contacted authorities. Someone from the morgue called to tell him there was a body that could be Jackie. It wasn't. After four days Jackie returned, saying she'd been with a friend. On the way back to Sacramento, her plane stopped in Chicago. Rather than catch her connecting flight, Jackie vanished again. And "a family member finally informed Reggie that Jackie was addicted to cocaine."

Under a multitude of burdens, Reggie collapsed emotionally and entered a counseling center where he was treated for depression and alcohol dependency. In 1988 he returned to the Lions as a sober and recently-engaged young man carrying two hundred ninety chiseled pounds and ready to perform as expected. His progress was satisfactory until he injured an ankle in October. With too much spare time again, he resumed drinking, and three weeks later he drove to a bar.

"The next thing Reggie Rogers knew, he was waking up in a hospital with a broken neck and a severed thumb, his head immobilized in a metal halo," Harvey writes. "The police soon arrived to inform him that he'd be arrested upon his release from intensive care. Bewildered, he asked... 'Why? What did I do?'"

He'd broadsided a car and killed three teenagers. He spent 1989 recovering from his wounds, 1990 in prison, and played two more injury-interrupted seasons, for Buffalo and Tampa, before being waived out of the league.

The tribulations of the Rogers family have been publicized because of the athletic talent of Donald and Reggie, but until *One Moment Changes Everything* there hasn't been a sustained look at the family's medical problems – depression, alcoholism, and drug addiction, which plague tens of millions of families worldwide. Most of the time these inextricably-linked illnesses are treated as moral hurdles every righteous person should be able to overcome through willpower alone. That's a dangerous delusion. The brain of an intrinsically depressed person is a chemically flawed brain. In a majority of cases only medical intervention can save people from unrelenting pain. And those in pain often medicate themselves with alcohol, tobacco, marijuana, cocaine, and other perilous drugs.

Last week, following his first book signing, Sean Harvey wrote me this email about someone with an untreated problem: "The (TV) appearance on 'Sacramento and Company' went really well. Fun, easy, positive. I'm at Barnes & Noble, perhaps twenty people there, when in barges this giant woman screaming, 'Who wrote this book?'

"Jackie.

"Stoned and drunk out of her mind. Profane. Hysterical. She charges right up to the front of the gathering and begins yelling, 'You don't have no right to write a book about my family. You don't have no right to write about my motherfucking brother.'

"Right in the middle of the bookstore.

"A well-meaning friend of hers had seen the segment on TV and took Jackie to the signing as a surprise. The friend was so incredibly nice, and came up and pulled Jackie away (just as security arrived) and, crying, told me how sorry she was – that she wanted to buy three books right then, that this was my moment…

"Jackie grabbed a book and left. My girlfriend spoke with Jackie's friend for several minutes. She thought Jackie would be happy… She told my girlfriend that Jackie hasn't been off drugs once in twenty years… It's really sad. You could see just what an astoundingly beautiful woman she had been."

If Jackie Rogers reads this article, she'll be angry with me, too. But she shouldn't be. I liked her brother and still think about him. And since reading Harvey's book, I've been thinking about her, too. I hope she understands. She needs professional help. No one should try to climb out of a dungeon alone.

April 2007

Another Tragedy

A few minutes ago my girlfriend, who's not a sports fan, tapped my office door and asked, "Do you know Reggie Rogers?"

"I knew his brother, Donald, but didn't really know Reggie," I said. "Why?"

I sensed what had happened, as did most who knew the story of the Rogers family. Reggie Rogers was dead at age forty-nine. Authorities haven't released the specifics yet, but we know the cause. His heart gave out because he drank too much and killed three people while driving drunk and had six DUIs and twice spent time in prison for the crimes and sometimes took medications for depression and often groggily spent days in bed and he and his body didn't want any more.

This is news because Donald and Reggie Rogers were two splendid athletes whose exploits and travails have been chronicled above. Donald died almost twenty-seven years ago.

Most who'd known him were shocked, not for moralistic reasons, but because he always seemed like the most relaxed guy around, the one who makes good decisions. Reggie appeared less stable. Sister

Jackie has also battled the intrinsic two-headed terror: depression and alcoholism. I don't know how Jackie's life has been going, but I'm sure today she's grieving another lost brother.

April 2013

Message to Donald Rogers

Donald,

How's it going? I hope you remember me from 1978 to 1980 when as a newspaper correspondent I witnessed and wrote about your career in high school sports, and sometimes played basketball with you the summer before you went to UCLA.

I can't fathom it's been thirty years since you left, and many feel the same, especially those in Sacramento where you were raised. We miss you and the special qualities you had, the charm and quiet magnetism that endure.

Take it easy. And, please, let us hear from you.

Tom

June 2016

Rigors of Football in Seattle

I'm going to Seattle this Christmas season, and in that regard a few months ago received an email from one of my hosts urging me to accelerate my schedule and fly out of Bakersfield to catch a connecting flight in time to attend the Seattle Seahawks game against the Baltimore Ravens on December twenty-third. Since I'd already quietly purchased airline tickets designed to safely deposit me in the Emerald City on the twenty-second, and the football fans would be fetching me at the airport, I could not plead tardiness. I'd have to try something else.

* * *

Last December I'd joined these robust citizens of the Northwest for a game against the San Diego Chargers. In a sturdy SUV, they hauled me to their favorite parking area – "good for avoiding after-game traffic" – more than a mile from the stadium and some four hours before kickoff. Upon backing into a space we noted the pickup truck to the right featured a side-view mirror held on by vice grips. That was an inauspicious indicator. Within minutes we discovered someone had forgotten to pack the tri-tip. We jumped in the vehicle, and as we rolled through downtown Seattle, looking for a market, I made a few modest inquiries about real estate and learned a studio apartment goes for half a million bucks. I might be able to buy a downtown bathroom, if one were independently for sale. Even in this rarefied district the first two markets we found, both Chinese, did not have anything resembling tri-tip or the kind of Chinese food consumed in restaurants. Eventually we spotted a downtrodden place probably called Joe's Market, and purchased their finest meat – pork chops. Those would be great with the red pepper hot links that had been packed. We rushed back and recaptured the prime parking space.

Only the most ardent military commanders amass as many supplies as football tailgaters. From the back of their SUV this crew unfurled a canopy and under it placed a fold-out table with benches and crowned the table with a barbecue. An eighteen-piece barbecue tool kit promptly appeared, a propane heater ignited, padded chairs unfolded, a portable TV flashed football, pigskin sailed into our hands, and beers started going down. As a retired imbiber, I declined the suds and began devouring mounds of corn and potato chips.

"Did you hear Terry Bradshaw on Imus in the Morning?" asked Sam. "He was moaning about eight years of loneliness after all his divorces."

"I have no sympathy for him," said his friend Billy. "I've been alone longer than that."

"Terry Bradshaw is a whiny tit," Sam said. "He turned down his Super Bowl invitation all the other most valuable players are accepting (except Joe Montana) because they wouldn't pay him an appearance fee. Those guys are getting round trip transportation to the fortieth anniversary of the Super Bowl, free rooms in a great hotel, and several hundred dollars spending money. And Bradshaw won't go."

"Glad I brought my umbrella," I said, peering at a darkening sky and zipping my coat against the breeze.

"No one in Seattle uses an umbrella," said Claude, Sam's father. "Look around. Everyone just wears a baseball cap or uses the hood of their coat. They'll laugh at your umbrella."

"Bakersfield only gets seven inches rain a year. When it rains you see umbrellas all over. Up here no one minds forty inches?"

"Rain's nothing," said Sam. "Little more than a week ago we had winds eighty miles an hour that knocked out power in a million and a half homes. A week later a hundred thousand still didn't have electricity. Some people used generators to keep warm, others used their barbecues inside. Carbon monoxide's been a problem. Twelve people died."

About ten-thirty that morning it started to rain a little. No one said anything. We were chewing juicy pork chops, sausages, and horse-size bratwurst. Fuel was needed for the long hike. Not wanting to appear a weakling, I didn't mention my regret that locals had blown up the almost-warm Kingdome and replaced it with sky-open Qwest Field. Before entering, my hosts said I had to see Tailgater Heaven, under the

Alaskan Way Viaduct, a wobbly-looking double-decker many expect to crumble during the next earthquake. We hadn't tailgated here, they explained, since post-game traffic was horrific. Our walk through Heaven revealed waves of mobile homes and canopies, hundreds of drunken fans, lots of painted faces, and several chest-beaters adorned with T-shirts about queers in California. Those title-starved fellows must be forgiven their envy of California's eight Super Bowl championships, five owned by the San Francisco 49'ers and three by the Oakland Raiders (one while lost in Los Angeles.)

Inside Qwest Field we loaded up on peanuts plain and salted, and took our end zone seats, mercifully sheltered on top, in the final row of the grounded section of the stadium. Unless you're standing on the sidelines or sitting fairly low between the 30-yard lines, you're really not going to see much football. In fact, no one at any game sees as well as television viewers plied with stunning live shots and a stream of instant replays. People go to football games to feel the event, commune with thousands of other fans, exchange manly barbs, slurp brews, curse referees, boo opponents, berate the home team when it struggles, and roar after it makes a play.

Some fans say they prefer end zone seats, commenting how they love watching the holes open. On a sunny day I might've enjoyed such intricacies but as slashing winds drove wet air into my bones, I concentrated less on man-to-man blocking than the sheltered snack bar where three times I escaped to buy food that, back in my seat, numbed me as I gazed north at surrealistic skyscrapers close enough to touch yet from a distant world where numerous lit windows suggested mysterious secretaries traipsing around desks.

"Where does Paul Allen sit?" I asked about the team owner who, with Bill Gates, had founded Microsoft before retiring young to confront (and conquer) cancer while the computer revolution transformed his stock into billions.

"Anywhere he wants," said Billy.

"He ain't outside," I concluded.

With indifference wrought by growing discomfort, I watched Phillip Rivers' pass in the waning seconds sail over a Seahawk defender and into the grasp of a game-winning receiver. It was time to go.

Seventy thousand faithful converged. Walking in massive halls I was consumed by a horde that moved ever on, carrying my companions away and forcing me to think – my god, what if I were a child? Parents couldn't find a kid in this mass if someone wanted to run away with him. Several minutes later Sam eased back and took me by the sleeve. When reunited with everyone, I mentioned my concern.

"That's right," said Claude. "A parent's got to take hold of the child's hand and keep holding it."

I haven't checked the wind patterns in Seattle but this day the big blow was attacking from the south. Whatever energy we'd used walking to the stadium, we spent several times more on the way back, pushing into a black storm that battered my umbrella all over as rain froze my face and soggy legs and feet.

* * *

Studying the email, and considering the forgoing experience, I pressed reply and wrote, "We'll take a look at that. But for me the best place to watch football is in front of a big screen." Claude has one six feet wide in his den and a full-scale theater next door.

"That sounds like a no...which is fine...so be it...no worries," he replied. Seattle's not that bad. "In Denver last year Sam's beer froze twenty minutes after he bought it in the stands."

December 2007

Bill Walsh Remembers

I want to emphasize I'm writing this from the viewpoint of a competitive and even Machiavellian coach in the National Football League, not merely the genial elder statesman who in retirement kept an office at Stanford and watched film with and drew plays for some of the young coaches and begged their indulgence if I'd spoken a bit too long. Honestly, I saw their enthusiasm and knew they were under my spell, and their respect enchanted me in equal measure. That's the irony of my coaching career, the most gratifying times – excepting transitory moments of Super Bowl exhilaration – came when I wasn't on the sidelines anymore, when I didn't have to worry about who to draft or cut or how to win in the regular season and ultimately capture the Super Bowl. Anything less than absolute victory invited people to impugn me.

Many wonderful things have been said and written about me in the two weeks since my passing, but one thing most people knew, but suppressed during this solemn period, was that I really did enjoy being called a genius and in fact resented it when lesser status was implied. I'd felt that way a long time. At the latest, I considered myself a revolutionary force in 1970, when, as a Cincinnati Bengals assistant, I designed a quick-strike offense of short passes for our weak-armed quarterback, Virgil Carter, and by 1971 had him completing a high percentage of his attempts, which he wouldn't have done – and never did do – under the guidance of anyone else. I then took Ken Anderson, a kid out of Augustana College, not a noted quarterback factory, and by 1974 transformed him into a precise passer. He was comparably efficient the following year, but, after owner Paul Brown "stabbed me in the back" and hired someone else as head coach, I left town and Anderson's passing efficiency plummeted for several years.

Really, it was a humiliating time. I was already in my forties and had not been a head coach in the NFL and felt the call would never come. Many less-able men my age and younger had been given a chance. What's wrong with me, a tormenting voice continually asked?

My opportunity finally arrived in 1977, when I was forty-five, not with a professional team but at Stanford, an elite university qualified to appreciate my creative temperament. We had two good seasons and twice won bowl games, and Eddie DeBartolo, the cocky owner of the woeful two and fourteen San Francisco 49ers, hired me to coach the team I'd followed as a young man in the Bay Area.

In 1979, during the first draft I controlled, I made the most important professional decision of my life, selecting quarterback Joe Montana. My career and Joe's would likely have been quite different had I not made him a 49er, and for the rest of my life I enjoyed praise for acquiring him. Yes, I'd studied film of Joe at Notre Dame, and later said I had considered him poetry in motion and known he was going to be one of the greatest ever. Frankly, if I'd really realized that at the time, I would have seized him in the first round rather than the third. But that isn't the point. I took Joe Montana before anyone else, and kept him safely on the bench most of his rookie and my inaugural 49er season during which opponents tattooed us with a two and fourteen record that prompted fans to call me foolish and overmatched.

I worried they might be right. Really, I knew they weren't, but my record made their catcalls credible. We had to get better. In 1980 I might've stayed too long with Steve DeBerg, who completed lots of passes but threw more interceptions than touchdowns, prompting me to comment, "He plays about good enough to get us beat." Then I announced Joe Montana would be our starter, and felt optimistic as we won some games and improved to six and ten. But we had the worst pass defense in the league, and most observers felt that deficiency would take a few years to resolve. I couldn't wait that long. Moving decisively in the 1981 draft, I took defensive backs with our first three picks.

Ronnie Lott was the critical choice. He stormed in and hammered receivers and running backs, energizing our team and warning opponents the 49ers were no longer patsies. Rather suddenly, we had the best quarterback and finest defensive back in football. On first downs I often called short passes that worked like long handoffs, and we went that way when defenses expected this way, and struck long when others were looking short, and ran when they expected passes, and confused and dissected defenses while our own controlled opponents. During this sublime season we rolled to a thirteen and three record, best in the league. The entire football world, and indeed many who followed other sports, were stunned by this bold turnaround and delighted by the graceful maneuvers of our offense.

That's when people in the media, as well as fans, began to publicly call me a genius. I didn't have time to discourage them. Both arms raised, I was being carried off the field after our Super Bowl victory over the Cincinnati Bengals who'd rejected me. Around the nation one heard the same compliments that have been offered lately: Bill Walsh is "an extraordinary teacher...a great pioneer...an innovator...a master of preparation and detail..." Some also noted I was frequently an unpleasant taskmaster. After the 1981 opener, for example, I cut a rookie kick returner because his two fumbles inflicted defeat.

All coaches say they don't like losing. It burned my insides and darkened the horizons. In 1982 the players went on strike and shortened and above all distorted the season, and we finished three and six. People enjoyed my struggles and again claimed I couldn't sustain a high level, that I must've been lucky, that after all I'd had three losing seasons out of four in the NFL. I told the media they'd been "awfully good...about tolerating us" this season and I regretted their suffering. They were mere spectators. The 49ers were the show, which I enhanced by taking high-knees running back Roger Craig in the 1983 draft. In 1984 we were supreme, losing but one game all season and in the Super Bowl shredding the Miami Dolphins of celebrated coach Don Shula, who'd actually believed he could win.

The accolades returned in even greater measure, and I felt wonderful. This was the life I'd always craved. Soon I purchased a beautiful house in the bucolic community of Woodside, within minutes of Stanford and our Redwood City training site. And in the 1985 draft I again demonstrated why many have called me an "incredible personnel executive," trading up to take Jerry Rice, a certifiably superior football player. The Chicago Bears won the championship that year, but in 1986 I counterpunched with my most celebrated draft, trading down to acquire more picks and selecting an astonishing eight players who would become starters.

Our 1986 season nevertheless ended on a gusty winter day in New York City where the Giants crucified us forty-nine to three. We had so much talent, but they'd overpowered us. I responded in the 1987 draft by taking a big offensive tackle, Harris Barton, who could battle brutish defenders. That plan and all others worked during a regular season we consummated with impressive victories, including a forty-one to nothing pasting of the Bears and mulish Mike Ditka. Our unmatched record earned home field advantage for the playoffs when the Minnesota Vikings swaggered into Candlestick Park and, on a soggy field, began abusing us. Joe Montana, who'd had back surgery the year before, was not maneuvering well in the muck, so in the third quarter I benched a man many already considered the finest quarterback in history – and certainly one of the top three – and inserted his talented understudy, and now rival, Steve Young, a sturdy young man who ran like a halfback. Steve generated some offense but we still lost twenty-eight to sixteen.

Joe was angry, our players and fans dispirited, and team owner Eddie DeBartolo hysterical. I thought he was going to fire me, and broke down and said go ahead if that's best for the team. I couldn't withstand much more pressure, anyway. Go ahead, give this miserable job to someone else. I've already climbed the mountain twice. Eddie was a great motivator, always ready with maximum legal money and more for a champion but a tyrannical runt when his athletic superiors weren't number one.

We decided to move ahead into 1988. Responding as an adroit leader must, I'd forced some once-key players to retire and alluded to wielding the axe on others. Our team wasn't overpowering and barely made the playoffs with a ten and six record but began to execute in the playoffs and was a strong favorite in the Super Bowl against the Cincinnati Bengals. They weren't intimidated and played more sharply to lead us late in the fourth quarter. That's when Joe Montana, standing confidently in the huddle, said to a teammate, "Check it out."

"What?"

"Check it out. There's John Candy."

Joe threw strikes and Jerry Rice made great catches against tight defense, and that set it up: Joe over the middle to John Taylor, one of those 1986 picks, and we'd won our third Super Bowl of the eighties. After the game, emotionally embracing one of my sons, Craig, I knew my era had to end. I resigned and became a rather uncomfortable TV analyst. Our championship team the following year was coached by George Seifert, a veteran of my staff, and I think everyone feels that Super Bowl also belongs on my resume.

In 1992 I returned to the sidelines at Stanford and guided the team to a ten and three record and a bowl victory, but in 1994, after two losing seasons, some of the players threatened to revolt because I'd made some harsh remarks about their athletic deficiencies. This time I took off the headphones forever, unwilling to endure 49er-like pressure at a great university whose lofty academic standards precluded annual gridiron excellence.

I didn't divorce myself from the game. I communicated with my battalion of former assistant coaches who had become head coaches in the NFL and at major colleges. I'm particularly proud of assistance I gave African American coaches Dennis Green, Ray Rhodes, and Tyrone Willingham. I concentrated on developing coaches as well as players. I also understood contracts and salary cap restrictions. In the late nineties the 49ers recalled me as general manager to rebuild a losing team soon back in the playoffs. Perhaps I should have stayed on as an executive.

That's a daydream. In November of 2001 I turned seventy and didn't want daily duress. I had a great life as sage, speaker, and celebrity as well as husband and father. Then my son Steve died of leukemia. And my wife Geri was incapacitated by a stroke. My war with leukemia began in 2004. Tragedy destroyed paradise, and now only the memories endure.

August 2007

Walsh Lectures Harbaugh and Kaepernik

Bill Walsh – Sit down, both of you. This is a classroom, and I'm the teacher.

Jim Harbaugh – You were, and I respect that, but I'm in charge of the 49ers now.

BW – Remember, Jim, I had complete control, creating a new model of management, drafting, trading, and cutting players, coaching them and calling the plays. Trent Baaltke's unquestionably in control of 49ers' personnel. Your tasks, compared to mine, are rather limited. Nevertheless, I consider you a great young coach, albeit now a year older than when I won my first Super Bowl, and that's why I've agreed to talk to you and Colin, who would've made a fine backup to Joe Montana.

Colin Kaepernick – Don't presume, Coach Walsh. I'm bigger, stronger, faster, and tougher than Joe.

BW – You're also prone to throwing incompletions and interceptions at critical times such as the final drives of the Super Bowl against Baltimore and the NFC championship game versus Seattle. Joe would have thrown perfect passes for title-winning TDs. But I'm not here to rebuke either of you. I'm here to edify.

JH – I don't like your tone.

BW – I'm the eternal 49er. Pay attention. I'll start with Colin. You must settle down so you can concentrate. You can't keep stumbling around, mentally, as the play clock expires and the team is assessed costly five-yard penalties.

CK – I've been working on it. Some problems are because the offensive coordinator doesn't get plays to me in time.

BW – Jim, that's also your responsibility as well as that of the offensive coordinator.

JH – I didn't tell the coordinator to bumble.

BW – Did you tell him to deemphasize the running game? You shouldn't be passing so much. Your offensive line's allowing far too much pressure on Colin. I know they've had a holdout, and an injury, and an all star not playing as well as expected. But most of those problems impact your pass blocking. Though I'm a master of creative passing, I direct you to start running the ball more.

JH – We ran a lot last week when we came from behind to beat the undefeated Philadelphia Eagles.

BW – Keep emphasizing the run to set up the pass. I was the first in history to pass to set up the run but, for the aforementioned reasons, you must be traditional. That should be a relief, Colin. You won't be expected to win the game by yourself. You're temperamentally unsuited for the task. Last week I was shocked by your cat-eyed hysteria. For goodness sake, we're talking about an early regular season game against an average opponent.

Once you relax and see the whole field, you'll pass the ball properly. You're missing receivers on very short patterns that should be almost like handoffs. You're also missing receivers in motion on intermediate patterns, often throwing behind them when well-delivered passes would lead to big gains or touchdowns.

CK – I just haven't been getting time.

BW – Even when the protection's good, you've made tense, imprecise throws.

JH – I've been working with Colin on his passing game.

BW – That worries me.

JH – I beg your pardon.

BW – I think you're turning a potential franchise quarterback into a journeyman. This you're doing by transmitting some of your bad habits. Let's be forthright, Jim. You threw almost as many interceptions as touchdowns in your career. That's completely unacceptable and reminds me of Steve DeBerg, whose untimely interceptions would've ruined my career if I hadn't drafted Joe Montana and taught him to be great.

What I'm telling you, Colin, is not that you should try to be Joe or anyone else but that you must learn from the great ones. When you watch films of Jim Harbaugh or Steve DeBerg, note their mistakes and stylistic infelicities. Then, in games, make better choices about who to throw to and when. And quit throwing the ball so hard. I think you believe, at least unconsciously, that velocity is a substitute for accuracy. It isn't. An inaccurately thrown pass is an abomination.

Now, Jim, you must also relax. Deion Sanders tells me you're losing your team. They resent your condescending manner.

JH – Your players resented your arrogance, as well.

BW – Jim, and you too, Colin, take a look at my hands here. These are the hands of an artist, and you'll note that three of my fine fingers are adorned by special rings. Get a couple of these, and the heat on you gentlemen will subside, until the following season.

October 2014

Notes: Despite leading the 49ers to three straight conference title games, and a narrow Super Bowl setback in 2012, Jim Harbaugh lost an internal struggle with Trent Baaltke and was forced to walk the plank after the 2014 season. Two years later, Colin Kaepernik and Baaltke were also banished. Only the owner's unsteady son Jed York seemed safe until he provided six-year contracts to coach Kyle Shanahan and general manager John Lynch.

Hiking at Stanford

Don't you love the Bay Area? It's the greatest megalopolis on earth, featuring the Pacific Ocean and San Francisco Bay and wooded hills surrounding blue water and boats and ominous Alcatraz and the Golden Gate and Bay Bridge, and there are all the major league sports and concerts and countless museums and parks and universities and tech firms and creative energy that even from afar, a hundred miles southeast on I-5 in the hideous Central Valley, must have disoriented me as I glanced at the Highway 152 sign, gateway to my South Bay destination at Stanford University, and blithely ignored it, heading north about twenty miles before realizing – I missed the damn exit I've taken a hundred times. I confessed the error to my wife, a good-natured sort who didn't upbraid me, and declared, "No way we're heading back. Hand me that map…" Okay, we'll just take 580 west toward San Francisco but stop well short of Oakland and go south on 680 and then west on 137 right over by old Moffett Field and our motel in Mountain View just a few miles from the farm of Leland Stanford.

My dreaminess had cost us a half hour and precluded unpacking but, thankfully, didn't prompt me to forgo a quick layer of sunscreen, which would be more essential than I'd reckoned. If I'd had more foresight, I would've also taken tranquilizers. I was already a bit nervous and ambivalent. After decades of unabashed enthusiasm for the traditionally talented Trojans of USC, I had in recent years, as Stanford began to establish gridiron excellence under Jim Harbaugh and then became a perennial power guided by David Shaw, started liking the Cardinal almost as much as the men of Troy. And when an undermanned and unprepared USC team was disemboweled by top-ranked Alabama, fifty-two to seven, in the opener this season, I admitted that I might be changing allegiance. Christian McCaffrey, a short, fast, and elusive halfback is simply too exciting to root against. Not that I'm a frontrunner. I still resent the stout Thunder Chickens defense and quarterbacking prowess of Jim Plunkett and the late Don

Bunce who guided the upstart Indians, as they were then called, to consecutive Rose Bowl wins in 1970 and 1971. The Trojans rebuilt – they almost always rapidly reloaded the talent chambers – and fielded some of the finest teams in college history under John McKay, John Robinson, and Pete Carroll, born in San Francisco and raised in Marin County, who led USC the first decade this century.

That is history. This Saturday Stanford was ranked seventh, and their increasingly confident fans, and thousands of vehicles, packed hundreds of yards of informal dirt parking lots surrounded by big trees. As the cognoscenti dined and drank in their forest, I drove around and learned I had to be a VIP or season ticket holder to park here and there and elsewhere nearby, so kept heading north on El Camino Real and finally, far from Stanford Stadium, pulled into a dusty clearing where they had a single space left for the righteous price of forty bucks. I dared not complain about such a pittance in a community where buyers pay the median price of two and a half million dollars – fourteen hundred per square foot – for nondescript suburban homes.

"Okay," I told my wife, "I'm writing this down: Palm and Arboretum, northeast corner. Without that information, we'll never find the car. Do you understand?"

"Yes," she said. She understands directions as well as I speak her native Tagalog.

We set off on a long and dusty trail, battered by sun less intense than in Bakersfield but still pretty damn hot, and in about ten minutes sweat oozed down my temples. Some of the discomfort must have resulted from inexperience: I hadn't attended a game here since 1968, when scintillating (and still pure) O.J. Simpson carried the ball forty-seven times and USC edged Stanford which also thrilled as Jim Plunkett fired strikes to premier target Gene Washington, and I yearned to get back inside a stadium now modernized and reduced in size. We prayed our seats would be on the west side and relegate the sun to our backs. To find out, we'd have to wait. At the entrance, the ticket taker passed us on but a Praetorian Guard said to my wife, "Your purse is too big. Are you parked close?"

"We're about a mile away," I said.

"Okay," he said, pointing, "you can go to the track stadium for bag check."

"They've already scanned our tickets."

"Here, I'll un-scan them."

I wondered if we'd miss the five-fifteen kickoff. Arriving at the track, we presented the offending purse, and its cache of fresh fruit, and a teenage attendant said, "Your notebook's too big."

"No way," I countered, opening it. "This is just to take notes. Besides, it's already been okayed at the gate."

And back at the gate, I presented my ticket and walked in until the man said, "She needs a ticket, too."

"Where is it?" I ask.

"In my purse at the track stadium," she said.

"No problem." I take three computer-printed sets of tickets to every major event, and still had two. We were in, and I told her, "No more football in person, only basketball." The preceding December we'd seen the Cardinal host Texas and Sacramento State in Maples Pavilion, and there'd been no long marches or parched skin.

In our sheltered west-side seats, opposite fans staring into sun, we soon stood for kickoff, and with four-eighteen left in the first quarter Christian McCaffrey caught a pass moving toward the left sideline, turned on the genetic jets – his maternal grandfather won 1960 Olympic silver in the hundred, his father caught passes in the NFL – and sped to a fifty-six-yard touchdown. USC kicked a field goal later in the quarter to trail seven-three, but Stanford had established itself as the more physical team. The Trojans used to steamroll opponents with a bevy of future first round picks and other imminent pros, but charismatic Pete Carroll is now in charge of the Seattle Seahawks, and his three "permanent" replacements – Lane Kiffin, Steve Sarkisian, and, now, Clay Helton – have demonstrated neither the star power nor stability necessary to recruit as many blue chip recruits as elite opponents.

The Cardinal's big offensive line continued to pound smaller Trojans up front, McCaffrey tunneling inside and darting outside, and late in the first half he broke through the line, high-stepped in open field, faked defenders, and charged thirty-three yards deep into USC territory. He then ran once, twice, and on the third attempt leaped toward the end zone but was hit in the air and stopped a foot short. Stanford, leading ten-three, decided to test itself, as well as the Trojan defense, and McCaffrey again leaped over the line, this time landing in the arms of a defender in the end zone. The second half had the same character as the first – McCaffrey eventually rushed thirty-one times for a hundred seventy-two yards – and Stanford won twenty-seven to ten, less impressive than Alabama's punishment of USC but more encouraging, certainly, than the Crimson Tide's surrender of forty-three points to Mississippi earlier this day. Be assured. Coach David Shaw and Christian McCaffrey and everyone else associated with Stanford football believe the team is a national title contender. That's an astonishing goal for a school whose academic requirements annually force it to ignore many top prospects.

After letting the exiting hordes thin a little, we headed back to the track stadium to retrieve the purse and began a dark journey, aided by electric lights in the forest, toward my car. We walked and wondered where we were and continued walking until my wife began saying, "I think the car's over there."

I retrieved my note from that afternoon and said, "Look, Palm and Arboretum, northeast corner. First, we've got to reach Palm."

As endless cars crawled out of the campus, we began to ask fans, "Can you tell me where Palm Street is?"

Most couldn't. Two navigators pointed north and said, "That way."

Okay, there's Palm. Now where's Arboretum? I began seeking people in uniforms. Fine, here's the corner, and there's the northeast quadrant. We started heading down dim, dusty roads. The lots were well enough lit we saw my car wasn't in this one or that one or in any other lot we could find. Where's my damn car? I worried someone had stolen it and feared we'd soon be in total darkness. Hailing a policeman, I asked, "You aren't going to turn off the lights out here, are you?"

"Oh no," he promised.

But what if they did?

"I know the car's over there," she said, pointing to the southwest quadrant.

"It can't be."

"Where is it then?"

I huffed and took her hand and pulled her across the busy street where the car couldn't be, unless I don't know north in a place close to north-south artery El Camino Real. "Sir, excuse me," I said to a young student. "We can't find our car."

"There aren't any lots over this way," he said.

"I told you," I said to my wife, and angrily turned to step on grass that wasn't grass but vines that snared my foot and tackled me, my face landing several inches short of a concrete curb.

After thanking the heavens for not crushing my skull, I marched to the northeast corner of Palm and Arboretum and was heartened a few other people wandered around in search of their rides. Either by cool thinking or reflexive luck I walked past the last lit parking area I could locate, and found a place where the lights had gone out and through dimness saw my lonely car. In silence we rode back to the motel.

September 2016

Notes: Staggering with a one and three record after the Stanford game, USC benched ineffective quarterback Max Browne and inserted redshirt freshman Sam Darnold who performed well in a loss to a fine Utah team and then began bombarding opponents with passes that generated thirty-one touchdowns and three thousand eighty-six yards. Darnold threw five TD passes against Arizona and California as well as Penn State during a Rose Bowl comeback that produced the Trojans' ninth straight victory. Let's be restrained about this large, cool, and athletic lad, and say he projects to be an All American and a pro football star who'll earn a bust in the hall of fame.

Ryan Mathews in Touchdown City

In the bleachers before the football game a startlingly youthful student smiled at me and said, "I know why you're here."

"Yeah, I gotta see Ryan Mathews play."

"You a scout?"

"No, just for fun."

"What's your prediction?"

"Three hundred yards rushing," I said.

"More than that, I bet."

No, we hadn't been dining on magic mushrooms from Oaxaca, just soberly assessing the statistical devastation likely to be wrought by the nation's leading rusher, a senior quarterback who takes direct hikes in shotgun formation and immediately dashes right or left, or fakes one way before sprinting the other, or charges up the middle to propel two hundred pounds helmet-first into the chests of defenders. Admittedly, Mathews' task for West High School two weeks ago did not figure to be onerous. Lined up against him would be North High – north of Bakersfield and the Kern River in Oildale, Merle Haggard's hometown – a team with a solitary win and many rather slow players.

The shellacking of North began on the first play from scrimmage: Mathews sped to his right then cut inside before darting outside, powering past defenders, an adult against adolescents as he sailed down the sideline fifty-one yards for a touchdown. On the next possession he rushed several times and completed a pass before running twice more, the last a three-yard touchdown. Early in the second quarter he feinted a run, stopped abruptly, and threw a touchdown pass over befuddled defenders, then soon followed with a thirty-one-yard scoring run, and a sixty-five-yard touchdown pass to make it thirty-four to six late in the first half. I jotted this in my notebook, closed it, leaned back and prepared to watch the cheerleaders dance at halftime. But, suddenly, West got the ball again. I don't know how; I hadn't written down every play as I did years ago when covering prep football.

"No more scoring this half, Mathews," I said. "I'm through

working for now."

The ambitious lad refused to stifle himself. He knows talented players generate lightning, and is perhaps aware they're also likely to get lucky: he floated a wobbly pass down the middle, a pass crying to be intercepted, but it was tipped, high and softly, into the hands of one of West's several fleet receivers, and the touchdown made it forty-one to six when halftime entertainment began. Mathews opened the second half by running several times, pouncing on his fumble, overcoming a penalty, and dashing ten yards into the end zone before, mercifully, he was taken out. In little more than two-and-a-half quarters, he'd rushed for two hundred forty-four yards and four touchdowns, and passed for three.

Those startling numbers are actually modest for Matthews this season. In the preceding four games he'd rumbled for three hundred thirteen, three hundred seventy-four, three hundred eighteen, and four hundred fifteen yards, scoring seven touchdowns one game and six another. And last week in the regular season finale, he galloped for three hundred seventy-four yards and three touchdowns against Centennial to propel West to the league championship. For the ten-game regular season, he rushed for two thousand eight hundred forty yards and scored thirty-seven touchdowns. That's the gridiron equivalent of a politician grabbing eighty percent of the vote against a popular incumbent.

After the upcoming playoffs, Ryan Mathews will have to choose a college. Arizona State and Colorado have already beckoned him. UCLA, where he'd most like to perform, surprisingly has not made an offer, and may be waiting for results of Mathews' SAT test, which he's confident will be sufficient. Or perhaps the proud Bruins have already forgotten their running game was moribund three weeks ago in the loss that should have been a win at Norte Dame.

I'm going to step in and send this column-cum-scouting report to coach Karl Dorrell and other members of the UCLA football staff. I'll note this young man was raised by his mother and they decided to come down from Tehachapi in the mountains so Mathews could test himself against good competition. I'll stress he's already mature and his mother trusts him to live in his own apartment with his adopted brother, also age 18, a friend he'd once brought home for a visit that became a familial commitment. I'll remind the Bruin coaches he plays best in big games, and his team is undefeated since two early-season losses and his move from halfback to shotgun quarterback. And I'll suggest they could've beaten Notre Dame if Ryan Mathews had been running for the big blue.

November 2006

Notes: Mathews starred at Fresno State three years, and in seven NFL seasons has rushed and received for more than six thousand six hundred yards and scored forty touchdowns. His production, though commendable, has been diminished by injuries forcing him to miss twenty-six games. He will earn five million dollars in 2017 unless the Philadelphia Eagles cut him to save money and clear more time for younger players. At age thirty Mathews is rather old for a pro running back.

Showdown in Fresno

For two months I'd been teaching and writing most of the time and hadn't left Bakersfield and wanted out but was reluctant to break the numbing routine and only considered doing so because in the summer I'd purchased an escape ticket for the late October game at Fresno State against Boise State, the now renowned "Out of the Blue" Broncos who in January had thrilled fans during their battle against Oklahoma in the Fiesta Bowl. I couldn't buy a forty-yard line seat for a big game and stay home. The day before, I compelled attendance by packing a bag and neglecting to cancel my reservation at the motel a short walk from Bulldog Stadium.

Right after school, early that Friday afternoon, I pointed my little 1990 Honda Civic north on Highway 99 and accelerated. When you live in Bakersfield, going to Fresno is a move up. As brown farmland sped by I used up my Bakersfield radio-range on AM redneck talk shows and FM country music then, in the middle of one hundred ten miles separating the cities, I was bombarded all over the dial by the pious voices of Christian broadcasting. It's never easy to determine if these sacred souls are in ecstasy or pain or both, and intolerable to listen more than several seconds, so I kept punching the scan button until I got a PBS station playing an excerpt from a documentary about the current war in Iraq. The narrator was building his case: politicians and media members had clasped hands to deceive the public, bang the drum of aggression, lambaste those who protested, and parrot sterile slogans to make disaster less unpalatable. One of the quaint and oft-used phrases was collateral damage, a euphemism for civilian casualties. PBS in the Central Valley is rarely this edgy.

What station dared? It was KPFA, in Berkeley, proving again that radio programs in beautiful places offer thoughtful commentary while in barren stretches they preach carpet bombing and pray like hell. In the next documentary, after pledge break, an evolutionary scientist discussed the essential contrast between science and religion. The former is founded on evidence and sustained by an eternal search for more knowledge; the latter is based on faith, a ritual embrace of mythology. The British scientist played his interview with televangelist Ted Haggard, George W. Bush's spiritual adviser, who was appalled anyone could doubt the sacred truths of the bible, which marks the earth as having been Created merely six thousand years ago. This scientist-preacher exchange had occurred before gay-bashing Ted was unveiled as a meth-snorting customer of a male prostitute.

Such considerations were soon superseded by Fresno, a burgeoning metro area that features about eight hundred thousand people, lots of agricultural money, plenty of poverty, suburbs with expansive homes, a Save Mart Arena big enough to attract the Rolling Stones and Madonna, and more than forty thousand red seats in Bulldog Stadium. I was headed that way, rolling north through the city on Highway 41 and exiting on Shaw Avenue, gateway east to Fresno State University.

I tried to keep driving past that Chinese buffet, where undisciplined customers interpret literally the all-you-can-eat sign and slowly depart rubbing distended bellies, but a steering malfunction caused an unanticipated turn into the parking lot where I bounded out and hustled inside. About twenty minutes later I'd already twice encircled the long rectangle of entrees then walked the dessert line, and was urging myself to stop when an energetic fellow approached and began talking, and within seconds I said, "You're all the way down from Boise for the game?"

"Right, I'm doing color commentary for ESPN2 and spotting the Broncos' players – in Spanish."

"A Spanish broadcast for Boise, Idaho?"

"There are a hundred thirty-eight thousand Hispanics in Idaho and their growth rate is the highest in the nation."

"Why is this college game on a Friday night?"

"Because Thursdays, Fridays, and Sundays are when we've got TV slots for schools like these."

"Just a second," I said. "Let me run to my car and grab my notepad."

"Fine, I'll get a business card."

I assured the conscientious cashier I'd return and then did so and asked the announcer to join me. While he ate his dessert, I wrote.

"I'm Ron Prado," he said.

"When I was a kid our family's favorite restaurant was called the Del Prado, in south Sacramento. Are you from Idaho?"

"I'm from East LA."

"That was my next guess. What're you doing in Boise?"

"I'm one of the owners of radio station KWEI."

"What's the population there?"

"About a hundred forty-five thousand."

"Boise State's football program has really been doing well."

"Since 2000 we've won more games than any other team in the country, USC is second, and we've scored more points than anyone, Texas is second. During that period our Western Athletic Conference record is forty-two and one. The only loss was right here two years ago. This season we were allotted three thousand two hundred tickets for this game and they sold out in two days."

"I imagine, like the Pacific 10 schools, your key recruiting area is in California."

"We recruit heavily here. About forty guys on this year's team are from California. We do well in Idaho and Washington, and we've also started to get players from Nevada, Colorado, Texas, and Louisiana. As the program has grown we've been able to recruit more freshmen, instead of junior college transfers, and those four-year kids are better academically."

"Who're Boise's best players?"

He cited quarterback Taylor Tharp, offensive tackle Ryan Clady, a three-hundred-fifteen pounder, and running back Ian Johnson. "Johnson's one of the top backs in the country, but he won't play tonight. He's got a bruised kidney."

"Isn't that the guy who dropped to a knee and proposed to his girlfriend on TV after the Fiesta Bowl against Oklahoma?"

"Right," he said.

"That was the most exciting game I've ever seen."

Boise State had landed a series of improbable haymakers to surge to a twenty-eight to seven lead, but Oklahoma's more physical athletes asserted themselves and tied the game at twenty-eight then returned an interception for a touchdown and a thirty-five to twenty-eight advantage late in the game. The Broncos, who coach Chris Petersen said had been wearing down, soon faced fourth and long and desperately reached into the gridiron magic bag to pull out the legendary (but seldom used) hook and ladder play. Quarterback Jared Zabransky threw to a receiver who, instead of trying to advance, pitched the ball back to a speeding teammate who got the first down and kept motoring unopposed until near the goal line where he dove into the front corner of the end zone. The conversion kick knotted the score at thirty-five, and time expired. The Sooners offensive line began overtime by hammering Boise's defenders as Adrian Peterson churned twenty yards to score. (A year later, as a rookie, Peterson rushed for an NFL record two hundred ninety-six yards in Minnesota's win over San Diego.)

Right away the Broncos had again faced a convert-or-lose fourth down play, and coach Petersen ordered a reluctant reserve halfback to enter the game, take the direct snap, and, while sweeping right, throw a pass, which stunned Oklahoma's defenders and resulted in a touchdown. Petersen decided his Broncos were too tired to tie the game with a kick and continue the war of attrition against increasingly-potent Sooners, so he ordered a two-point conversion attempt. Make it and win. Fail and lose. Boise's players were aghast at this most unorthodox gamble. Oklahoma's defenders were worried but aggressive as quarterback Zabransky prepared to pass and hurled the ball – where? He'd thrown the ball, hadn't he? No. He'd faked a pass with an empty right hand then with his left handed the ball behind his back – the Statue of Liberty – to Ian Johnson who bolted around the left side into hysteria. Obscure Boise State had felled the Boomer Sooners. Fans of underdogs celebrated across the land. And fame increased with the release of *Out of the Blue*, a documentary about the undefeated season of a team whose home turf is seriously blue.

This fall, the Broncos came to Fresno with a single loss, to Washington, and were undoubtedly confident in the locker room. Outside Bulldog Stadium fans of both teams and thousands of others gathered for twenty-first century tailgating. Traditional diners and wine sippers sat in shade outside mobile homes or under vast tents where restaurants had established temporary quarters and were serving chicken, steak, shrimp, Italian food, and a lot more. A rock band played from a large stage while nearby ESPN2 interviewed people on radio and television as the U.S. Army recruited next to its black Hummer brightened by a yellow design in front. Kids and adults soared on a trampoline and crowded into booths to throw footballs at targets and shoot free throws and whack golf balls against a movie screen that registered how far the drives would've gone.

Quite a few revelers arrived late for kickoff but were seated as twice-beaten Fresno State jumped on Boise to lead fourteen to seven, and at halftime trailed only seventeen to fourteen. Thereafter, the Broncos' formidable offensive line, averaging three hundred seven pounds per player, manhandled the Bulldogs' defense. Boise's defensive front also overpowered its adversaries, and the Broncos controlled the rest of the game and won thirty-four to twenty-one, climbing into the top twenty-five nationally.

The Broncos may not be in the midst of another miracle season but I'll remember this team as the one I saw the night before my car almost didn't start, for the fiftieth straight morning, and as I drove back to Bakersfield I knew the next day I'd lurch to a dealer, take what the salesman offered on a trade in, and get my first new car – a Fit, hottest selling car in Japan and soon a star in the States.

November 2007

Notes – Ryan Clady, Boise State's mammoth offensive tackle, made All American, and in 2008 the Denver Broncos selected him in the first round. He made four Pro Bowl teams while playing for the Broncos and in 2013 earned an eight-figure contract with thirty-three million guaranteed. Foot and knee injuries forced Clady to miss most of one season and all of another before Denver traded him to the New York where he injured his shoulder playing for the Jets. In the world of pro football he's considered aged at thirty, and battered, and is a wealthy free agent looking for a job. Ryan Mathews of Fresno State, now comparably affluent, scored a touchdown this game against Boise State.

O.J. SIMPSON

Continuing Decline of O.J. Simpson

Once, there was a better O.J. Simpson. I first learned about him in the mid-sixties when he starred two years as a running back for City College of San Francisco. I was a teenage student in Sacramento and daily devoured the San Francisco Chronicle's renowned green sheet sports section. And in certain editions, buried beneath the exploits of Willie Mays, John Brodie, and Rick Barry, I'd see short pieces about this guy with a cool name who was tearing up the turf on long and exciting touchdown runs. That was enough: O.J. Simpson, still unseen, became my premier college player, and that feeling intensified in the spring of 1967 when he transferred to the team still my favorite, the mighty Trojans of USC.

It was unnecessary to wait until gridiron autumn to see O.J. perform. Right away he joined the track team that came to the Bay Area for a dual meet against Stanford. I attended and made sure to check Simpson out, noting he looked muscular and fit. But he wasn't the main show on perhaps the finest college track and field team yet assembled. I was studying Bob Seagren as he sprinted down the runway and pole vaulted into the sky. He would win the 1968 gold medal in Mexico City. Earl McCullough ran like the wind, skimming over high hurdles, and also took gold in 1968. Sprinter Lennox Miller was even faster than Simpson, and sped to hundred-meter silver the following year and bronze in 1972. The quarter mile relay team, featuring Simpson, Miller, and McCullough, was progressing toward a world record.

O.J. Simpson, handsome, personable and astonishingly athletic, had become a star before he first tucked a football into his side and dashed USC Student Body Right and Left behind offensive linemen destined for the National Football League. In the fall of 1967 the Trojans began overpowering and outrunning opponents as Simpson amassed nation-leading yardage and carried his team to the top ranking. The chant began: "All the way with O.J." And on the way the Trojans were coming to Berkeley to play Cal. I had to go see a guy already faster and more elusive than any professional running back but O.J. had sprained his ankle the previous game. Maybe he wasn't going to play. No, that couldn't be. There he was on the sideline in Memorial Stadium, wearing uniform number thirty-two and looking ready. He must have been there to distract Cal, which on the field was hammered by a stocky former high school All American – USC had many then as now – named Steve Grady who rushed for more than a hundred yards. McCullough, the hurdler, caught two touchdown passes and USC won by that margin.

O.J. Simpson recovered rapidly and played well in mud the following week in Corvallis where Oregon State, already known as the Giant Killers, stifled the Trojans three to nothing. That setback could still be overcome against crosstown rival UCLA in the final regular season game: the victor would go to the Rose Bowl and probably play for the national championship. This would also be a Heisman Trophy showdown between Simpson and quarterback Gary Beban. Before kickoff the Los Angeles Coliseum was abuzz with pageantry and anticipation. As the game unfolded and the teams battled each other with a special level of intensity, I feared the Bruins were good enough to win. And they would have except for two plays that still amaze. In the first half Simpson, blockaded by a horde of defenders, slashed through several who almost brought him down and charged in for a touchdown. In the fourth quarter UCLA led and appeared one play closer to victory as Simpson ran to his left and was sealed off and about to be buried before he instinctively cut back to the right, sprinting by one defender then another and another, gliding into history as he covered more than a hundred yards on a score some two-thirds that length. No one else at any level of football could have made that play. USC prevailed, and then won the Rose Bowl to seize the national title. In a preposterous slight, the Heisman Trophy was awarded to Gary Beban. That proved irrelevant. In 1968 Simpson won the award without debate – I saw a typical performance as he shredded Stanford for more than two hundred yards – and in 1969 he was the most coveted player in the NFL draft.

In Buffalo O.J. Simpson entered one of the coldest and most unglamorous cities in America and one housing a forlorn team. During his first three seasons two dim coaches sabotaged their careers by declining to give him the ball much and the Bills won only eight games, a two-month total at USC. Lou Saban then took command and over the next five years put the ball in Simpson's hands more than twenty times a game and allowed him to burst, fake, twist, power, and speed through defenses. He won four rushing titles and in 1973 lifted his artistry to the sublime, confounding opponents as he became the first to reach two thousand yards in a season. No one has since done so in only fourteen games.

The already enormous celebrity of O.J. Simpson expanded and so did what most at the time thought was confidence. We now understand arrogance prompted him to tell an interviewer his first (and then current) wife knew he was "selective" about which women he went out with. That surely upset the lady who'd been his sweetheart at City College of San Francisco and borne their two children. People do grow apart, though, and sleek Simpson was drifting away from his rather matronly wife. Why not, he figured? He had his choice of groupies and others. This was his entitlement as Heisman Trophy winner and now officially the finest football player in the world. The media and fans loved him. So did the camera. Hollywood and Madison Avenue wanted him on screen. He looked great but couldn't act and spoke inarticulately. So what? O.J. Simpson had charm and charisma, and if you've got those and superstar stats, you believe you can do what you want.

On the field a knee injury in 1977 forever damaged Simpson's athletic options, and he immediately plummeted from best to average. In 1978 the Buffalo Bills sent the biggest star they ever had back home, to the San Francisco 49'ers. He hobbled two seasons for teams as bad as those in his early Buffalo years and was forced to retire in 1979. The transformation did not appear to be difficult. He had a new woman, the stunning blonde Nicole Brown, twelve years his junior. And he got a job as a TV football analyst. It was another competitive endeavor for the man who'd always been a champion, but he still spoke so poorly comedians parodied him as a mumbler.

Most fans still enjoyed O.J. Simpson because he lit up every space he entered, and was friendly and gracious to everyone from bellhops to power brokers. It must not have indicated a mean streak when, as a Monday Night Football commentator, he sniped that former quarterback Jim Plunkett, standing next to James Garner on the sidelines, looked about as old as the actor, born a generation before Plunkett. It was likewise no big deal when he commented that "those Alabama shores are tough on (Ken) Stabler," as the gray and somewhat haggard quarterback stood on the sidelines. Many had been taking shots at Stabler and the effects of his partying. Simpson's partner in the booth, ever-acerbic Howard Cosell, on another occasion referred to "the passing years" as he and America looked at Stabler. Many fans criticized Cosell for cruelty.

But O.J. Simpson wasn't that way. He was a great guy. It wasn't outrageous he beat his wife, Nicole Brown, in the nineteen eighties. Police summoned to their home said Simpson was intoxicated and arrogant before he got in his car and drove away. Why did they let him leave? It must've been because he was O.J. After his conviction for spousal abuse it certainly helped being O.J. The judge sentenced him to counseling. He took care of that obligation by phone. What a farce. If he'd been a salesman or a less appealing athlete, he'd have had to do more. He needed the counseling, didn't he? At least nine times Nicole Brown called nine-one-one to plea for help because O.J. was either beating her or threatening to. She told friends and others he was going to kill her and get away with it. That was the privilege of a hero pursued by women, admired by men, and idolized by USC football recruits ritually brought to his Brentwood mansion to listen as the legend told them why they too should become Trojans. Look what playing for USC did for him. People were required to notice. If they weren't paying attention when O.J. walked in a room, he'd often speak loudly or clear his throat to take the stage.

By 1994 O.J. Simpson and Nicole Brown had divorced and she and their two children received about twenty thousand dollars a month in support and alimony and lived in a luxury condominium. She spent her days and nights dining, shopping, exercising, and being romanced by men not named O.J. He'd been prolifically unfaithful during marriage but Nicole evidently had no right to a private life. O.J. stalked her on dates, crept outside her condominium in the dark, and told people he was doing so because he was a "proud man." The correct term should have been an "obsessively-ill man," who that June wielded a long knife to murder Nicole Brown and her friend (and potential witness) Ron Goldman. Should we be surprised the man who then kissed Nicole's cold face in the coffin at the funeral would try to publish his book *If I Did It?* Public outrage has prompted Rupert Murdoch to burn his edition of the book, but it will be reincarnated under someone else's imprint which will use the blood of victims to sewer-pipe money to their killer.

O.J. Simpson's chief legacy, ironically, will not be his savagery or even athletic achievements. It will be that his criminal case forced examination of issues most would prefer to ignore or deny. After the murders, when all physical and circumstantial evidence pointed to one man, most whites thought this crime was easy to solve. They had no idea the case was really about race and only learned when many blacks started calling radio talk shows and giving TV and newspaper interviews to lament that a racist white society was trying to frame their great, obviously-innocent O.J. He'd long ago extricated himself from most black society and immersed himself in an essentially white environment, but that which had long been resented was now forgiven with gusto. O.J. wouldn't have done it, and he couldn't have; old football injuries precluded such an attack.

Justice might have prevailed if the trial had been held in the West Los Angeles jurisdiction where the murders were committed and where educated and reasonably impartial jurors could have served. Instead, publicity-hungry Angelinos – in this case, district attorneys – insisted on a larger courtroom. What for? Seating was limited downtown anyway, and most reporters and the rest of the world watched on TV. The trial that began as a media and gossip circus became more absurd when black jurors who'd been removed from duty insulted the victims and praised the accused. The jurors who remained proved unqualified to absorb even a scintilla of the DNA evidence and incapable of convicting a popular black man of murdering his blonde ex-wife.

When the acquittal was announced, numerous blacks, gathered in the streets and around TVs and radios, erupted with cheers and pumping fists. Part of this was pay back, of course. Pay back for slavery.

Retribution for Jim Crow. Revenge for many trials when white jurors acquitted obviously-guilty white defendants of killing blacks. There is, however, an essential difference: when white killers walked free, most whites were appalled.

As for O.J. Simpson, while he awaits his opening in the literary world, he'll play a lot of golf in Florida, cash his twenty-five grand a month NFL pension checks, do ghoulish autograph shows for cash his minions will hide from the families of Ron Goldman and Nicole Brown, winners of a huge wrongful death civil suit, and he'll continue to overuse food and alcohol to a degree that's fattened his face and begun to make him look like a felonious Porky Pig. That ain't life-without-parole but will do until the day of reckoning.

November 2006

Cruising O.J.'s House

In 1995 I squirmed through long and boring academic lectures at UCLA and dreaded a direct return to my motel room to await more punishment Sunday. I guessed it would be all right to drive over to O.J.'s house on Rockingham Avenue in Brentwood. I wouldn't be as bad as fools who a year earlier had converged to gawk right after his estranged wife and her friend were slashed outside her condominium. Carefully I eased around do not enter signs and newly-installed cement roadblocks into the neighborhood but didn't join tourists parked and loitering outside the house. I also kept driving by a crowd in front of the murder scene, a condo on Bundy Drive, hoping I was a little less ghoulish.

April 2012

You're O.J. Simpson

You're O.J. Simpson and most of the world knows you're an unconvicted killer. You say you don't care what people think because you're innocent. But you don't feel innocent, and your guilt has long been eating you and left a hollow core inside a fattening and increasingly ridiculous man.

You weren't satisfied merely to beat the criminal justice system, and prompt misguided African Americans to publicly cheer the appalling verdict, nor were you content to live at ease on your fat monthly pension. How could you have lived at ease? While once you were everywhere gazed upon with affection and respect, since 1994 you have been glared at with hatred and contempt. We understand why you've been tormented but will never grasp why you were angry enough to butcher two people. Millionaire celebrities, after all, generally don't use knives to deal with anxiety.

Equally confusing, though entirely less serious, was your decision last year to use force to seize various sports mementos, some of which were probably stolen from you. Don't you know, law-abiding people call the police to deal with such matters? Of course you realize that's a rhetorical question. Even if all that property had been stolen, none of it really belonged to you, not anymore. It belongs to the families of Ron Goldman and Nicole Brown. They won millions from you in a civil trial, and you've been concealing assets ever since. The pre-1994 O.J. Simpson would have indignantly called the police about a theft, and for you, a football superstar, they'd have proudly drawn their guns and barged into that Las Vegas hotel room.

You instead recruited five assorted criminals, punks, and pimps, ordered two to bear arms, and all six of you invaded the room occupied by two sports memorabilia dealers. During the siege, an enterprising member of your gang recorded threats that reminded jurors of your curses after Nicole had called nine-one-one. You really are quite primitive, and no longer sly enough to work alone. Four of your accomplices testified against you so they wouldn't have to join you in the dock. The other intruder was, like you, convicted of burglary and kidnapping, and will likely endure many years of incarceration.

Did even one person look good in this tawdry affair? The pimp said God ordered him to cop a plea. The memorabilia dealer with the recorder, who set all this up, made a couple hundred grand, and the dealers you and your accomplices cornered immediately started contacting the media and planning to grab big money.

Maybe you'll get another trial on appeal, though it's doubtful the verdict would be overturned. Most people don't care. This isn't the riveting case of the century. You're too old to be box office anymore, and people around you aren't as intriguing as your supporting stars like Johnny Cochrane and F. Lee Bailey from the glory days. Any interest in you now centers on when you'll hit three hundred pounds and whether you ever get out.

Whatever happened to you, number thirty-two?

October 2008

The People v. O.J. Simpson

I'm not watching that O.J. Simpson miniseries, not a single episode much less ten. They're crazy offering more of something people saw too much of a generation ago. Why do they think there's any interest? There isn't, not on my part. I must've reflexively put *The People v. O.J. Simpson* in my Netflix queue but will surely delete it soon.

Later this Friday night, bored with my Kindle after a day of writing and reading at the computer, I think, hell, I've watched a lot of foreign films lately, I need something from my cultural experience, but only one episode, forty or fifty minutes . Then I'll move on. I don't know exactly when I start watching – my timeline may be as imprecise as those presented during the trial – but let's say about ten-thirty. When I press the remote play button I release into my system medications as powerful as those administered before an invasive medical procedure.

All the characters entertain me, whether or not I agree with the way they're portrayed. I'd thought Robert Shapiro, originally the lead attorney of Simpson's dream team, was a smooth and competent legal mover albeit not a courtroom gunslinger. Instead, I learn, at least from John Travolta's portrayal, that Brentwood Bob is pompous, vain, legally light, and deluded that he's a boxer. Even if Travolta isn't quite accurate as Shapiro, he creates an intriguing character, and this is Hollywood, not journalism central.

Marcia Clark, Shapiro's courtroom adversary, is played by Sarah Paulson who convinces me I must've wanted to ravish Clark during the trial, though I don't recall such feelings. Paulson seamlessly captures Clark's anguish as millions around the nation call her a bitch who's got the hair of Medusa. Paulson responds with three stylistic changes, at the urging of her boss, attorney general Gil Garcetti, portrayed by Bruce Greenwood whose appearance verily shouts: here comes former governor Pete Wilson, rather than hi, I'm Gil. Trust me, the real Gil looks different. From a few feet away I once saw him as he studied French Impressionism at the Los Angeles County Museum of Art. A polite lad, I did not interrupt.

I don't know what episode I'm on. It doesn't matter. Like an addict out of dope, I keep pressing for another episode. The clock's marching into early Saturday morning. I don't care. There's Sterling K. Brown as Christopher Darden, the black face of the prosecution brought in to counter inner-city hero Johnnie Cochran played by Courtney B. Vance. Brown is real and tormented as Darden was when Cochran's flamboyance and courtroom instincts overwhelmed him. These two despise each other, but Darden bonds with Clark in a way that surely drifts into the romantic.

And what of O.J., the man whose handsomeness and charm, far more than his lost athleticism, mesmerized a nation eager to convict or acquit him for the murder of two people. Cuba Gooding is okay as O.J. but his rather high voice collides with memories of the Juice's deep baritone effusions, and Gooding's stature is that of a soccer player rather than gridiron stalwart. Still, Gooding evokes the maniacal suspect who shoves a pistol to his temple and inside his mouth as lifelong friend Al Cowlings, represented by Malcolm-Jamal Warner, long ago Bill Cosby's TV son Theo Huxtable, drives the white Bronco on the ultimate L.A. freeway adventure. Gooding's O.J. isn't merely addled and suicidal, he's guilty.

Amazing, I've watched seven episodes and it's four-thirty in the winter morning. No problem. Let's watch some more. I pray Kenneth Choi never enters a darkened bedroom to crawl in next to Judge Lance Ito's wife or she may receive him. She might not know the difference in daylight. Choi also sounds like Ito, who's generally portrayed as a stable and authoritative courtroom manager.

Nathan Lane well plays F. Lee Bailey but the actor looks too much the clean liver to fully evoke the alcohol-sodden and once-celebrated Bailey, defender of The Boston Strangler and Patty Hearst. Bailey's brief return to stardom occurs during his cross examination of Mark Fuhrmann, depicted by Steve Pasquale, who's probably following directorial orders to portray the n-bombing detective as the incarnation of evil. Those who read Fuhrmann's book about this case may judge him less severely.

There are many other people. Anguished but telegenic Fred

Goldman, mirrored by near twin (in makeup) Joseph Siravo, still suffers in the background. Rob Morrow's Barry Scheck distorts science to confuse the jury and free the murderer. And Evan Handler, as eternally overpublicized Alan Dershowitz, enjoys pontificating why the only man who could've done it didn't do it.

The final character I'll mention is Robert Kardashian, Simpson's close friend and a dapper little fellow portrayed by much larger David Schwimmer, who's given unexpected screen time to brood about Simpson's blood at the Bundy Drive murder scene, and the victims' blood in the white Bronco and outside and inside the star's Rockingham Avenue estate. Kardashian knows who murdered two people but can't stop himself from helping the defense.

That's it, I've seen all ten episodes, and am going to bed. It's getting light and I can't recall the last time I've stayed up all night. I sleep or try to four hours – I generally need eight – and bound out of bed to fire up the internet. Didn't that documentary, *O.J.: Made in America*, get nominated for an Academy Award? It certainly did. But I can't stream it on Netflix. All right, what about YouTube? It's here, but partially blocked. I'll have to track it down later.

February 2017

Notes – Now I'm examining nude photos of Marcia Clark, from the late seventies, mentioned in the movie. She's hot, and the district attorney's office, instead of worrying about the exposure, should've highlighted this side of the stern prosecutor.

What's she doing these days? After receiving more than four million dollars for *Without A Doubt*, her book about the Simpson trial, she moved to Calabasas where large homes feature high ceilings and wide windows overlooking canyons and hills, and where Clark arises five mornings a week, though not five days consecutively, to write crime novels for seven-figure totals. After Simpson's acquittal she never returned to the courtroom or her office.

Chris Darden also quit his job and wrote a book. He taught at Southwestern University School of Law, alma mater of Marcia Clark, before opening his own law practice.

Robert Kardashian died of cancer eight years after the acquittal, shortly before his daughters Kim and company became reality TV curiosities. Some critics suggest that Robert's role may have been expanded to appeal to his daughters' young fans. He earns screen time because of his empathy for the victims.

In a filmed interview Cuba Gooding states he doesn't know if O.J. did it. Now that's acting, Cuba.

Nevada parole commissioners on July twentieth, 2017 voted four to nothing to grant O.J. Simpson parole, in October, after serving nine years for kidnapping, robbery, and assault with a deadly weapon in a Las Vegas hotel room.

PLAYING ROUGH

Women's Football

This wasn't an NFL battle for glory, money, and macho supremacy. It was helluva lot rougher flag football game between the junior and senior girls at my high school decades ago. At stake were the admiration of boys, feminine bragging rights, and something more fundamental: imagine a mother protecting her child and project that intensity to the line of scrimmage. This surprised most guys watching on sidelines.

Girls who'd rarely appeared in anything but dresses now hitched pants, rolled up football jersey sleeves, and altogether ignored flag-pulling as a means to end offensive plays. They instead transformed unprotected heads, shoulders, and chests into weapons, and growled and grunted while slamming bodies into each other as if clad in armor. Several players cried, not due to physical pain but emotional intensity. When some boyfriends insulted the opposition's hardest hitters, gridiron girls should've turned and pancaked the loudmouths.

No one remembers the score now nor did anyone know at time. Touchdowns were irrelevant. Only collisions counted, and years later they still signal that women's pro football would be a winner.

March 2013

Dolphin Brother Defends Incognito

Listen, I'm a brother, and white Richie Incognito's more my brother than "Big Weirdo" Jonathan Martin. Martin reminds me of a white ass wimp, the kind of guy who calls cops when he sees a crime. You don't go runnin to cops, and you don't rat out a teammate. Richie was trying to help Martin when he voice mailed, "Hey, wassup, you half nigger piece of shit. I saw you on Twitter, you been training 10 weeks. I want to shit in your fucking mouth. I'm going to slap your fucking mouth. I'm going to slap your real mother across the face (ha, ha). Fuck you, you're still a rookie. I'll kill you."

Richie was trying to make a man out of Martin, and he tried harder than most brothers to relate to this weird dude who played at Stanford and had two parents who graduated from Harvard. That was the problem when Martin joined our Miami Dolphins. He felt he was better than us. He may have read more books but he knew a lot less about football and life. A brother knows how to carry himself and respond to trouble, but Martin usually acted like a shy ass punk. We'd try to talk to him. We wanted to be friends, well, not exactly friends but at least friendly enough to get him to play aggressively, like a guy six-five and three-twenty should. Richie was our leader and responsible for making Martin better.

But Jonathan Martin just didn't understand real men like another teammate who said, "We're going to run a train on your sister... She loves me. I'm going to fuck her without a condom and come in her cunt." Martin didn't fit in. Now he's crawled into the psycho ward and hired lawyers and shit in our locker room. Believe me, he ain't welcome back. He's no brother. He's no football player. Richie Incognito's our honorary brother and the kind of guy we love in the ghetto. Martin's the kind of guy we roll. Guys like Richie we high five and say nigger and fuck a lot. We can't wait for Richie to come home.

November 2013

Notes: Richie Incognito didn't play at all in 2014, returned to action the following season for the Buffalo Bills, performed and behaved well, and in early 2016 signed a three-year contract for almost sixteen million dollars. Jonathan Martin played one year for the 49ers before being waived. Several months later, hampered by an injured back, as well as depression and anxiety which predated his experiences in Miami, he retired from the physical and emotional violence of football.

The Human Brain

John Mackey left the football field four decades ago and most fans today don't know his name or his game but they should. He enlivened highlight reels when most tight ends labored as blue-collar blockers. After catching the ball, Mackey simply ran over people: he busted defenders with his legs, bruised them with shoulders and arms, and battered them with his head, transforming short gains into long touchdowns. I remember worrying about opponents in Mackey's path. It seemed sadistic to ask anyone, especially much smaller defensive backs of the era, to try to stop a man so strong and swift.

A few years ago, on *60 Minutes*, I saw John Mackey again. He wasn't running and he wasn't talking. He stared into an abyss as his wife answered questions about his ailment, frontotemporal dementia, which is degeneration of the frontal lobe of the brain. Despite having been president of the NFL Player's Association and an essential force in increasing pensions and benefits for players, Mackey was deserted by his former organization, which at first denied his family's request for medical help. His problem wasn't positively related to football, the association ruled, but later relented – because of shame as well as mounting medical evidence about dangers of playing football – and provided funds for convalescent care Mackey needed during his final years. He died in 2011 at age sixty-nine.

Perhaps dementia would've overcome John Mackey if he'd been a career accountant, but that's doubtful. Maybe Junior Seau, one of the best and most ferocious linebackers in history, would've battled depression if he'd never played football. Astonishingly, many fans still don't understand about ten percent of people worldwide suffer from depression, often biological in origin, and that Seau was under emotional siege despite being strong and fast and rich and handsome. Those attributes are unrelated to the biochemistry of the brain, which when awry can make any man consider permanent escape.

There were two major signs Junior Seau needed ongoing psychiatric care. Hours after being arrested for assaulting his girlfriend in 2010, he sped his car off a cliff near San Diego and landed, slightly injured, on the beach a hundred feet below. He denied this was a suicide attempt, and most believed him. Some of those closest to Seau, including a new girlfriend, knew he had severe insomnia and was treating it with the powerful sleeping medication Ambien, which often exacerbates depression. Seau greeted friends and fans effusively but, inside, he was stressed and exhausted. Evidently, he never told anyone how bad he felt. He may have believed a legendary linebacker couldn't admit to being depressed. During two decades on the gridiron he never acknowledged being concussed. That, too, would've undermined his superman image. He was tough and talented but also overwhelmed by an illness too often undiagnosed and untreated. That's why a vigorous father of four, age forty-three, decided he had to shoot himself.

June 2012

Pat Tillman, Army Ranger

We are in our mid-twenties and professional athletes of uncommon talent, toughness, and dedication. We're also bright and have excelled in the classroom as well as on the gridiron. Men yearn to be like us, and women are stirred by our masculine faces and physiques. And we've just been offered more than a million dollars a year to continue playing games we've loved since childhood. We're living in a world of privilege and eternal promise, and with our wives we plan to embrace this special place forevermore.

We know that's we'd do. It wouldn't occur to us to do otherwise. We can state that empirically. In three decades since the military draft was abolished and successful professional athletes automatically became wealthy for life, not one of us has forsaken our good fortune and picked up a rifle to defend the nation. Are you kidding? Why would we do that? Don't tell us that's what you'd do. We know damn well you'd do what we're doing if you were one of us. And not one of us is Pat Tillman.

Pat Tillman didn't want to say anything publicly about why he was going to leave football, fortune, and family, and try to qualify for the Army Rangers, a specially trained group of soldiers among the finest in the history of warfare. Most guys don't make it. They're tough but not tough enough, smart but not quite sharp enough. Pat Tillman? He must've known he had the stuff, and he made it. He was an Army Ranger fighting in Afghanistan, and now he is dead.

It has already been emphasized that the death of one soldier should not be officially mourned more than the passing of any other soldier. That is certainly true and fair, but we can't help feeling the loss of Pat Tillman a bit more. That's because we knew him a little. We knew enough to feel it even more than we do when daily watching the television roll pictures of young people who have paid the ultimate price. Every one of them did it for us.

Pat Tillman wouldn't want special attention. But we can't help it. We're moved by what he gave up even before his first day of duty.

April 2004

Notes: The public much later learned what the United States Army knew right away. Friendly fire killed Pat Tillman.

Dogfighting and Michael Vick

Wouldn't it be reassuring to view the estimated forty thousand human participants in dogfighting in America as merely enthusiastic sports fans who seek compelling entertainment to escape their mundane worries? There is some strained logic to support this assertion, which many of those involved believe and indignantly assert. After all, the dogs are prime athletes, bred for excellence and in their youth selected for encouraging levels of strength and aggression. Then many are given steroids and trained on treadmills and "crude carousels" and thrown into pits to practice against other fledgling pros. I hope it doesn't seem I'm alluding to the regimen of young football players – or competitors in wrestling, boxing, and many other sports wherein the outcome is settled in a pit.

Beyond refutation, there are fundamental differences. The pit bulls training on carousels are chasing horrified cats placed just beyond the jaws of the prospects, and most of those cats will never emerge from practice sessions which they at any rate did not consent to. Furthermore, human athletes do not have their ears cut off before competition to prevent them from being bitten off, nor are they chained to the ground between games while their oozing cuts are ignored. Indeed, human gladiators recuperate under the care of doctors, trainers, coaches, bartenders, and groupies delighted to be near those who are cheered while earning millions of dollars. Alas, dogs will never really be our best friends. But their former enemy Michael Vick is going to help make things better for them.

Federal charges had been filed in July 2007, and Vick recently pled guilty to "interstate commerce for the purpose of dogfighting" but at the same time was permitted to assert he didn't make side bets – as opposed, presumably, to making big bets in a nationwide web of gamblers who wager a half billion dollars a year. The former Atlanta Falcons quarterback, whose astonishing runs (far more than his passing) made him a hundred thirty million dollar celebrity, was also allowed to state that he didn't "kill any dogs at this time," that being when Vick and his three felonious friends, two of whom had already done prison time for drug dealing, decided that six to eight dogs didn't have the right stuff and should be drowned, electrocuted, shot, or hanged. Vick was forced to acknowledge his "collective responsibility" for these gruesome acts since his buddies had told authorities he was directly involved. At this stage the legalistic contradictions don't matter. Michael Vick has promised to cooperate with federal investigators and provide information that will lead to other dogfighting rings.

This is a worthwhile tradeoff. As a wealthy celebrity with a kennel of more than forty fighting dogs, Vick was likely beckoned into the bowels of a secretive business he must now illuminate for prosecutors and the public. It will be fascinating to learn about a subculture in which fights aren't announced until doomsday, and then only to clients who've been investigated to verify either their bloodthirstiness or at least their addiction to gambling. These quite diverse people – from hicks to dudes to dealers to babes – are often further confounded by being taken on "circuitous routes" to the venues, which, rather than glistening stadiums and arenas in great cities, are barns in the mountains or square wooden kill zones in the country. The wood floors are covered with blood and walls nailed with rotten carpeting are splattered red.

Enterprising promoters ensure maximum entertainment by scheduling most big events in the coolness of autumn and winter when dogs won't rapidly overheat and can battle an hour without cease. Panting, growling, biting, gnawing and tearing, the pit bulls attack each other until one dog has crushed another's vital bones or torn out a throat or ripped off part of a face. Losing dogs deemed too injured or incompetent to successfully compete again are done away with, often immediately, sometimes by gunfire. Michael Vick must've learned early it was a callous business. People who know him stress that growing up he survived in a Newport News ghetto known as Bad Newz. Vick took that attitude to his estate in the Virginia countryside and established hell in the hills.

Now, what kind of people are federal authorities going to discuss with Michael Vick? They'll want to know about guys like David Tant of South Carolina who in 2004 was charged with sixty-eight counts that included animal fighting and assault and battery with intent to kill. His conviction on several charges resulted in a sentence of thirty years in prison. Ten of those years, as well as dogfighting sentences of unprecedented severity, were prompted by Tant having set up booby-traps in the fields surrounding his estate. A shotgun, rigged to fire when someone intruded, blasted pellets into the legs of a surveyor, who called the police. Otherwise, David Tant probably would still be profiting from the slaughter.

While many convicted of dogfighting are released on probation, sentencing is generally at the discretion of judges. In 2002 in southern New Hampshire, after forty-three of his pit bulls were seized, Christopher DeVito was sent to prison for two to five years. An increasing number of people involved in dogfighting, like Vick's friends, are also dealing drugs. And their pit bulls segue into service as crack house guards.

If Michael Vick can deliver enough men like Tant and DeVito, he could be granted house arrest. Whatever his sentence, Vick has now begun the process of rehabilitation. His undeniably repugnant acts have evoked condemnation, destroyed his reputation, jeopardized his freedom, imperiled his National Football League career, gotten him indefinitely suspended without pay, nullified millions of dollars of endorsement contracts, and made his life a nightmare.

That is sufficient punishment, once he has fulfilled what the court orders. Then it will be time to go back to work. I'm always appalled when fans scream that Vick, and many other athletes in trouble – especially if they're black – should never be allowed to play again. What abject nonsense. Don't these loud and self-righteous fans understand almost all people sent to jail will emerge? And when they do, their most essential need is to find a job. What is Michael Vick to do? Sit around? No. He is a football player, and at age twenty-seven he's likely to be legally free to play again while still in his twenties. Will the National Football League give him that chance? If not, toward what line of work would it direct a repentant man who has earned millions for the league and its sponsors?

Vick's charitable activities must also be considered. In his old Newport News neighborhood he has provided school supplies, athletic uniforms, and home air conditioners for people needing relief from summer swelter. This charismatic young man has many admirable qualities and those would be enhanced by letting him earn a carefully-monitored return to his profession. To deny him a reasonable job would manifestly increase the odds of further trouble.

And what of Michael Vick's good friends, the ex-cons and drug dealers and fellow dogfighters who long accepted his money and shelter and then shoved him into the arms of authorities? They too deserve a chance to be rehabilitated because they will also be on the streets again. For everyone, it'll be better if they have good jobs.

August 2007

Notes: Michael Vick served twenty-one months in federal prison, and a legion of creditors, attorneys, relatives, friends, and hangers-on pounced, forcing him to file bankruptcy. He returned to quarterback in the NFL in 2009 and played seven more seasons, thirteen total, and set the record for most yards rushing by a quarterback – six thousand one hundred nine.

Vick now does a lot of volunteer work helping children avoid trouble and promoting the well-being of animals.

WHAT'S THE NCAA?

The BCS is BS

Don't bother closing all the windows or shoving cotton in your nostrils. That won't help. From Bangor, Maine to Chula Vista, California the stench of bullshit is upon us, and its source is as unavoidable as it is predictable – the people who run college sports. Their purpose, as ever, is to perpetuate their power and influence and increase their wealth, both personal and institutional, while those who generate the glory and support them, the best college athletes in the nation, often struggle in a system that forbids them to have more than a few bucks to go on a date or take a trip home. These latest officious fat asses call themselves the bozos of the Bowl Championship Series. And the mess they unloaded earlier today is ultimately going to weaken their stranglehold on college athletics. Oh, they'll always have their ever-grasping hands somewhere near the golden gridiron, but now the people who love sports in this country have had enough. You can feel and hear them everywhere. They're angry and they're shouting no more b.s.

Coherent fans are disgusted some arcane computers declared that Boise State's victory over Hawaii, which is light years removed from relevance, was what ultimately determined top-ranked USC, laden with great players and the overwhelming winner of all its games since September, is somehow unworthy of playing for the national championship. Why the aforementioned game? USC had long ago dispatched Hawaii, and that always less than significant victory became less so, at least in the bizarre world of computer determination. So who, dear computer, has amassed the necessary data and is therefore more worthy? Why, Oklahoma, of course, a team that last night was outrun, out-passed, out-hit, and knocked out thirty-five to seven by Kansas State. The BCS computers, evidently programmed by those with fanatical allegiance to the Big 12 Conference, have now twice in three years declared that a team demolished in that conference should play for the national championship. Two years ago the great beneficiary was Nebraska, which had just surrendered more than sixty points and miles of yardage on the ground to Colorado. Then unqualified Nebraska was predictably and quite boringly dismantled by Miami, while second-ranked Oregon, a hot and exciting team, had to play elsewhere.

Those who understand and care about sports – as opposed to those who benefit because so many do care – want to see the best and most-deserving teams play for the national championship. For decades we were told this couldn't happen because university presidents didn't want a playoff system. They supposedly felt it would require Division I student-athletes to miss too many classes. Bullshit. There is and has long been a sixteen- and an eight-team football playoff in Division I-AA, and Division II, and in the NAIA. Didn't those university presidents also care about the academic health of their students? Of course they did. But at the smaller schools there weren't millions of dollars on the table, and under it, for those who control access to and profit from the big bowl games, nor was there the national attention and prestige.

The irony is this: the same flabby hypocrites who run things now could make even more money and get more attention if there were a championship playoff. Such an event would be huge, and its excitement and cultural significance would certainly rival, and perhaps even surpass, that of the NFL playoffs. If an eight-team playoff is too sane and wonderful for these limited men to embrace, then let's make it very simple and establish a one game national championship showdown to be played the week after the major bowl games. The power boys are soon going to have to do something right or they'll get the boot. Somehow, that's what they'll get. Fans are tired of holding their noses.

December 2003

Letter to Division I Personages

Dear Personages,

I wanted to simply address this letter to athletic directors but that would have been inadequate. They often don't make the critical personnel decisions. Instead, university presidents and provosts and trustees and even boosters, influenced by pouting students, interact and confer and decide what to do. So I'm going to refer to all you individuals – who make up this tribunal – as personages. It's likely you feel comfortable with that designation. You know you deserve it. You have great power and only the very powerful, for example, would be able to perpetuate the fatuous BCS system of combining human votes with computer data to determine who plays for the national championship, while suppressing the popular and rational proposition of settling matters on the field in an eight-team playoff.

You have many other difficult but no doubt satisfying tasks. Looking very serious, you recently felt compelled to fire at least a dozen of the hundred seventeen head coaches in Division 1-A football. That mortality rate indicates you've been quite productive in your deliberations. Someone must be blamed when a football team doesn't win enough games, and the coach is frequently a not unreasonable choice. So let's concede you've been doing what had to be done, removing the insufficiently successful from gridiron leadership.

Tyrone Willingham of Notre Dame was the most recent and by far the most publicized coach you judged unworthy of maintaining his job. He compiled a twenty-one and fifteen record in three years, comparable to two predecessors – Bob Davie and Gerry Faust – who you granted the opportunity to fulfill the final two years guaranteed by their original contracts. Willingham's merits are by now well known: he is a man of intelligence and integrity and, more pertinently in the coaching business, his Fighting Irish this season beat damn good teams from Michigan and Tennessee. Willingham's shortcomings have also been widely discussed: he's a rather austere and uninspiring individual who failed to stir the blood of the troops in the manner of Knute Rockne or some of the contemporary coaching stars like Pete Carroll and Bob Stoops. Of course, Carroll of USC and Stoops of Oklahoma don't have to limit their recruiting to the most scholarly athletes. Playing swifter and more-gifted opponents, Willingham and the Irish lost five games by at least thirty-one points, three of those to traditional rival USC. Before Ty, such lopsidedness had occurred only fifteen times during hundred and fifteen years in the land of the Golden Dome.

Perhaps we should feel as bad for Old Notre Dame as we do for Willingham. You Irish personages so expeditiously – during that "emergency meeting" late at night – shoved Willingham through the exit because you'd fallen in love with someone else, Urban Meyer, slayer of all eleven foes at Utah this season, ten and two the year before, and once a Notre Dame assistant who now held the cherished contractual right to leave Salt Lake City should the Irish ever offer him a job. But Urban Meyer spurned you, deciding it would be less troublesome to win at talent-rich and academically-laid-back Florida. Willingham must have chuckled, and not unkindly, about that.

There remains an issue that no one is likely to find humorous. Among the recent firings were Fitz Hill of San Jose State and Tony Samuel of New Mexico, and their departures, along with Willingham's, reduce the number of black football coaches at Division 1-A schools to two. Those who don't follow college football probably think that's a misprint. But you personages know numbers like that are in granite. You chiseled them there. And why is that? Forty-four percent of the players at the top hundred seventeen football schools are black. A large group of former players, and not merely those who played for major schools, now work as assistant coaches. Surely a lot more than two of them are qualified to lead a football team. Isn't that logical? The current secretary of state, Colin Powell, is black. And you certainly recall that Powell also served as Chairman of the Joint Chiefs of Staff, the highest military authority in the most powerful nation. There are in fact a lot more black generals and mayors and members of Congress and corporate chiefs and surgeons than black head football coaches.

Why is that? I had to read about forty articles about football this week to confirm what I suspected. The explosive nugget was found in an ESPN.com article by Gino Wojciechowski. He wrote that "a prominent athletic director for a BCS-conference program" told him "the pool of qualified minority candidates for head coaching positions wasn't as deep as you'd think." And why didn't this eminently qualified athletic director use his name? I suppose he didn't want to be the Al Campanis of this generation. In the eighties Campanis, you will remember, was the Los Angeles Dodger executive, and a decent fellow, who on national television stated, based on his decades of association in baseball, that he was convinced blacks didn't have "the necessities" to manage major league baseball. Campanis did affectionately concede they were nice people and had wonderful musculature.

There have since been a number of successful black managers, professional football coaches, and innumerable basketball coaches at all levels of college play and in the pros. So the next time you, a nameless white athletic director speaking for your fellow personages, says there just aren't any black football coaches worthy of taking charge, go jump in the pool and take a better look.

GTC

December 2004

Congress Mandates College Football Playoffs

Don't worry. Though we United States senators and representatives eagerly kiss fannies of major donors, vacillate on critical issues, kowtow to presidents, and squander the nation's wealth and prestige on maniacal defense programs and unwarranted aggression, we at least are resolute and farsighted about the most urgent issue of our era, and proved so today by dismantling and forever burying college football's psychotic BCS system of determining the national champion and replacing it with the College Football Playoffs that from inception will soar to unparalleled popularity in this land.

Those who have long presumed to be inherently more qualified than football players to determine the best team have been neutralized. Hypocritical and dollar-crazed university presidents who blathered that a playoff wasn't workable were subdued by police and National Guard units before dawn this morning, fitted with straitjackets, and locked into isolation at the nearest detention facilities. These expeditious tactics also snared corpulent bowl-game executives and conference commissioners whose parasitic proclivities have for more than a century, long before the BCS, deprived fans of seeing a compelling series of football games.

We didn't have to arrest coaches who've been voting in this farce, since today they embraced competitive rationality and vowed to play to win rather than pray for victory by arcane vote tabulation. The diabolically programmed BCS computers, which regularly declared that lambs would slay lions, were unplugged, battered with sledgehammers, and donated to junk yards. As for media lackeys who've been part of the process, they now are the process. A tad less biased than coaches of the teams involved, these scribblers and televised blabbermouths will have an unequivocally easy task: identify and rank the top eight major college football teams.

Since playoffs already exist for Division I-AA, Division II, and other football teams, and in fact for virtually all teams in all sports, amateur or professional, we're positive the College Football Playoffs will be easy to implement, even at this juncture. In the future, incidentally, the regular season will start no sooner than the first Saturday in September and end no later than the final Saturday in November. Teams will play no more than eleven games, and, of course, there will be no more debilitating, and generally repetitious, conference championship games. How many times per season do you want to watch one team slap another around? Or, as in 2003, do you really wish to witness a team disemboweled at the conference dance and then mysteriously voted one of the nation's two title participants?

This whole stinking BCS system is as absurd as preventing Ali and Frazier from entering the ring because power-crazed voters have already determined the winner. No need for Tiger Woods to show up at Augusta every April. BCS officials and their aberrant computers will tell us when he might be worthy of raising the trophy. They'll also vote to determine who wins Olympic track races, World Series titles, Super Bowls, and marital arguments. Don't bother to experience life. BCS chest-thumpers crave to tell you what it's like. They've always been that way, and that's why they're now in the pokey.

Start celebrating the world's preeminent event this Saturday, December eighth, as the top four seeds host five through eight, the first playing the eighth, the second meeting the seventh, and so on. That'll set up two blockbuster bowl games for December twenty-second. Then, on January first in The College Bowl, we'll have our first real national champion.

That's the College Football Playoffs, seven intense, soul-boosting contests that will generate much more sacred cash than a few politically-made BCS games drained of meaning.

December 2007

Time to Pay College Athletes

Howls in the sporting world have resumed as they always must since those making the disgusting noises cannot do much else. I am primarily referring to white sportswriters and talk radio grunts, a snaky and jealous lot, who have recently called Tiger Woods scum and a bum because he enjoys sleeping with attractive young women. Many of these same scavengers have been screeching that LeBron James is a coward because for seven splendid years he lifted an otherwise mediocre Cleveland Cavaliers team into NBA title contention, but couldn't get a ring with the help he had, so opted to play with better teammates in a more appealing city. Now, the unforgivable scoundrel is Reggie Bush, who during three seasons at USC electrified fans nationwide and generated tens of millions of dollars for sportswriters, football coaches, athletic directors, NCAA parasites, bowl game leeches, television executives, and advertisers. While doing so, as long rumored, Reggie Bush was accepting money from prospective agents. In other words, he was being paid, not by those who were already guzzling the profits from his talent, but by those who hoped to do so when Bush became a professional.

Reggie Bush had a job. Let's call it a part-time job. He was a college football player. It is a farce when, in sacred tones, those who never could play proclaim that "scholar-athletes" must remain pure and that somehow means unpaid. The hypocrites should suck their thumbs. For their edification, most college students with jobs do get paid. They bus tables on campus and off. They make deliveries. They work in construction. They work in department stores. They work in hundreds of jobs to make money. If those in the sanctimonious set don't think work warrants pay then let them work without compensation. Mow Reggie Bush's lawn for free.

True, many college athletes receive scholarships that pay for their education and room and board. But thousands of the country's finest young athletes don't have enough money to visit their families on holidays, unless their parents pay for it. And many parents of elite college football and basketball players cannot afford to send their sons money. Oh, and the majority of these future NFL and NBA standouts are African American. That makes it particularly painful for white media scolds, who proclaim their love for all humanity until a young black athlete earns something, monetary or social, that was and is beyond them. Then the howls begin, and howls boost ratings.

There is another elementary point. The United States is a free market country. People sell their talents and are paid for them, regardless of age. As a child in the nineteen thirties Shirley Temple earned hundreds of thousands of dollars, millions today, from her work as an actress and merchandising Shirley Temple dolls and other products. Other examples abound. Kurt Russell and Ron Howard were successful child actors. Musical prodigies Little Stevie Wonder and Michael Jackson reached stardom before puberty.

Why shouldn't the nation's best college athletes, in sports and at universities that generate money, be paid? Why should those who benefit from their excellence make countless millions, make that billions, while the stars – the athletic counterparts to Shirley Temples and Stevie Wonder – scrounge for money to visit their parents?

The system is ridiculous. It's an inherent contradiction. It stinks. USC has been punished by pious bloodsuckers in the NCAA, and the contrite university has returned the Heisman Trophy of Reggie Bush and is now removing all other trophies and likenesses of a young man who brought the program great wealth and glory. If the NCAA demands that Bush return his copy of the Heisman, he should say, "Sure, drop your drawers and bend over."

July 2010

Champions of Sleep

BCS voters evidently believe LSU and Alabama are incomparable football teams from the same conference and no one else is qualified to play them though in regular season neither scored a touchdown against the other and the second time they numbed the nation with another electoral championship.

January 2012

A Real College Football Playoff

A Sixteen Team College Football Playoff is needed.

Get rid of meaningless conference championship games, and limit all schools to only eleven regular season games. That way only two teams would play fourteen games and four would play thirteen. They're already playing that many: but that's to line greasy pockets of NCAA thieves and corporate coconspirators.

Every year several good teams are denied the chance to compete in real national championship playoff millions of fans would love to see. If NCAA goons don't like it, too bad. Either stand aside or face criminal antitrust charges and more.

December 2014

THE TROJANS

Reggie Bush Electrifies

They are defensive ends with whiplash, linebackers eating turf, defensive backs chasing a comet. They're confused, frustrated, and ever-empty handed. They're groping for Reggie Bush who explodes from the backfield like an Olympic sprinter. But, really, it's much more problematic than that. Reggie Bush, you see, frequently does not travel in a straight line. When defenders close in, he cuts, twists, hurdles or dives, and no one including Reggie knows what's next. Ultimately, of course, everyone understands he's going all the way, flying into the end zone at altitudes high and low.

Reggie Bush will next perform for the University of Southern California football team in the Rose Bowl on January fourth when his top-ranked Trojans play the University of Texas for the national championship. Both teams average fifty points a game and are undefeated. Last year's Heisman Trophy winner, Matt Leinart, is the man who hands (and sometimes throws) the ball to Bush. Their principal opponent is another Heisman candidate, sleek and powerful Texas quarterback Vince Young. Perhaps next year Young will win the highest award in college football.

This season the trophy belongs to Bush, who dashed nearly eleven yards a carry in the desperate win at Notre Dame, amassed an astonishing five hundred thirteen yards of offense against Fresno State, and who could've rushed a half-mile against rival UCLA. As Leinart and Young and others shake his hand, Bush will collect his prize tomorrow in downtown New York. This individual honor is a mere prelude to what should be the most widely-watched game in college football history.

Reggie Bush is only a junior and could play another year of college ball, but that is a quaint notion, like Bill Gates staying in school instead of starting Microsoft. Bush will assuredly charge off campus to become a top pick in the National Football League draft and collect an enormous reward. Last year the number one selection, quarterback Alex Smith – Bush's high school teammate in San Diego – received a bonus of twenty-four million dollars. Negotiations for Bush will start higher, yet the deal probably won't take long to close. Urgency compels the new team to be generous.

So where will Reggie Bush play next year? The franchise with the worst record gets first choice. Those eligible for the Bush Sweepstakes are the once superlative San Francisco 49'ers, now struggling with a weak defense and callow quarterback Alex Smith, the hapless-since-inception Houston Texans, and the lowest scoring team in the league, the New York Jets. Will Bush leverage his prestige and refuse to go where he doesn't want to play, as John Elway spurned the Baltimore Colts in the early eighties and Eli Manning recently nixed the San Diego Chargers? That seems to be the rare prerogative of disenchanted quarterbacks. Halfback Bush will probably sign with the team that takes him and report to a gridiron environment fundamentally different than he's enjoyed at USC, where prodigies are plentiful and future pros often spend time as backups. His last collegiate setback was a prehistoric thirty-four games ago. In the National Football League, his team will frequently lose. But excitement and hope are guaranteed every time he maneuvers past falling foes in ways no one else can.

December 2005

Notes: During eleven NFL seasons Reggie Bush rushed, received, and returned kicks for fifty-eight touchdowns and almost ten thousand yards.

NFL Scouts Assess Vince Young

Team One – We love the way University of Texas quarterback Vince Young shucks off opponents as if they were kids at a family picnic. Add some weight to Young's current two hundred thirty-three pounds, and we project him as the fastest and most athletic defensive end in the NFL and a man likely to set season and career records for quarterback sacks.

Team Two – There's never been a linebacker prospect like Young. He's faster than the incomparable Lawrence Taylor and, at six-foot-five, just as big. On every play he'll either blitz timid and immobile pro quarterbacks or use long strides to glide back into pass coverage and smother tiny wide receivers.

Team Three – Vince Young will revolutionize the way defensive backs play the game of football. If we get this young man, we'll turn him into a terror who on consecutive plays can plant quarterbacks, flatten halfbacks, and intercept passes he'll return for touchdowns.

Team Four – It's time for a new kind of offensive lineman, one who's the fastest guy on the field. The only man with the requisite size, strength and speed for that role is Vince Young. We have calculated he's quick enough to block the left and right defensive ends on the same play and then rush downfield to bury any defender approaching our end-zone-bound receiver.

Team Five – Imagine, if you can, that your primary wide receiver is the strongest man on the field. We've processed this image and will offer inducements both legal and illegal in order to obtain the draft rights to Vince Young. Our strategy is simple but profoundly original. We'll throw the ball to Vince immediately after every snap and let him dodge or bulldoze the two closest defenders before breaking deep into enemy territory. If teams place four or five adversaries on Vince, that opens up the field for our other guys.

Team Six – We simply are not going to pass much after we pull a few deals and obtain Vince Young. For us he'll play halfback and carry the ball forty times a game, battering defenders and blowing by them as he ensures we start winning Super Bowls.

Team Seven – We plan to use Vince Young at quarterback. He completed thirty of forty passes during Texas' forty-one to thirty-eight national championship victory over USC in the Rose Bowl last week, and none of his aerials was intercepted. Few quarterbacks have ever thrown the ball so many times against a fine opponent in a big game and not had at least one picked off. We therefore aren't worried by some complaints about Young's unorthodox throwing motion.

We're also delighted by his ability, even when his team trails and action is chaotic, to spot openings in defenses and charge through them. With nineteen seconds remaining against the Trojans, Texas trailed thirty-eight to thirty-three and faced elimination on fourth down and five at the USC eight-yard line. A composed Young surveyed his passing options and saw only blanketed receivers before he tucked the ball into his ribs and dashed untouched for his third touchdown in an historic victory. He had scored four times against Michigan last year, and on all seven TDs in Pasadena he entered the end zone upright.

We of course realize that in the headhunting NFL, where running quarterbacks are treated like cattle rustlers, Young won't be able to carry the ball as much as in college. We therefore establish this limit: though our new quarterback could lead the league in rushing, he will not be permitted to do so. He'll be allowed to top the passing charts, but statistics aren't the point. We want Super Bowl victories and have already determined his ring size for every finger and both thumbs.

January 2006

Notes: Sometimes great all-around athletes aren't the best passers, and issues of inaccuracy troubled Young in six professional seasons during which he threw fifty-one interceptions but only forty-seven touchdown passes. He was then released by teams three straight seasons before play began. In 2017, six years after his final pass in a regular season game, Young signed with the Saskatchewan Roughriders of the Canadian Football League.

Pete Carroll Departs

Admit it. You've chosen the wrong profession. You should've been a head coach in the National Football League or at an elite gridiron university where you've long pulverized opponents or, at minimum, convinced school presidents, athletic directors, and boosters you'll soon deliver championships. Then you'd be the object of an ardent courtship placing you at the epicenter of wealth, glamour, opportunism, greed, and betrayal – the stuff of drama.

Pete Carroll, blessed with a cool quotient hotter than most L.A. celebrities and a resume featuring revitalization of the formerly great but then moribund USC Trojans, initiated recent excitement when he listened as the Seattle Seahawks secretly offered him the platter of gold and power he'd always craved. The incumbent Seattle coach, young Jim Mora, thought he'd made moderate progress with a five and eleven record during his first season and assumed he was being summoned to discuss the team's future. Instead, he got the guillotine. His severance ironically recalls that Carroll at about the same age, in 1994, was poleaxed after a single unsatisfactory campaign, six and ten, for the New York Jets. He was also fired by the New England Patriots in 1999 after three seasons and a commendable yet intolerable record of twenty-seven and twenty-one.

Now Pete Carroll at age fifty-eight is moving to the rainy Northwest as a savior. For that task he'll be paid about seven million dollars a year – a hundred forty grand a week – for five seasons. If he doesn't win at least one conference championship and play in a Super Bowl, he will thrice be considered a bust and forever removed from elite coaching. Carroll, a man of astonishing energy and optimism, probably envisions only imminent glory. He's body surfing a tidal wave of seven straight superb seasons, 2002-2008, featuring two national champions and at least four other teams, ignored by provincial and generally redneck voters, that should have played for the still-mythical national title of college football. The politics infuriated him, though he sometimes denied it, and more damaging still were the howls: "He failed in the

NFL." He didn't fail except to enshrine himself in the pantheon of pro coaches: Vince Lombardi, Chuck Noll, Bill Walsh, and – no doubt tormenting Carroll – Bill Belichick, his successor at New England.

Pete Carroll couldn't ignore the only opportunity he'll ever have to determine who plays for him on a professional team, and thus have a chance to engineer two or three Super Bowl titles. If he does that, he will be embraced as an immortal leader of men in athletic combat. If he does not, he'll be a wealthy retiree much desired for television and speaking appearances.

Lane Kiffin, still cherubic at age thirty-four, abandoned the University of Tennessee late one recent weeknight, enraging Knoxville fanatics who police had to barricade, so he could return to USC where he assisted Carroll six years and was endowed with the sheen of success. As a head coach, Kiffin has been less stellar, registering a five and fifteen record in little more than a season with the dysfunctional Oakland Raiders. Kiffin was a mere babe of thirty-one when he agreed to work with the once-shrewd Al Davis, who, upon firing the lad, publicly read from letters and notes purporting to prove Kiffin was a lout and that Davis was both righteous and still a winner, and by implication not a neurotic who'd squandered his energy in ceaseless courtroom confrontations and personal battles well before the aging process destroyed the rest of his talent. Today, one of Davis' most startling complaints, from the fall of 2008, was that he had earlier rebuked Kiffin for not wanting to draft quarterback JaMarcus Russell in the 2007 first round and informed his coach the Raiders would certainly be doing so. During three seasons Russell has regressed and may be among the unfortunate half of highly-drafted quarterbacks who fizzle in the NFL.

That's the point about Lane Kiffin: he can assess talent. He was an ace recruiter as an assistant at USC. And during his fourteen months at Tennessee, where he inherited a five and seven team and improved to seven and six, he twice attracted top five or ten recruiting classes, perhaps better than the last two groups Pete Carroll signed for the Trojans. Kiffin not only knows how to acquire dynamic players, he understands the requirements of celebrity, and, though not as dashing as Carroll, he excites fans when he appears with his stunning blonde wife. In Hollywood that helps.

January 2010

Pat Haden's Termination Plans

(An unnamed and unabashedly frightened member of the USC athletic department today released this document, liberated from an electrified safe in the bunker of athletic director Pat Haden.)

How I Shall Terminate Coaches

Football – This one's got my hands hot on the keys because I know I'm soon going to have to decapitate Lane Kiffin. This I shall do not with a guillotine, as I'd prefer, but in a way acceptable in this repugnant twenty-first century of weakness and handwringing. After our next humiliating loss, I shall stand at attention in front of the team bus as it prepares to leave the stadium, and when the driver turns off the engine and opens the doors I'll storm onboard, assume a three-point stance and propel myself at Kiffin's chest into which I'll bury my forehead. Whether this losing coach is conscious or not, I shall eject him from the bus and order our immediate departure.

(Internet flash: At Arizona State last week, following USC's sixty-two to forty-one loss, fellow administrators tackled Haden before he reached the bus and carried the athletic director to a van which took him to the Phoenix airport where he was sedated and stowed with the luggage. Upon arriving at the Los Angeles airport, a reawakened Haden ordered Kiffin off the team bus, handcuffed him in front of his players, told the driver to get lost, and in the airport holding cell upbraided Kiffin an hour before shouting to walk home and never return to the hallowed halls of Troy.)

Basketball – I'm tired of not winning national championships in basketball. We're a potential hoops giant and lack only a John Wooden to enshrine my name with the greatest of hardwood legends. When I discern the man I've hired for this task is lacking, I shall march to the bench and begin ripping his jacket apart. I may order all coaches to wear epaulets, as an expression of military fanaticism, and also to give me something symbolic to tear off. After my guards remove the former coach, I shall take command of the team.

Baseball – USC was once the New York Yankees of college baseball but now plays like the 1962 Mets. This I shall no longer endure. When the coach irrevocably shows he lacks the horsepower to get us into the World Series – and not merely the college version – I shall dash onto the diamond and fire fastballs at his feet. Only a sadist would target points higher. My arm, blessedly, is still strong from my college and pro passing as well as recent hardball workouts designed for this grand purpose.

Track and Field – A real track and field coach, even a real bad one, wears sleek sweat pants while coaching the team. Thus, when I conclude the Trojans cannot beat the U.S. national team, I shall yank the coach's pants down to his ankles where the pants will be taped prior to the coach being manacled to a pole vault stand.

Swimming – Once I've ripped off the trunks of a coach who isn't producing Olympic gold medal winners, I'll throw his lead ass into highly-chlorinated water. A less honorable AD would dispense with the water.

Volleyball – Standing over a coach who's headed somewhere other than the national title, I shall several times spike the ball into his or her face. I may even miss the ball and plant my wrist between evil eyes. `

Golf – I must be careful here. I don't want to go to prison though most great revolutionaries have done so and I'm willing to as well. Rather than whack the bogey-inducing coach with a driver, or a ball blasted by my long one, I shall simply shove one or more balls into his mouth and have him tossed into the nearest hazard.

Fight on, Trojans.

October 2013

Sarkisian Drunk at Rally

Let's start with the most important issues: protecting Steve Sarkisian's health, and that of the public, and perhaps saving his career as well. Most commentators and others who've held forth to date understand that last Saturday the USC football coach wasn't merely drunk and shouting, "Get ready to fucking fight on, baby," at the Salute to Troy football rally where wealthy boosters, fans, and students gathered to generate money and enthusiasm for the once unstoppable Trojans. Steve Sarkisian was proving, beyond deniability, that rumors he has a drinking problem are true. People who can control their liquor don't get intoxicated at work and rant that some of their top competitors "suck." In this case, Sarkisian was referring to Arizona State, Notre Dame, and Oregon.

I'm not going to preach. I can't. I've screwed up more than Sarkisian has to date and more, I hope, than he ever will. In other words, I'm an alcoholic. In my behalf, I can state that I never drank before or during any work shift, but afterward I consumed quantities and substances that could have resulted in tragedy. I suppose being a drunkard and an abuser doesn't automatically confer expertise, but the experiences of long-term excess, combined with medical treatment and independent study, certainly do give one greater insight, and have enabled me to build almost eighteen years of sobriety.

Steve Sarkisian will have to decide if he wants to change. At present he's learning about the consequences of public drunkenness. His boss, athletic director Pat Haden, escorted him off stage at the rally and rebuked him in private before publicly stating he'd delivered a message "loud and clear." The coach is also feeling the wrath of some players who were insulted by their leader's undignified behavior and stated that such conduct on their part would not be tolerated.

All right, what's next? Haden has probably already decided not to fire Sarkisian less than a fortnight before the season starts. He'll give the coach a season to redeem himself, and if he behaves while the Trojans win ten or more games the issue of drinking may not be terminal.

Irrespective of final scores, Steve Sarkisian should be required to attend AA meetings at least once a week for a year and be examined by a psychiatrist to determine if he may have an underlying depression he's self-treating with alcohol. If those terms are unacceptable to Sarkisian, he should immediately be relieved of his head coaching duties. People who drink too much and keep drinking always get worse. Anyone who doesn't know that is a fool.

I'd like to discuss a little football, which we could concentrate on if not for Sarkisian's problem, still publicly unacknowledged by him, and state that Rhodes Scholarly Pat Haden is less skillful as an athletic administrator than he was as a student, a college and pro quarterback, a college football analyst on TV, an attorney, and an entrepreneur. During the search to replace Lane Kiffin, Haden said they examined many candidates and "it always kept getting back to Sark." I've been a USC fan since 1962 and would like to know why it kept getting back to him. He compiled a thirty-five and twenty-nine record at the University of Washington. This mediocrity fails to suggest a worthy successor to the national championship regimes of John McKay, John Robinson, and Pete Carroll. So now USC has an average coach, at a university that demands football excellence, and one who sometimes drinks too much publicly and damages the Trojan brand. One suspects that Pat Haden's next big personnel move may be replacing himself.

August 2015

Paraphrasing Sarkisian

From USC football coach Steve Sarkisian's press conference of August twenty-fifth

Sark said – When you mix meds with alcohol you say things you regret.

Sark meant – Sure I drank too much but it doesn't sound as bad when I blame my behavior on unnamed prescription medications.

Sark said – I don't think I have a drinking problem.

Sark meant – I probably do have a drinking problem but am more comfortable being in denial than acknowledging the truth.

Sark said – Through athletic director Pat Haden and the University I'm going to find out if I have a drinking problem. I'm going to have therapy.

Sark meant – Haden and some other USC administrators insist that I have a drinking problem and must either get treatment or leave campus on Traveler, our great white Trojan horse.

Sark said – I don't know if I even need rehab.

Sark meant – Haden has already booked my therapeutic appointments.

August 2015

Rolling Hills Paradise

Sure, I've been lucky but also worked hard and produced some movies millions have seen. I already own a beautiful home in Bel Air but am tired of living amid show business people. They remind me of myself. I've been looking to the south, down around Palos Verdes, a beautiful peninsula reaching into the sea and home to folks who've made money doing things besides making movies.

My real estate agent is excited about showing me a place on more than five acres in Rolling Hills. I at once love the spacious grounds and expansive house, eight thousand square feet all in one story. I don't like climbing stairs or taking elevators no matter how pretty the house. I think I can feel myself living right here. Look at the city and the hills, the air's so clean down here, and the weather's great and there's a luminous swimming pool and a tennis court and putting green and koi pond and five hundred fruit trees.

Inside, it's elegant but not garish. It's California cool. There are many wonderful features, a pool table next to a huge TV, a den with a TV over the fireplace, an office with a TV opposite the desk, a TV above the fireplace in the kitchen, a TV next to the casual dining area appointed with stools at a bar, a TV over the fireplace in the master bedroom, a TV in the executive bathroom above the tub, a TV in the exercise room, a total of eighteen flat screens highlighted by a massive presence in the living room. I can watch movies wherever I want, and beforehand will step into my climate-controlled wine cellar and pull bottles of the finest stuff.

"How much does this place cost?" I ask.

"Eight and a half million."

"I'll take it. Who lived here before me?"

"USC's football coach and his family. The couple's divorcing and doesn't need such a big place anymore."

August 2015

Stop Drinking

I just reread three columns I wrote in late August about the problems of USC football coach Steve Sarkisian and am saddened the key issues covered therein are again in the news: Sark was intoxicated yesterday when he arrived at football practice. Here's a review of my earlier points.

1. After slurring a profanity-fueled speech to Trojan supporters in August, it was "beyond deniability" that Sarkisian had a drinking problem.

2. A couple of days later he said, "I don't know if I have a drinking problem," and I thought: he's in deep denial. When people deny there's a problem, they ensure the problem will worsen.

3. Steve Sarkisian must decide if he wants to change.

4. When he said, "I don't know if I even need rehab," I assumed that athletic director Pat Haden had already ordered him to get treatment or face immediate dismissal.

5. For rehab, I suggested a minimum of one AA meeting a week and that he be examined by a psychiatrist to determine if he suffered from an underlying depression and had been self-medicating with alcohol.

I see that my therapeutic recommendations were rather timid, probably like those of Pat Haden. It's now apparent that Sarkisian needs to attend at least one AA meeting every day for a long time. He also should be examined by two psychiatrists who, separately, may be able to determine if depressive factors are involved. Many medical professionals would no doubt recommend that Sarkisian be placed in a treatment facility for ninety days. Be assured that his brain craves alcohol, and unless your brain also craves booze you can't know what an utterly overpowering urge that is.

In a far less important realm, I still don't understand why Haden chose Sarkisian to try to carry the national championship sword of his three most distinguished predecessors. Sark coached unimpressively at the University of Washington and in five seasons his best league record was five and four. At USC Sarkisian and his team lost four games last season, and have already been defeated twice this year, most recently by his former Huskies who will probably have better teams led by current coach Chris Petersen.

I feel uneasy criticizing Pat Haden, a man distinguished in several disciplines, but it's probable he's miscast as an athletic director. I'm not saying I would fire him if I were the university president – I wouldn't. I think he deserves a chance to hire another football coach. Steve Sarkisian, now on indefinite leave, has surely coached his last game for the Trojans. He faces a far bigger game every day the rest of his life. He must figure out how to be undefeated in the battle for sobriety.

September 2015

JOHNNY FOOTBALL

Meet Johnny

I swear years ago I overcame many dastardly devices and am no longer addictive and in fact am a man of considerable restraint, and disdain those who contend I've relapsed. Am I drinking, am I smoking, am I overeating? No, they say, but you're addicted to Johnny Football.

That's preposterous. A month ago I hadn't even heard of the guy, and saw only the final quarter of the Alabama-Texas A&M game, thus missing most flashy-feet, laser-arm plays that dismantled the top-ranked Crimson Tide and created a cult. I don't like cults. They remind me of lemmings who follow bad guys off cliffs. I'm not doing that.

I'm only getting online a time or two a day watching videos of Johnny Manziel throw, run and receive, sometimes all on the same play, as he twists and spins and fakes and cuts making defenders grope. I'm stunned by his quickness and speed. Scouts say he's not a sprinter but he outruns fast opponents even when they have favorable angles. I marvel at his instincts. I applaud precise passes either fired or floated as needed. Hold my calls. Get out of my office. I refuse to stop watching. Screw the boss. I'll do my work later. Hell with the wife and kids. They should watch this too. Really, I only do this once or twice a day and don't consider time relevant in the world of Johnny Football.

December 2012

Sober Up

Dedicated critics of Johnny Manziel have recently blistered me with emails about the quarterback's latest personal struggle, and I immediately responded by rechecking and citing his high school and college exploits, which earned him a Heisman Trophy as a redshirt freshman, and noted he'd played fairly well during limited starts this, his second, professional season, and finally reviewed the long and lengthening list of personal problems which do indeed threaten his health and his career.

It's clear many people have overdosed on Johnny "Football" Manziel and want him to either shape up or disappear. That's a universal rule: cause too much trouble and you'll at some point be banished. Cleveland Browns head coach Mike Pettine is among the most disappointed. A week earlier he'd named Manziel starting quarterback for the rest of the season, a six-game stretch that likely would've confirmed or refuted that Johnny Manziel, age twenty-two, can soon become a prime time NFL quarterback.

Manziel meanwhile has reminded everyone he faces a more critical test twenty-four hours a day the rest of his life. Can he stay sober? I don't know if the official diagnosis has been released. It doesn't have to be. Johnny Manziel is an alcoholic, and all alcoholics are certain to suffer if they continue to drink. A review of Manziel's trajectory, since his June 2012 arrest for disorderly conduct while in college, proves he's headed for the tank unless he changes. During his 2015 rookie year in Cleveland I attempted to dismiss his frequent hangovers and lack of professional commitment as youthful indiscretions he'd soon outgrow.

The Browns knew the truth, and Manziel entered a rehabilitation center for two months. That's an unusually long stay for an alcoholic only twenty-two years old, and I admired him for going through treatment, even if he was compelled; most people who need professional help never receive it. Despite his efforts to heal, Manziel just several months later had "a couple of drinks" earlier in the day and, while driving, got into an altercation with his girlfriend who told police she initially "feared for her life." Her wrist and forearm were bruised and abraded. Manziel attributed this to his attempt to prevent her from jumping out of the car.

Meanwhile, on the practice field and in the film room, he'd worked much harder this year, and in his most recent start passed for three hundred seventy-nine yards against the Pittsburgh Steelers. For the season he has five touchdown passes and only two interceptions. The coach was correct in promoting Manziel, who promised the Browns he wouldn't embarrass them. A week later he was seen, and still can be, in an online video showing him drunk and holding a champagne bottle as he sings in a nightclub.

This binge not only cost Johnny Football his starting job; he was demoted to third string. Rather than acknowledge the obvious, Manziel said videos can be old and he's not sure this one was taken last week. Horse feathers. People know whether or not they got drunk in a night club last week. And if Johnny Manziel didn't, he simply would've guaranteed the video was old, not that it might be. His evasion is called denial. Manziel has a bad case of it, and it will worsen if he keeps drinking. Guaranteed.

November 2015

Johnny Goes Vegas

I'm always eager to discover and sign gifted young actors, those with the "it" factor, so I scour hotspots in Manhattan, Miami Beach, L.A., and Las Vegas, places you've got to be cool to get through doors. Tonight I go to my favorite Vegas nightclub where last year I met a couple of stunning ladies now starring in adult films. I do regular films, too. In fact, I prefer them. I just have to find the right talent. And I think I see a guy with presence. I'm not sure if he's a leading man but sense there could be roles for him. He isn't Hollywood pretty but's nice looking and has striking blond hair under his hoodie and a cute dark mustache. His glasses confer authority.

I approach his table, smile at a couple of young men and two ladies, nod at the main man, and say, "Hi, I'm Vic. Here's my card. I'd like to make you a star."

He doesn't rise but offers his right hand and says, "Billy."

"I'm friends with lots of producers and directors who'd love to give you a screen test. Ever done any acting?"

"I act all the time."

"Movies, TV, or plays?"

"Just making everyday life different. Can't handle boring routines."

"Can I ask you to take off your glasses? I need to see what the camera will."

He takes them off, putting them in a sweatshirt pocket, and smiles. "What do you think?"

"You've got potential. What pays your bills?"

"I'm a combination entertainer, actor, conductor, and athlete."

"Where do you perform?"

"Gotta keep that secret a few days or the media'll be all over it."

"You're already a star?"

"He's a big star," says one lady.

"Great," I say, "we can use what you're already doing as entrée into movies."

"Don't screw me," Billy says.

"People in Vegas know better than to screw each other."

"Okay, I'm a quarterback."

"Really?"

"Yep."

"In college?"

"Pros."

"You're kinda small."

"Like to arm wrestle?"

"No, I can see you're built. Billy who?"

"Johnny."

"Johnny who?"

"Johnny Football."

"Johnny Manziel?"

"Have a drink," he says, and finishes his, holding his glass high for a smiling, mini-skirted waitress to take and soon replenish.

I order a dry martini and say, "I read you got a concussion a few days ago. You shouldn't be drinking, should you?"

"Takes away my headache."

"I don't know, Johnny," I say.

"The doctors don't, either. They expect me back in Cleveland tomorrow for a checkup. I won't be there. Maybe I'll make it back for the exit interview. My season's done."

"In movies, Johnny, it's a team, just like in sports. Everyone's got to work together and show up on time."

"I usually do that, then something inside starts taking over."

"I'm no Pollyanna, Johnny, but under the circumstances I think you should drink orange juice the rest of the evening."

"That ain't the message my brain's sending."

January 2016

Notes: Johnny Manziel did not play or even attempt to play anywhere in 2016 when he was periodically spotted holding drinks and champagne bottles while talking to fellow revelers. Now he says he's sober, training every day, and ready to sacrifice to return to the NFL. Let's see what Johnny Football actually does.

IN THE NEWS

Why is Fisher DeBerry Apologizing?

Last week a fleet and strong group of Texas Christian University football players enveloped and routed the future military officers of the Air Force Academy. The score was forty-eight to ten. A couple of days later losing coach Fisher DeBerry, who has long guided modestly talented teams to overachievement, said TCU "had a lot more Afro-American players than we did and they ran a lot faster than we did. That doesn't mean Caucasian kids and other descents can't run, but it's very obvious to me that (blacks) run extremely well."

Since that was reported, DeBerry has been barraged by criticism and called insensitive and anachronistic and perhaps even racist. The new academy superintendent ordered him to report for a reprimand. Like a good civilian soldier, DeBerry complied. Afterward, the coach said, "I have made a mistake and ask for everyone's forgiveness." The solemn athletic director then proclaimed, "The academy has a zero-tolerance policy for any racial or ethnic discrimination or discrimination of any kind…It was a seriously, seriously inappropriate comment."

In fact, it was an accurate statement, and one that should have been interpreted as a compliment, which is likely how the TCU players received it. No forthright viewer of sports can logically refute DeBerry's observation. One desperate-to-sound-righteous reporter from Sports Illustrated tried, noting that some white guys are fast and some black guys are fast and so are some people from every race and after all white Jeremy Wariner won the 2004 Olympic gold medal in the four hundred meter dash. Please – reporter, superintendent, athletic director – stop pretending.

Black athletes are demonstrably superior in every sport they commit to en masse. Every four years almost all the Olympic finalists in the hundred, two hundred and four hundred meter dashes are black. The distance events are dominated by Kenyans. Have you ever seen a boxing match? Name the ten greatest heavyweights of all time; anyone who includes a white fighter either doesn't know boxing or is challenging Pinocchio. How about basketball? The eight finest players ever are, in chronological order, Bill Russell, Wilt Chamberlain, Kareem Abdul Jabbar, Magic Johnson, Larry Bird, Michael Jordan, Shaquille O'Neal, and Tim Duncan. Only Bird is white. Out of the top one hundred performers in the game today, at least ninety are black.

How about football? Ask yourself who's putting the ball in the end zone. Roughly eighty percent of touchdowns are scored by blacks. Who's trying to prevent that? Defenses loaded with the most qualified (i.e. fastest) people. How many white cornerbacks do you see in the National Football League? I don't see any. And the notion has actually become ludicrous – a white cornerback Maybe there'll be another one someday, but probably not this century.

Well, look at baseball, some folks breathlessly say. Most players are white. That's true. Baseball doesn't interest young blacks like football, basketball, and track. Nevertheless, ask an easy question: who are the finest baseball players since 1947 when Jackie Robinson modernized the game and energized the civil rights movement? The first three eternally great players after that point were Willie Mays, Mickey Mantle, and Hank Aaron. Mantle was white. Who are the preeminent players today? They're Alex Rodriguez and Albert Pujols. But Pujols is from the Caribbean and Rodriguez is of the same ancestry, it is eagerly stated. That doesn't matter. If Judge Kennesaw Mountain Landis, the segregationist who ruled Major League baseball in the decades before World War II, were here, he'd tell you: they're black. They wouldn't have been allowed in the game in his era. (Parenthetically, wouldn't it be nice to bring that bigot back in a time machine and let Bob Gibson throw a high hard one under his chin?)

How many professional black golfers are there? There is precisely one. His name is Tiger Woods. In his twenties he won ten major championships and frequently made even great golfers look inadequate. How many players of African descent play pro tennis? Very few. Two who do are Venus and Serena Williams. Both have been ranked number one in the world. Serena once won four straight Grand Slam titles.

Any sports fan could write pages about the above information. That's not necessary. The point is clear. But, as DeBerry indicated, that doesn't mean people from all other races can't run and play very well. They can. They do. One has to be careful with generalizations, but

I'm wholesomely comfortable with this one: all peoples are talented in all areas.

When candid souls make public statements like DeBerry's, the outraged and righteous responses really are not related to sports. The concern, instead, is this: if the obvious is acknowledged, that blacks are better athletes, then some, perhaps many, will infer, will perhaps even trumpet that logically there must be other intrinsic differences between the races. Maybe, some will say, there are natural differences in intelligence.

Don't worry about that one. Millions of us may be sports experts but no one has discovered the most profound secrets of evolution. We know only this: children who are well fed and cared for and who study hard do well in school and, later, in any profession they choose. All peoples have the capacity to do well in all endeavors. And in most pursuits, unlike sports, there's no reason to keep score.

November 2005

Pete Carroll Called What?

Pete Carroll is a great coach and dynamic person but this evening he made – rather allowed his offensive coordinator to make – the worst call in the history of championship football. Many of you probably just saw it. As seconds waned the Seahawks, trailing by four, had second down and goal from inside the one-yard line and powerhouse running back Marshawn Lynch ready to drive the ball into the end zone and secure victory. Lynch had just gained four yards the previous play. It was a no brainer. Why did Pete Carroll allow his team to throw the ball, and throw it on a slant pattern into a compressed goal line defense? After the game he said he was thinking about third and fourth downs. What? He and the Seahawks could've won the game outright on second down.

Perhaps in their self-destruction there is poetic justice. Two weeks ago they were outplayed by the Green Bay Packers who imploded down the stretch. Tonight they were outplayed by the New England Patriots and only in position to win because of a most unlikely and quite lucky bounce off a defender's hands had delivered the ball into the astonished hands of a receiver, prostrate on his back, two plays before the mental meltdown. As an admirer of Pete Carroll, I appreciate his stellar performance at USC, transforming my favorite college team into the nation's finest, and, after the elimination of my beloved 49ers this season, I hoped he'd coach his second Super Bowl champion, and then catch Bill Belichick. That will now be impossible. Belichick got his fourth ring while Carroll still has but one. Several people called to commiserate this evening, and one aptly noted, "It's not watching someone die." It isn't. It's just a damn emotional letdown. We all take seriously our entertainment.

February 2015

Belichick Zaps Carroll

My career in the Central Intelligence Agency frequently forced me to analyze and surveil unsavory individuals but none so nefarious as Bill Belichick, with whom I've dueled in my later capacity as secret agent for the National Football League. I doubt even Saddam Hussein, in the brotherhood of coaches, would have used hidden cameras and other electronic tricks to spy on opponents at practice. This Bill Belichick indisputably did several years ago, and when I confronted him with evidence he slit his throat with two sharp fingers, and soon thereafter a knife-wielder set upon me and I survived only because of my rapid draw and straight shot.

I vowed to get Bill Belichick but couldn't prove the sly fellow ordered the hit or deflation of all four tires on my vehicle, the egging of my family home, the kidnapping of my wife, or, most vexing, the sudden cancellation of my cable service moments before kickoff of the Super Bowl last year. This time, abetted by electronics wizards from the National Security Agency, we recorded audio and video as, hours before the conference championship game against the Indianapolis Colts, devious Bill leaned into the ear of an equipment flunky and ordered him to feign gastric distress, lug a dozen footballs into the john, and deflate them so the feminine hands of Tom Brady could better squeeze the pigskin. Belichick countered that his security tapes prove the man stayed in the can a scant thirty seconds. Nonsense. That tape was spliced and, yes, I've secured it in a vault. What perplexed me was why Belichick practiced chicanery against overmatched foes like the Colts, whom his team throttled forty-five to seven.

Surely his paranoia would increase before the Super Bowl and more so when his New England Patriots stumbled ten points behind the Seattle Seahawks in the second half. While the Patriots rallied to a precarious twenty-eight to twenty-four lead, I ordered additional agents onto the sidelines and into dressing rooms. Perhaps we could preempt any Belichick tricks. They didn't always work. After all, in their two most recent Super Bowls, the Patriots had twice squandered late leads and lost. I prayed this would be super setback number three. And that it was certain to be when Seattle penetrated to the Patriot five-yard line as time dwindled and Marshawn Lynch hammered inside the one and would inevitably score on the next play.

I looked at Bill Belichick who was studying Pete Carroll. Belichick checked his wristwatch before rechecking Carroll. Our cameras enlarged each coach. Why was Belichick watching Carroll instead of second and goal with thirty seconds left? Carroll appeared disoriented, his eyes rolling as he staggered along the sideline and onto the field. Assistant coaches grasped shoulders and arms to steady him, and gasped when he said, "Dudes, Lynch ain't getting the ball. I'm throwin a slant pass into traffic short of the goal line." Carroll and his triggerman, Russell Wilson, did precisely that, and the preposterous pass, as you know, was intercepted.

Speaking into my device, I told agents, "No way a great coach does that unless something's amiss. Close in."

I personally took Carroll into custody and tried to interview him but he gazed at the dressing room ceiling and said, "Look at all those stars around Jimi Hendrix's head."

Our surgeon at once withdrew blood from Carroll's neck, and you may surmise the result: the crazed coach was zoned out on acid. How did Belichick do it, and when? We don't know since to date all video and anecdotal evidence is inconclusive. But, by god, we'll get that louse. I think we will.

February 2015

Faultless Frank Gifford

Frank Gifford died today of natural causes a week short of his eighty-fifth birthday. He was a great pro football player, won the most valuable player award in 1956 while helping the New York Giants take the NFL title, ran and caught the ball for nine thousand yards during his career, scored seventy-seven touchdowns, made eight all-star teams, earned first-team all pro honors four seasons, was almost decapitated in 1960 by hulking linebacker Chuck Bednarik, sat out a full season while his brain at least partially healed, and returned to play three more seasons before retiring in 1964.

Despite his on-field excellence, most people rarely thought about Gifford the player after 1971 when he joined insightful but vitriolic Howard Cosell and Dandy Don Meredith in the booth of Monday Night Football games, which every week motivated millions of fans to huddle with friends in living rooms across the land. Polysyllabic Cosell unleashed comments both helpful and insulting, usually the former, while Meredith Texas-drawled entertaining stories and when the game was decided sang, "Turn out the lights, the party's over," and Faultless Frank Gifford smoothly described the action and maintained order in the booth. All three men were huge celebrities, Gifford and Meredith beloved and Cosell often called the most disliked man in sports and television. Go back and watch some videos, especially in boxing. Cosell, quite simply, was the best ever. But this is Frank Gifford's story.

In the mid-seventies I watched a TV documentary about Burt Reynolds. He told about a screen test for young actors in the late fifties in New York. The makeup man asked Reynolds, "What color makeup do you want?"

Reynolds nervously looked around the room, pointed, and said, "I'll take whatever he's wearing."

"He's not wearing makeup," said the man.

Frank Gifford didn't need makeup to look like a leading man, and the ladies adored him and on this occasion we need say no more.

I live in Bakersfield, where Gifford was raised, played high school and one year of junior college football before moving to USC, and early in his pro career, in the mid-fifties, resided here during the off season. I know an art teacher, older than Gifford, who still teaches a couple of classes a week and lived across the street from the young star in northeast Bakersfield. Years ago the teacher told me, "One morning I got up and couldn't find my little boy. I looked everywhere and was very worried so I ran to Frank's house. That's where my son was, eating breakfast with Frank Gifford."

August 2015

SHORT STORY

Cal Tech v. Notre Dame

"What in heaven did we — and do we — really know about Hedrik Macintosh?" asked Professor Kingsley.

"We knew, and it was and is absolutely verifiable, that he was one of the most brilliant physics students in the history of MIT and that he became its youngest professor ever," said Professor Marx. "Furthermore, he distinguished himself as a very fine, at times even a compelling, lecturer, and published many respected articles about the most ecologically efficient way to launch a humane nuclear first strike."

"His work wasn't of Nobel quality."

"True. But isn't that the quintessential point? He didn't quite have MVP ability, so he went into administration."

"Damn it, stop the sporting analogies, will you, Professor Marx? I didn't come to Cal Tech for jock talk."

"Don't you understand? The very fact that Dr. Macintosh is here means Cal Tech has a chance to survive."

"We'd flourished for decades."

"That was decades ago, at the turn of the century, Professor Kingsley. You can't deny Cal Tech was a nanosecond from terminal status when Dr. Macintosh arrived."

"I believe a turnaround was imminent even without Macintosh."

"That is unsupportable, unscientific, and manifestly absurd," said Marx. "So many of you traditionalists were unwilling to adapt to dynamic and challenging new realities. Mired, as you've always been, in the arcane and unreal world of the laboratory, you would've preferred to gaze into test tubes until liquidators backed trucks up to your doors. The super-universities had been bleeding us for years, offering outrageous salaries to our most esteemed colleagues, forcing Cal Tech to either pony up or lose them. And whenever necessary, the academic carnivores doubled or even trebled their original stratospheric inducements. It damn near destroyed my spirit, seeing former Cal Tech professors develop cures for herpes, baldness, impotence, and hysteria, and their new institutions reap trillions of dollars. Those Nobel-caliber studs have got to be paid years before their work reaches fruition, and there was only one way we could hope to do so."

That's right. Dr. Hedrik Macintosh had resurrected football at Cal Tech in 2051, promoted it with evangelical zeal, demanded four quarters of excellence every game, reaped two straight undefeated seasons, announced that his coach was unsatisfactory and fired him, declared that only a Rockne or a Lombardi would suffice, and then, in an ultra-secret speech to faculty members, he revealed even more astonishing ambition: "Today, my fellow scientists, I proudly tell each of you that merely lowering our academic standards for certain gifted student-athletes, though helpful, has not been sufficient. Therefore, from this day and forevermore we shall eliminate all academic standards. We shall obliterate them. We shall forget they ever existed, for they have imperiled our very existence. Yes, the great scientific super-universities, our adversaries, long ago forsook academic standards. That profound change in doctrine is the dynamic that drives them. No doubt you all realize that we must also improve exponentially, and we must do so at once.

"Our beating the pipsqueaks of the gridiron universe is inadequate. Look, if you dare, at attendance in our cherished home, the legendary Rose Bowl. For two seasons we've averaged a mere thirty thousand a game. Those seventy thousand empty seats are a plague to advertisers. They're an insult to recruits, many of whom have so often already been degraded by our blue nose admissions department. This is America, God bless every one of us, and we too shall have an equal opportunity to become our nation's greatest team."

The logistical aspects of Dr. Hedrik Macintosh's dream were surprisingly direct and unproblematic. Ten billionaires invested one hundred million dollars apiece in the Cal Tech Football Dorm, and in return received two-percent shares of future earnings from the scientific developments of every Cal Tech professor. Thus, the dorm was expeditiously built, and at once acclaimed for combining the most tasteful and luxurious traits of Beverly Hills and Las Vegas architecture. Great high school players would certainly come to look at a place like that. And the Rose Bowl really was the most picturesque football setting in the world. Lots of phenoms might be willing to play there if they could compete against the best. So there it was, again entirely up front. Cal Tech, buoyed by investments from several more billionaires, sent certified checks of eighty million dollars to each of the eleven most esteemed scientific powerhouses — Notre Dame, Michigan, Ohio State, Nebraska, Oklahoma, Texas, Alabama, Florida State, Miami, UCLA, and USC. For that kind of remuneration, they'd forget the quaint home-and-home tradition and in 2054 start coming to Cal Tech every year.

Recruiting became an objective of the most nerve-grinding urgency. Failure to attract nonpareil talent and produce a juggernaut would surely destroy Cal Tech, just as it had scores of universities around the country. Dr. Hedrik Macintosh was not going to fail. He allocated ninety-two percent of his time to courting prep stars, and in this mission he was joined by the photogenic and driven William Johnson Jones, recently hired for seventy-five million dollars a season (plus research options) after coaching the Des Moines Diablos to an unprecedented four consecutive Super Bowl championships.

Fleet, and hulking, and hulking and fleet high school players from California to Florida to Massachusetts to Washington were mesmerized by the sermons of Dr. Hedrik Macintosh and/or Coach William Johnson Jones, and the men privately told each recruit: "Son, if you're uncomfortable being a hall of famer, just tell me now, and I'll understand." No one admitted to that, and Cal Tech stunningly signed all fifty of its supreme blue-chippers. They comprised, by computer analysis and rational assessment, the finest freshman recruiting class in the annals of college football, and numerous spurned coaches made unsavory comments and several leveled the most horrific accusations.

"I pity these overmatched men," said Dr. Hedrik Macintosh.

"Those coaches are more content embracing failure than tightening their jock straps," said coach William Johnson Jones.

Rival coaches were even more outraged when Cal Tech convinced fourteen All Americans to defect.

"Yuh know goddang right that ain't right," said Bobby Bowden IV, coach of defending national champion Florida State, which lost three All Americans to the Researchers. "Why should a kid, who's already receivin the best NFL preparation here, go out to some pansy ass school, so he can sit out a year? I'm findin out why. That's what."

These were the sentiments within every big time program in the nation — not just those on the 2054 schedule. University presidents and coaches and players publicly challenged the NCAA to force the Researchers to explain how they could have done it. Generous donors, a nice stadium, an enticing schedule. That's not enough to so quickly accomplish so much. Opponents were positive that investigations would be followed by revelations and humiliations and the death penalty.

"I welcome the most thorough and ongoing inquiries," said Dr. Macintosh. "Cal Tech will immediately drop its college football program if there's a single impropriety, even a minor one."

The football season of 2053 was certainly entertaining, but it was not transcendent. Cal Tech had its third straight undefeated season but did not qualify for the sixteen-team championship playoff since it had not navigated a sufficiently difficult schedule. This was a just ruling. Other than Division One opponents Fresno State, Utah State, and Brigham Young, Cal Tech had only trounced inappropriate victims such as Harvard and Yale, which were studying (not investigating) Cal Tech's astounding gridiron rise, as well as Army, Navy, Air Force, Mills College, and Chico State.

When the most anticipated year ever, 2054, at last eased into late summer, Cal Tech's All American transfers had blended with the sacred sophomores, and opponents were probably scared and indisputably petulant, clamoring louder still for the NCAA to rescue them. Fans throughout the nation were outraged by such raw and flagrant timidity. "Play Cal Tech or play with yourself," they chanted. They were tired of politics. Politics should not matter on the field. Neither should the polls. There could never have been a debate about supremacy. Cal Tech became the finest and most widely watched college football team ever, and eviscerated eleven regular season opponents, ranked two through twelve, with an assaultive defense and a slashing offense. The cumulative score was six hundred ninety-two points to twenty-four. No team scored more than once. Seven didn't score at all. The college playoffs were going to be an unmitigated slaughter. Las Vegas quoted odds only on what the Researchers' margins of victory would be.

Though no team could control this magnificent Cal Tech machine, one man ignored mortal threats and the most personal insults, and tried. He was Edward Teller, the superb but rather dour and portly coach who'd led Cal Tech in its first two flawless seasons before being dismissed. At his press conference early Christmas morning he stated: "My heart and my conscience will not permit me to suppress the truth any longer. Cal Tech has defecated on decency while breaking every rule, and has in fact done things so horrible that no rules existed for them because no one could have fathomed such outrage.

"My attorneys have compiled a list of seven hundred twenty-three gross violations — we don't have time for the minor ones — and you can all purchase bound and autographed copies after I make a few general statements. God, where do I begin? Cal Tech — represented principally by Dr. Hedrik Macintosh and his institutional henchmen — paid young aspiring actresses five-figure sums per night to have sex with recruits who were still undecided as deadlines approached.

"What's worse, the institution, and its unscrupulous scientists, provided mega-steroids and other dramatic and dangerous growth supplements to many of the players. You're all idiots for not recognizing that. Have you ever seen offensive linemen who average four hundred pounds and every guy's fast and mobile?

"Also, the institution gave every player on the team a minimum of twenty grand a week in cash. If any player paid taxes, it was solely because he wanted to."

"Why didn't you do anything?" shouted a reporter.

"Because I wouldn't have collected my fifty million dollar bonus."

"Are you going to return the money?"

"I'll return the twelve million I still have. I'm so sorry. I can't continue."

Edward Teller placed beefy hands over his face and stumbled off stage.

Within minutes, Dr. Hedrik Macintosh was confronted by regular phones, cell phones, video phones, emails, still photographers, TV cameramen, documentary filmmakers, newspaper reporters, and two district attorneys. He promised a press conference in one hour. At the right time he stepped to a podium under beautiful trees in front of his office.

"All the allegations, I'm delighted to say, are utterly true," he pronounced. "And I'm not going to wait — Cal Tech is not going to wait — for a death penalty from the NCAA. That would be deceitful. We own the NCAA, and they'll be part of our management team when the Cal Tech Researchers next year become L.A.'s first NFL team in nearly a century."

SOURCES

Short stories "Therapy" and "Cal Tech v. Notre Dame" first appeared in the collection *The Bold Investor.*

"Hiking at Stanford" is an excerpt from a much longer feature titled "Bay Area Delights."

"Odom to the Hoop" first appeared in *In Other Hands*, a collection about prostitution, human trafficking, and prostitution.

Made in the USA
San Bernardino, CA
27 August 2017